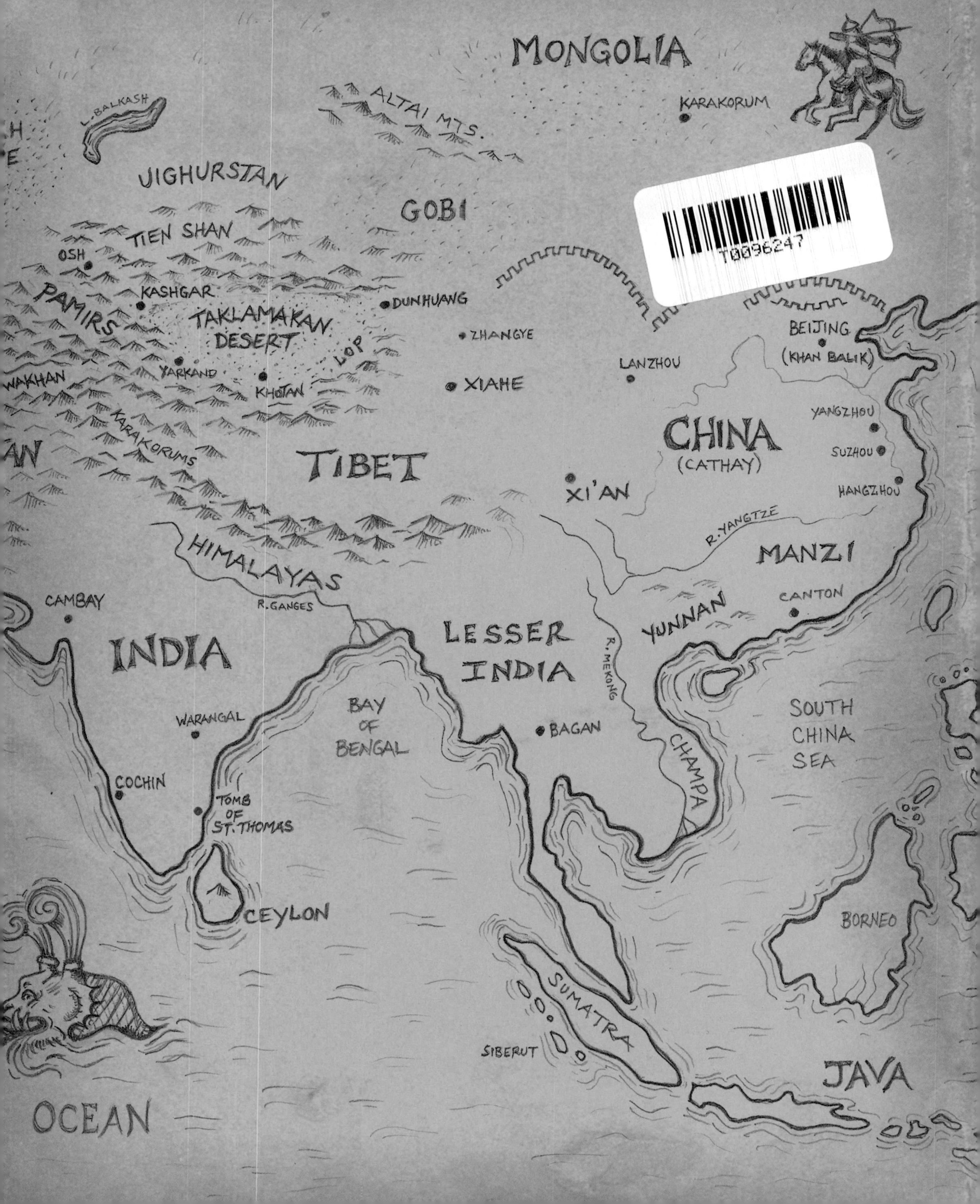
MONGOLIA
KARAKORUM
L. BALKASH
ALTAI MTS.
UIGHURSTAN
GOBI
TIEN SHAN
OSH
KASHGAR
PAMIRS
TAKLAMAKAN DESERT
DUNHUANG
ZHANGYE
LOP
YARKAND
KHOTAN
WAKHAN
XIAHE
LANZHOU
BEIJING
(KHAN BALIK)
KARAKORUMS
TIBET
CHINA
(CATHAY)
YANGZHOU
SUZHOU
HANGZHOU
XI'AN
R. YANGTZE
MANZI
HIMALAYAS
R. GANGES
CAMBAY
INDIA
LESSER INDIA
R. MEKONG
YUNNAN
CANTON
BAY OF BENGAL
WARANGAL
BAGAN
CHAMPA
SOUTH CHINA SEA
COCHIN
TOMB OF ST. THOMAS
CEYLON
BORNEO
SUMATRA
SIBERUT
JAVA
OCEAN

IN THE
FOOTSTEPS
OF
Marco Polo

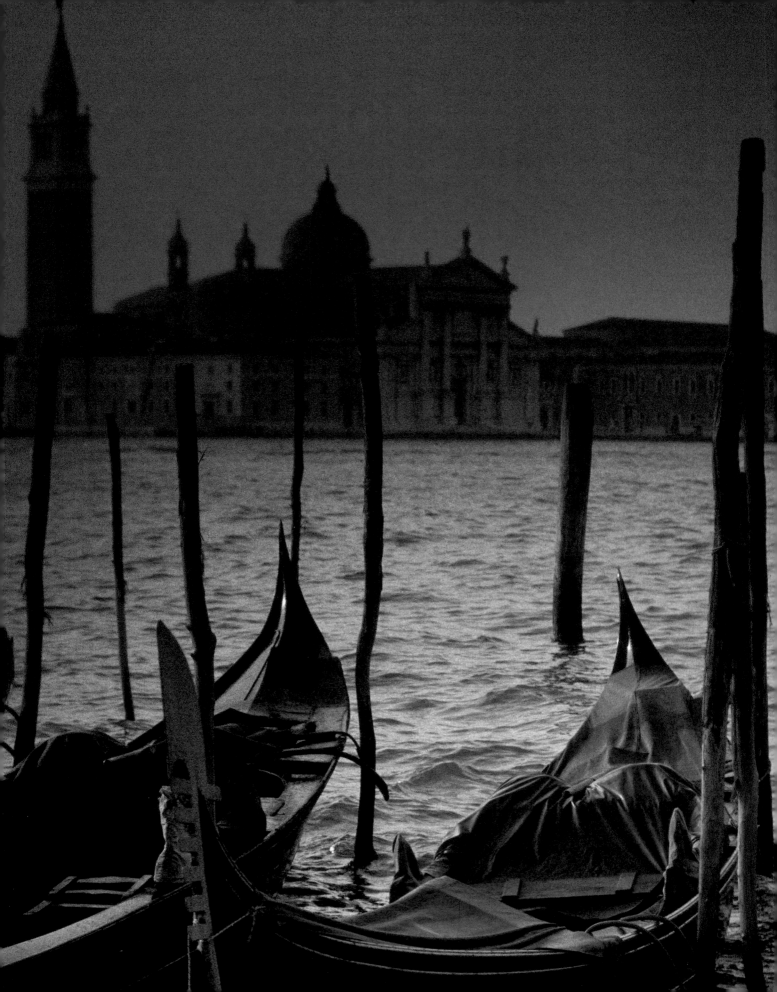

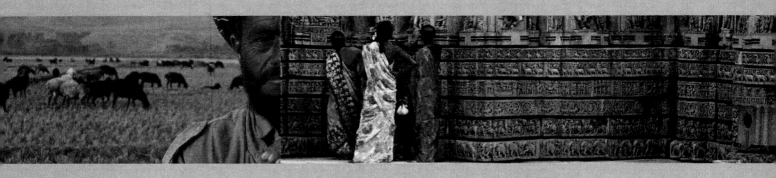

IN THE
FOOTSTEPS
OF
Marco Polo

DENIS BELLIVEAU & FRANCIS O'DONNELL

ROWMAN & LITTLEFIELD

Lanham · Boulder · New York · London

This book is dedicated to the memories of
Daniel O'Donnell, 1927–1994
and
Robert McAdam Smith, 1970–1992

馬哥孛羅

Published by Rowman & Littlefield
A wholly owned subsidary of The Rowman & Littlefield Publishing Group, Inc.
4501 Forbes Boulevard, Suite 200, Lanham, Maryland 20706
www.rowman.com

Unit A, Whitacre Mews, 26-34 Stannary Street, London SE11 4AB, United Kingdom

Distributed by NATIONAL BOOK NETWORK

British Library Cataloguing in Publication Information Available

The hardback edition of this book was previously cataloged by the Library of Congress as follows:

Belliveau, Denis, 1964–
    In the footsteps of Marco Polo / Denis Belliveau and Francis O'Donnell.
        p. cm.
        Includes bibliographical references.
        1. Asia—Description and travel. 2. Polo, Marco, 1254–1323?—Travel—Asia. 3. Belliveau, Denis, 1964– —Travel—Asia. 4. O'Donnell, Francis—Travel—Asia. I. O'Donnell, Francis. II. Title.
    DS10.B38 2008
    915.04'2092—dc22
    [B]   2008023411
    ISBN: 978-0-7425-5683-6 (cloth : alk. paper)
    ISBN: 978-0-7425-5684-3 (pbk. : alk. paper)
    ISBN: 978-0-7425-5737-6 (electronic)

Interior design by Piper F. Wallis, typesetting by Andrea Reider.

♾ ™ The paper used in this publication meets the minimum requirements of American National Standard for Information Sciences—Permanence of Paper for Printed Library Materials, ANSI/NISO Z39.48-1992.

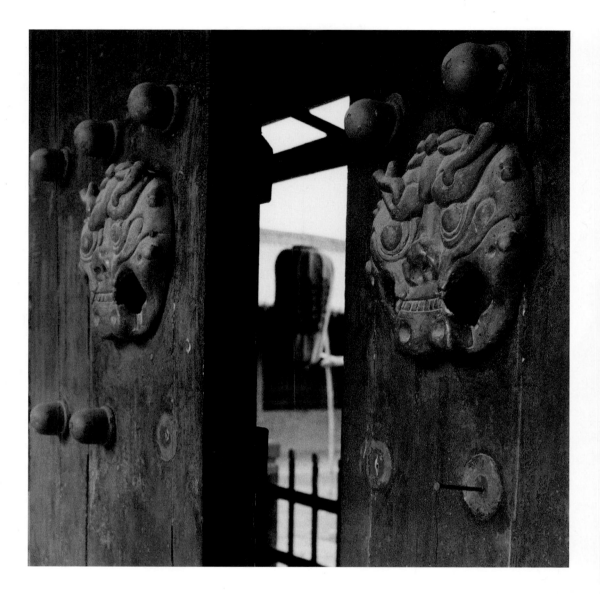

AT THE END OF THE THIRTEENTH CENTURY a book was written that would change the course of history. In its prologue, the author claimed to be the world's most-traveled man, igniting a controversy that has lasted for over seven hundred years.

> *Emperors and Kings, Dukes and Marquises, Counts, knights and townsfolk, and all people who wish to learn of the various races of men and of the diversities of the various regions of the world, take this book and cause it to be read to you. . . . For ye shall find therein all the great wonders and curiosities of Greater Armenia and Persia, and of the land of the Tartars and of India, and many other countries . . . as they were described by Messer Marco Polo, a wise and noble citizen of Venice, who has seen them with his own eyes.*

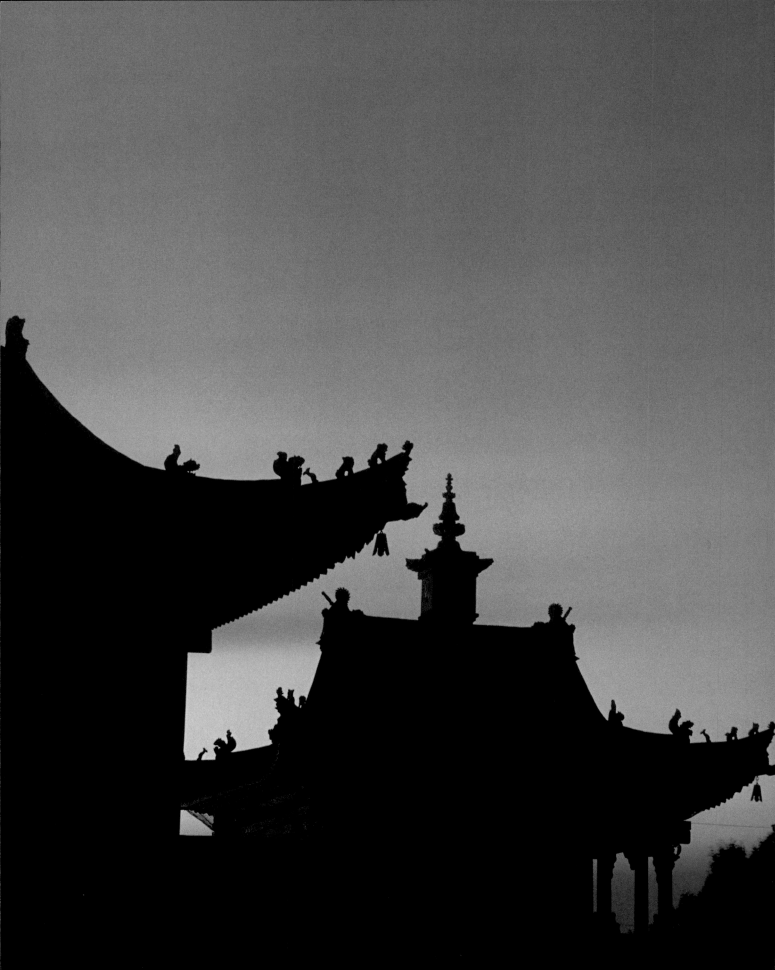

CONTENTS

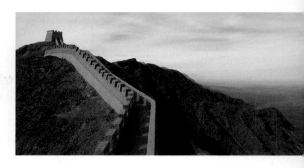

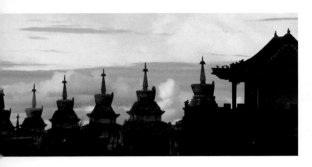

PREFACE

IN 1958 RONALD LATHAM WROTE in his much-respected translation of Marco Polo's *The Travels of Marco Polo*, "Some stretches of the trail he blazed were trodden by no other European foot for over six hundred years—not, perhaps, till the opening of the Burma Road during the last war. And the task of putting it on the map, in the most literal sense, is not yet complete."

In the spring of 1993, when Fran and I were both around thirty years old, we read these words over and over again for inspiration. We had taken it upon ourselves to try, "in the most literal sense," to put Marco Polo's journey on the map.

Perhaps the two are inseparable, but with a dash of reckless bravado and a lot of testosterone, we set out on our mission to see as many places Polo described without resorting to aircraft. We have tried to keep the story you are about to read "in the moment," and aside from a few historical updates, the words have come directly from the journals kept during the two years we were gone.

To maintain a cohesive flow to the narrative, we have chosen to tell the story as if from a single vantage point, but it reflects both of our experiences and insights.

The greatest learning experience of our lives wouldn't have been possible without the countless people who sheltered, fed, nursed, and guided us along the way. Their numbers are too great to mention here, so we'd like to thank from the bottom of our hearts just a few. To the brave and underappreciated people who work in the field for the UN, whether at UNHCR like Terry Pitzner and Raja Wickremasingh or as a peacekeeper like Sgt. Mick Travers, who was kind enough to smuggle us across a border in his car; to Bob Zincone for believing in the idea; Lisa Taylor for everything, especially putting up with the houseguests; Dave Smith for his keen eye; and Cecile Maurin, Nancy Grillo, Gary Hess, Vettor Giusti, Cere Berlin, and Marge and Bob Smith, we'll never forget your help.

To the people at WNET, especially Josh Nathan and Kathleen McGivern, and the staff at Rowman & Littlefield, especially Janice Braunstein for her diligent work, Piper Wallis for her excellent designs, and Susan McEachern whose kind patience and guidance this past year have turned our efforts into the gorgeous book you are now holding. And finally to our families, whose love, support, and belief in us never wavered—thank you all.

NOTE TO READERS

Throughout the body of the book you will find gold-colored type, which highlights Marco Polo's original descriptions from *The Travels of Marco Polo*. Excerpts are also included in several photo captions, but there we have put Marco Polo's observations in quotation marks.

In addition, the four Chinese characters—repeated throughout the text to signal transitions in the narrative—represent Marco Polo's name.

New York

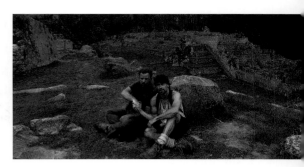

Stepping Off the Edge

"YOU'LL NEVER GET OUT ALIVE," Barney Rubin declared, thumping his desk for emphasis. "There's a civil war raging in Afghanistan! Even the kids carry guns. Believe me, you can't get in, but even if you could . . ."

It wasn't exactly "bon voyage," or even "good luck." But we weren't surprised. Ever since we began thinking of retracing Marco Polo's entire route in time for the 700th anniversary of his return, people had been giving us reasons why we shouldn't go—couldn't go—and why it would be utter insanity even to attempt a journey that would take us 25,000 miles through twenty countries and eight war zones. Barney Rubin, a distinguished Asia scholar at Columbia University, just added a few more.

All we wanted from him were some leads. Who could we talk to about traveling through Afghanistan? Who could give permission when there were no diplomats? Who could speak for the warlords who now fought each other for tribal domination? But the professor had little information to offer, and when we mentioned our Afghan contacts, he shot them all down. There was no way they could help. He spoke as if we were daydreaming boys in need of a reality check. In fact, we were way beyond daydreaming and well into obsession.

What does it mean to retrace the route of Marco Polo? There have been numerous attempts, with many inflated claims, but all have fallen short. One writer in the 1970s published a book and never even got into China! Another in the 1980s avoided Afghanistan altogether and was arrested before he reached Beijing. More recently, a photographer for a famous magazine claims to have achieved it, when in fact he only traveled 7,000 miles and flew to most of his locales. In other words, no one has taken the time to retrace the route of Marco Polo, all 25,000 miles of it.

Alone, without a crew, and using Polo's book as our guide, we decided to try to become the first to follow in his footsteps, for however long it took, nonstop, no flights, from village to village, city to city, and along the way see for ourselves whether or not Marco's words rang true.

We studied every version in print of *The Travels of Marco Polo*, and the book became our bible. For over a year we researched the route, charted maps, and read everything we could find about the journey and the countries we'd visit. Who else had traveled in his footsteps? How far did they go? Why did they fail? We consulted scholars of medieval Chinese and European history and attended lectures at the Asia Society, NYU, and Columbia University.

Despite all our research and hard-won knowledge, we couldn't seem to conquer the biggest barrier of all: bureaucracy. With the great Kublai Khan's golden tablets in their possession, the Polos could travel the vast Mongol empire at will, their only worry that bandits might rob and kill them—but at least they weren't strangled by red tape.

We knew we'd have unforeseeable delays, and because most countries issue visas for only one month, we decided it was best to obtain them once on the road. Afghanistan was different. It was in the throes of what historians now call "the warlord period." There were no visas.

Returning to our Afghan contact, we added a zinger to our plea for help by telling him what Barney Rubin had said: "His organization is a relief operation. They send food and clothes to Afghanistan. He can't do anything for you." It was a challenge and we knew it. He rose to it—and from his chair—and with deliberate movements picked up the phone. We anxiously watched as he spoke for a few moments in Dari and then handed the receiver to me. A deep voice asked why we wanted to go to Afghanistan.

I made our pitch: We weren't with the CIA, DEA, or any other government agency. Our project was historical, not political, and Afghanistan was a crucial part of our quest. When I'd finished, our contact took the phone and spoke again in Dari. He scribbled down "Mr. K" and a phone number on a scrap of paper and handed it over.

"This is the man who will get you into Afghanistan. You will have to go to Washington to meet him. When you get to the airport, call this number."

We flew to D.C. the next day, feeling as if we were living a chapter from a cheap spy novel, except that danger, real danger, still seemed far away. When we landed at National Airport, we called Mr. K from the first phone booth we found.

"Go to the Sheraton hotel," he said. "Then call me at this number in fifteen minutes." He gave us yet another phone number. We found the hotel in time and called again.

"We spoke to Mr. K; he told us to call."

"Okay," said a new voice. "Take a taxi to the Springfield Hilton. He'll meet you there. Do not take long."

A half hour later we sat down in the hotel lounge with Mr. K and told him about our plans, listing the regions that Polo traveled through. "Marco Polo, for most Americans, is a game you play in the pool," I told him. He smiled.

"Afghanistan, for most Americans, means war," he said. "I want people to know more of the history and culture of my country." He wrote out seven letters to various warlords on our route. "Do not get caught with these by a different faction," he said. "Make sure they go to the right people. Whatever you do, don't get them mixed up."

馬哥孛羅

As art school buddies from New York, we had never dreamed of making millions on Wall Street, had never even wanted conventional careers. Our jobs were just a way to finance what really made us feel alive: exploration, history, and adventure. I had met Francis on an archaeological dig in France sponsored by our school, and with a similar passion for art history we had become fast friends. Together we had climbed just about every pyramid in Mesoamerica, slashed through jungles to see cave paintings, and trekked in the highest mountains on the planet. We knew how to travel with little more than our cameras and the clothes on our backs, but for this expedition we would need new camera gear, film and processing, and enough cash to live on for two years. We could manage on a pittance compared to what a formal expedition would cost, but where would we find that pittance?

We started with Kodak. I'd won their prestigious Gallery Award and knew the head of the professional imaging department. "We only sponsor two projects a year," he said, showing me a thick pile of proposals. "One woman wants to photograph an iceberg as it melts in Antarctica . . . for a year!" He laughed. "Could you believe that?" I thought it sounded interesting, especially if she did a time-lapsed film, but said nothing, not sure if he was one of those knuckleheads who didn't believe in global warming. When he heard what we planned to do, his eyes grew big.

"It's right up Kodak's alley: it's apolitical, historical, and covers such diverse terrain— so many rich cultures, religions, and peoples," he said enthusiastically, repeating our pitch nearly word for word.

Once we had Kodak, the momentum snowballed. An international shipping company jumped on board to pick up and deliver our film. Donations flowed in for video equipment, foul-weather gear, boots, tents, sleeping bags, and even some cash. We could have used more, but it felt like the time was right to go and so we set a date.

Then, just before we were to leave, the unimaginable happened. My cousin Robert was senselessly murdered. He was just twenty-one years old. With the families of my mom's five sisters and brother living nearby, we cousins grew up more as siblings. I loved Robert; he was a little brother to me. I couldn't take in the reality that he was gone. He was young, happy, and had his whole life in front of him. An actor, Rob had just gotten his first big professional break, a traveling play that was to open in Dallas. He had been chosen over another up-and-coming actor, Edward Norton, for the role.

When we last heard from him, he was so excited about getting paid for work he loved to do. On the day he was killed, he was spending some of that money buying Christmas presents for his family. He and a friend were ambushed by a pack of teenagers in a parking lot. In what was perhaps a gang-initiation rite, a fourteen-year-old boy shot

Rob in the head. Rob died instantly. His friend was shot in the eye but lived. My family was destroyed.

When I saw the devastation Rob's murder had wrought on my aunt and uncle, I wondered what right I had to put myself in danger and cause my family years of anxiety while I was gone. Robert wasn't given a choice. His life was viciously stolen from him. I would be putting mine purposely at risk, knowing the odds. I didn't feel I could go on with the project.

After weeks of wrestling with my conscience, I met Fran in the Metropolitan Museum of Art at our usual spot in the Asia section. He was waiting in front of our favorite Buddhist fresco and we sat on the bench, thinking about the treasures in Polo's path.

I turned to my trusted friend. "I need to follow my bliss," I admitted, stealing one of our favorite lines from Bill Moyers's series of interviews with Joseph Campbell and one of the reasons we dared dream in the first place. "The heroes of all time have gone before us. It's what Rob was doing and what he would have wanted me to do."

Fran nodded knowingly and after a while just said, "It's better to live one day as a lion than a thousand like a sheep."

馬哥孛羅

Marco Polo was born in 1254, during a time of great upheaval. The Republic of Venice not only dominated European trade with the East but was also a major staging point for the Crusaders on their way to reclaim the Church of the Holy Sepulchre in Jerusalem. The Polos were rich merchants with connections in the Orient, trading in silk, spices, and precious stones.

> *In the year of our lord 1260 . . . Messer Niccolo Polo, the father of Marco, and Messer Maffeo . . . Niccolo's brother . . . men of good family, known for their wisdom and foresight . . . decided they would cross the Black Sea in hope of a profitable venture.*

After being away for years in the East, where they traded well and had the good fortune to meet Kublai Khan, the two brothers returned home to Venice. *There Messer Niccolo learnt his wife was dead, and there was left to him a son of fifteen, whose name was Marco.*

After a few years the Polo brothers decided to return to China, taking the wide-eyed seventeen-year-old Marco on a spellbinding journey, back along the fabled Silk Road. After a perilous three-and-a-half-year trek, they arrived at the summer palace of Kublai Khan, the Mongol emperor of China. The emperor instantly took a liking to the young Polo and for the next seventeen years Marco acted as an adviser to the Great Khan.

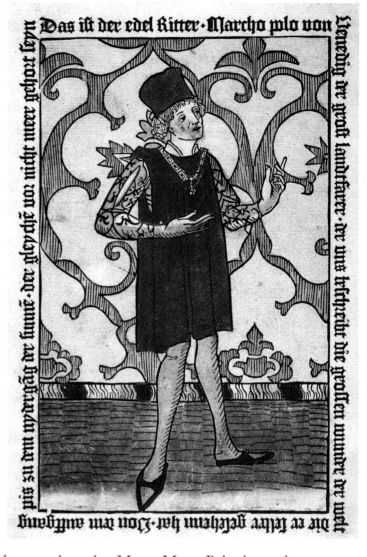

This, then, is how it came about that Messer Marco Polo observed more of the peculiarities of this part of the world . . . because he traveled more widely in these outlandish regions than any man who has ever been born.

馬哥孛羅

The night Fran called me with his insane idea, I was already planning a trip back to Nepal. I wanted to live there tucked away in some remote village in the Himalayas, getting to know the people, their language and culture, documenting their lives on film, and reading all the books I never had time for.

"Dude," he started, "I've been studying an old atlas, tracing ancient trade routes and contemplating kingdoms long gone: Carthage, Babylon, Rome, . . . and . . . I became lost in Marco Polo's route through the Mongol Empire and . . . like a beam of light it struck me! Seven hundred years ago, Polo astounded the West with his tales and discoveries, and

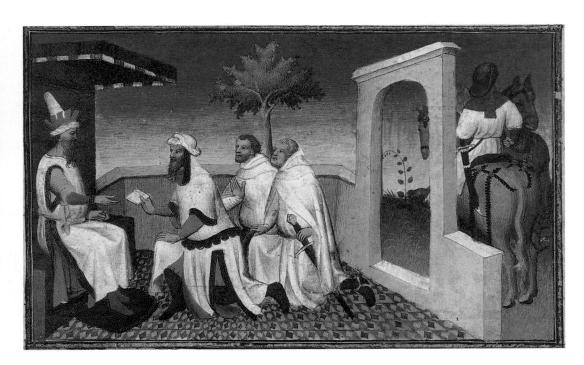

today, people still don't believe him. Wouldn't it be amazing to retrace his entire travels and try to prove him right?"

I was stupefied, lost in the magnitude of his proposal, and he couldn't wait for me to answer. "You're the only other person I know crazy enough to do it!" His words were tumbling out faster now. "So . . . what do you say? If we travel the way he did, overland and by sea, we'll see a lot of great things."

I thought he'd lost his mind. I'm always ready for an expedition, but this was way too big. I computed in my head what it would take. We'd need to traverse the world's largest land mass and back, climb its highest mountains, cross its most desolate deserts and seas—not to mention securing all those visas and somehow surviving a half-dozen war zones.

"No way, man. I want to live in one place, no traveling. I'm going back to Nep—"

"Just think!" he butted in. Then, almost in a whisper, "Jerusalem, Bukhara, Samarqand, Kashgar, Esfahan, Xanadu."

"It's just too big. I want to rent a little house in the mountains, grow my own veg—"

"Listen, listen," he jumped in again. "If we break it up . . . if we take our time . . . it's just a bunch of smaller journeys strung together. Just . . . do me a favor, think about it."

I tossed and turned all night, dreaming of exotic cities strung together on a map and the freedom that comes with moving on to the next place like a rolling stone.

The next morning I jumped out of bed and rang Fran's number. "It's a great idea," I said. "Besides, what's a little travel? How hard could it really be?"

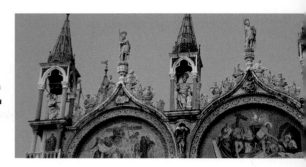

VENICE

Marco Polo Slept Here

AFTER BEING AWAY FOR TWENTY-FOUR YEARS, the three Polos returned to Venice in 1295. A few years later Marco was captured in a war with the rival city-state of Genoa. During his one-year imprisonment he dictated his fantastic adventures to a fellow prisoner, the romance writer Rusticello of Pisa.

Alternately titled *A Description of the World* and *The Travels of Marco Polo*, his book became one of the first international best sellers, hand-copied by scribes throughout Europe. There are over one hundred of these ancient texts still surviving that scholars cite. For centuries it remained the only source of information for Europeans about the magic of the Orient and the mysteries of the Far East, and it has never been out of print.

However, in Marco's own lifetime many did not believe his vivid tales about these distant lands, and because he conveyed the riches and population of China in the millions, he gained the nickname "Il Milione"—Marco Millions. Even today scholars debate the authenticity of Polo's account. Most recently, Frances Wood, head of the Chinese department at the British Library, suggested in her best-selling book, *Did Marco Polo Go to China?*, that Marco Polo only traveled as far as Persia, noting among other doubts that he failed to mention certain aspects of Chinese life.

馬哥孛羅

Well . . . did Marco Polo make it to China? The best hope we had of answering the question was to take on the quest ourselves. And as Lao-tzu famously once said, "A journey of a thousand miles begins with a single step."

The irony of landing at the Marco Polo Airport in Venice was not lost on us. "This is the first, last, and only airport we'll see in the next couple of years," Fran said as we waited for our packs to tumble down the conveyor.

"Just as long as we see it again," I shot back. "That'll mean we're alive, successful, and going home."

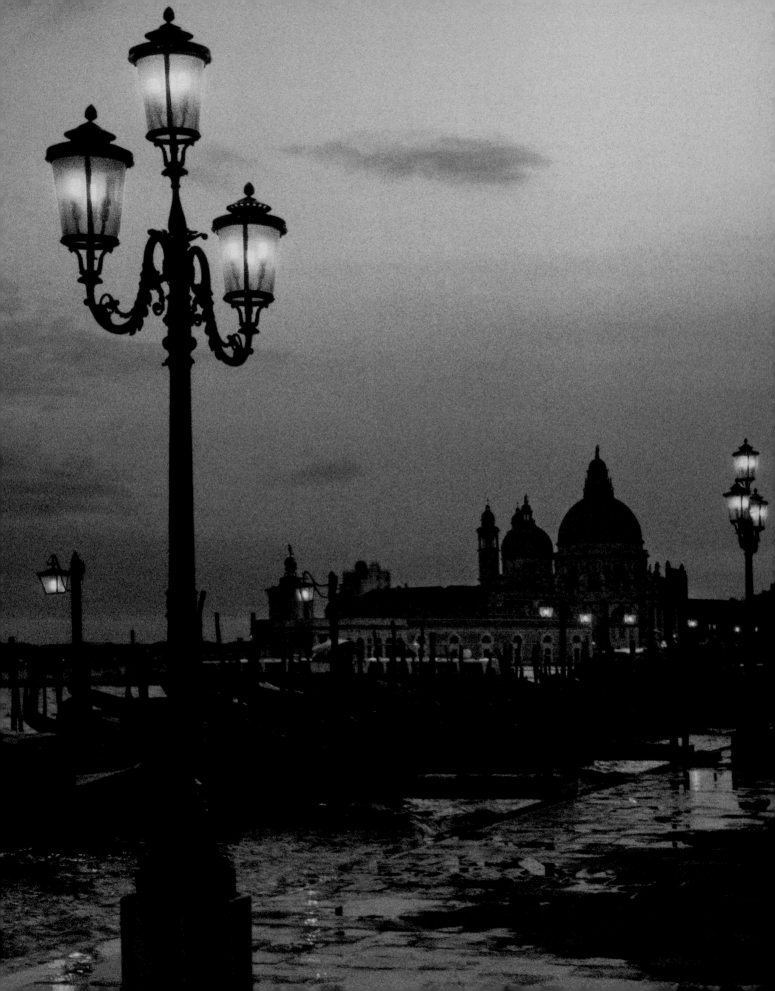

After checking into a cheap pensione, we went straight to work trying to find Marco Polo's home near the Rialto. A plaque above an archway that read *Corte del Milione* told us we had arrived. We slipped into the courtyard with silent reverence, as if we had entered a basilica. It was our first taste of walking in Marco's footsteps and we became, quite to our surprise, emotional.

It sounds corny, but I got the sense right there and then that we were setting out on something bigger than either of us had imagined. "Look," I said to Fran, "there are going to be times when we get homesick, when we can't stand each other, when we want to turn back."

He cut me off, his face full of purpose. "We're going to see this through no matter what."

After a long pause I added, "If something were to happen to me, I'd want you to get my body home, so my family could have some kind of closure."

"Okay." He nodded. "But if I go down you have to promise me you'll bury me where I fall and keep going."

We spent the next week or so trying to get permission from the Biblioteca Nazionale Marciana to see, hold, and photograph the only surviving document that we know Marco Polo laid his hands on: his last will and testament. After some initial promises, we were turned down. "You don't have the credentials," they finally said. "We can show you a facsimile."

"When we come back, they'll have to serve it to us on a silver platter!" I swore to Fran as we bounded angrily down the stairs into St. Mark's Square.

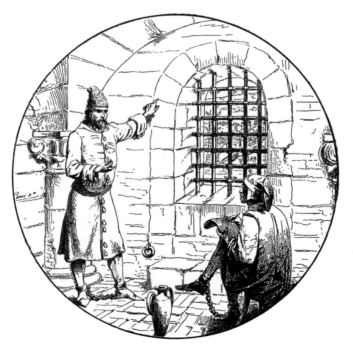

In one of the more fortuitous incarcerations in history, Marco dictated his tales to Rusticello of Pisa, a famous writer of Arthurian romances and fellow prisoner.

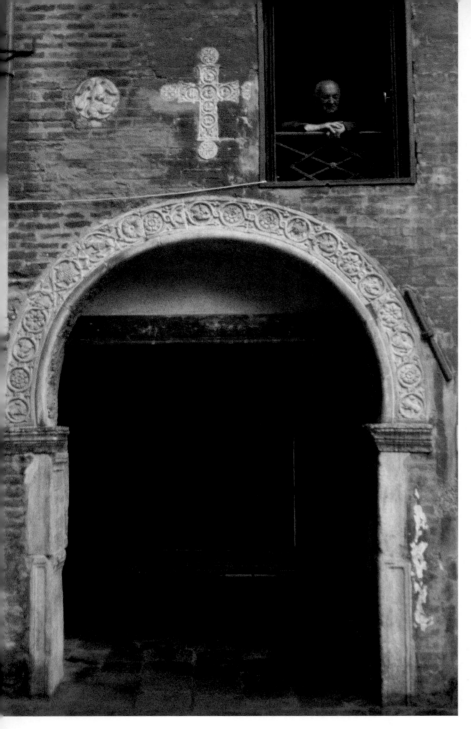

"It's time to hit the road," I bellowed, kicking the cobblestones for emphasis and scattering dozens of pigeons.

"No, bro," he corrected me. "From Venice, we hit the *waves.*"

> *So after Messer Niccolo and Messer Maffeo stayed at Venice about two years…they decided that if they waited longer it might be too late for them to return to the Great Khan. So they set out from Venice, taking with them Marco the son of Niccolo.*

HOLY LAND, HOLY FIRE

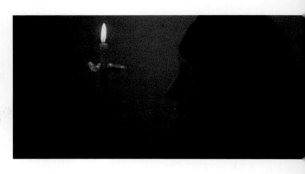

The Keys to the Church

For the Great Khan had directed the brothers to bring oil from the lamp that burns above the Sepulchre of God in Jerusalem.

PERHAPS NO OTHER CITY ON EARTH is more sacred or contested than Jerusalem. It is a place of incredible devotion, love, and piety but also a flashpoint of intolerance, hatred, and violence. At the Church of the Holy Sepulchre, believed to be on the very spot of the crucifixion and tomb of Jesus Christ, pilgrims from the various Eastern Orthodox traditions gather every year on the day before Easter to witness the ceremony of Holy Fire.

Because ownership of the church is hotly contested among all sects, the key to the holiest shrine in Christendom is not in the possession of any one of them. A century before the Polos arrived it was put into the neutral hands of a Muslim gatekeeper. We tracked down Wajeeh Nusseibeh in the older, more picturesque, Arab quarter of the walled city.

Wajeeh is a Palestinian whose family has held the key since 1187. Every day he rises before dawn to unlock the massive doors of the Holy Sepulchre and let the Christians flood in, as his forefathers have done for generations.

Kublai Khan had requested that the Polo brothers return to him with one hundred scholarly priests, hand-chosen by the pope, as well as with holy oil from a lamp that the faithful believe burns eternally inside Christ's tomb. Unable to secure the priests because the pope was dead and a successor hadn't yet been elected, the Polos' need to fulfill their other promise to Kublai—to bring back the holy oil—became essential.

Wajeeh not only helped us obtain a vial of this same holy oil, he procured us a spot just feet from the tomb on the day of Holy Fire. The noise of the surging crowd of pilgrims echoed down from the church's leaded dome, and it took a lot of pushing and well-placed elbows to hold such a good position. Arab Christians sang hymns dating back to Polo's time, when Jerusalem was in Saracen hands and the church was the only lawful place they could publicly profess their Christianity. They sat on each other's shoulders, loudly chanting "We are Christian. . . . We are Christian . . . and will be forever," to the beating of drums and rhythmic clapping.

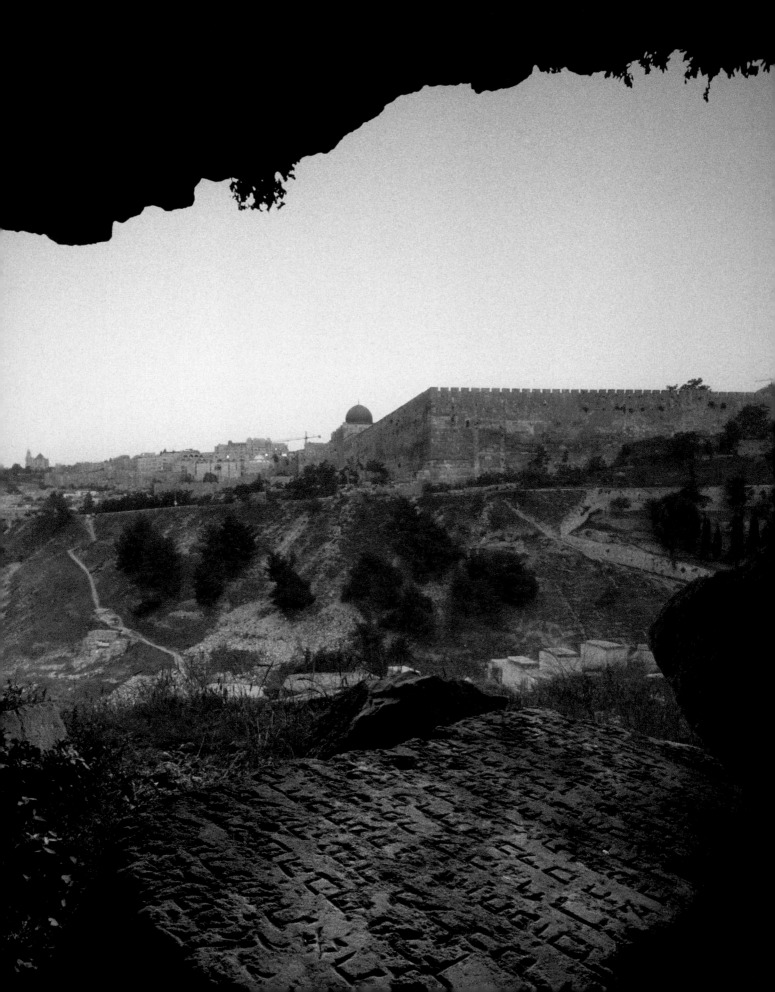

(opposite page) From a cave in the Jewish cemetery on the Mount of Olives, the leaded dome of the Church of the Holy Sepulchre rises above the ancient walls of Jerusalem.

That all changed when the Greek Orthodox patriarch entered the church and made his way to the tomb. The crowd froze in a hush as he was searched for a concealed lighter or matches. He was then sealed inside the tiny tomb with wax, where he recited ancient prayers as the throngs of pilgrims waited quietly for the miracle to occur.

He then emerged from the crypt with a symbol of the resurrection—candles believed to be miraculously set ablaze by the hand of God.

With a roar the crowd surged toward him, thrusting unlit candles to acquire the Holy Fire—the closer to the patriarch's original candle, the more sacred the flame. A scramble ensued as Armenians shoved Greeks, neither of them respecting the Arab Christians, and fistfights broke out. Israeli policemen held small fire extinguishers, ready to pounce on any pilgrim set ablaze by the inferno of candles, which could sweep through the cavernous church within seconds.

"Like these pilgrims today, the Polos left this church believing in miracles," I shouted to Fran as we made our way out the doors.

"We're going to need to pull off a few miracles ourselves," he hollered back.

"What about that scene? Somebody told me that a Greek priest actually stabbed an Armenian one last

Wajeeh Nusseibeh, the latest heir in a long line of Muslim gatekeepers, unlocks the doors to the Holy Sepulchre for us, just as Polo's Nusseibeh guide helped him gain access to the tomb.

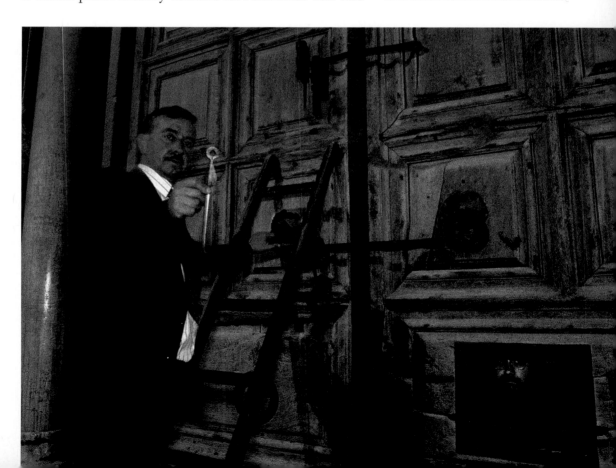

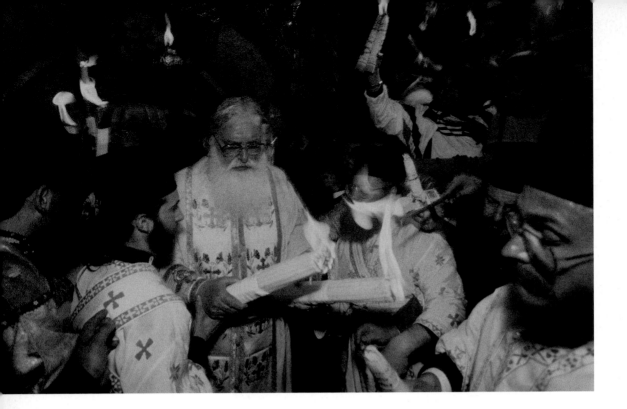

On the day before Easter, known as "Holy Fire," the Greek Orthodox patriarch emerges from the crypt with a symbol of the resurrection: candles believed to be miraculously lit by the hand of God.

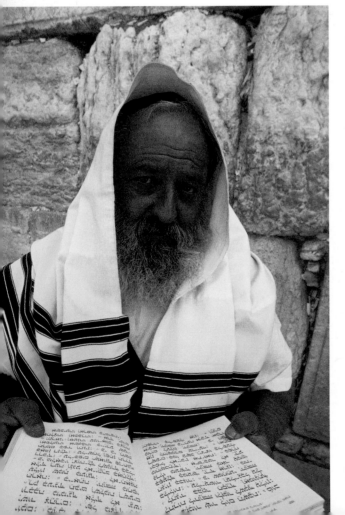

A rabbi prays at the Western Wall. In Polo's era Jews could pray freely in Jerusalem even though the city was in Saracen hands, but for the Christian Polos, a mission into the city would have been dangerous.

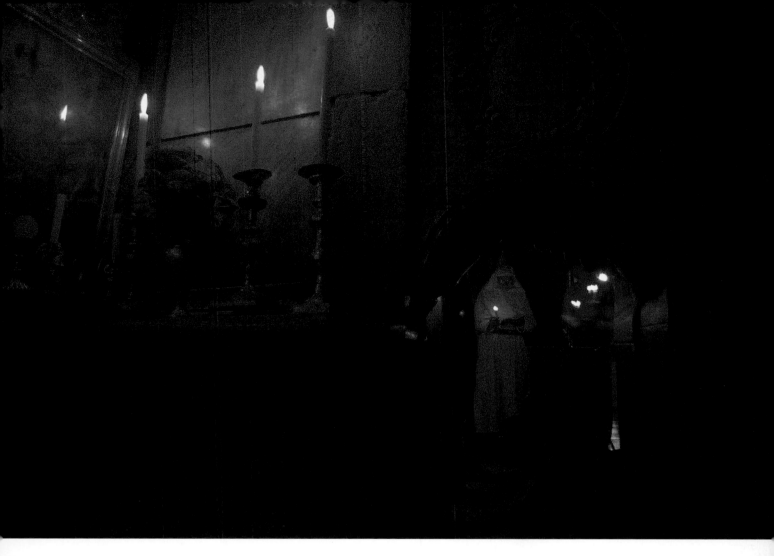

The inside of the tomb of Christ, or Holy Sepulchre, where the Polos obtained the precious holy oil requested by Kublai Khan, who believed it held miraculous properties.

year," I offered more quietly on the Via Dolorosa. "Right inside the church!"

"Intolerance just doesn't make any sense," Fran said. "If the Christians can't get along in their holiest place, how could we expect the Israelis and Palestinians to get it together?"

馬哥孛羅

Sneaking out of Muslim-controlled Jerusalem, the Polos continued back to Acre, the capital of the Christian Kingdom of the Holy Land and a major port on the coast of Palestine. Being inside one of the last strongholds of the Crusaders would have put them at ease, for it would have been filled with familiar faces, having its own Venetian quarter with churches, warehouses, and inns. Here, by chance, the three Polos met the man who would be elected the next pope. He gave them gifts and letters for the Great Khan.

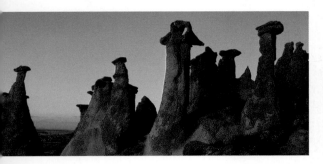

TURKEY

You Always Have a Friend

FROM ACRE THE POLOS SAILED UP THE COAST to Ayas in what was then Lesser Armenia. This now-unassuming Turkish fishing village was once the terminus of the great Silk Road. A bustling port in the Polos' time, it was the most important point of access for Europeans to the lands of the East.

> When they had got as far as Ayas, it happened that the sultan of
> Egypt came into Armenia . . . and wrought havoc in the country,
> and the emissaries went in peril of their lives.

Our ferry made landfall at Mersin, a stone's throw from Ayas on the Gulf of Iskanderun. We checked into a rugged sailors' hotel near the docks before setting out to find the offices of *Hurriyet*, the most voraciously read newspaper in a country full of newspaper readers. We barged in and befriended a group of journalists over endless cups of chai (tea). The Turks are incredibly hospitable people, and they were very patient as we bastardized their native tongue, yet clearly impressed we were trying. We spoke of our connections in New York's Turkish community and how we'd studied the language intensely for months before we left. We reminded them that Turkic-based languages were spoken by millions of people in Asia. "It is the lingua franca of today's Silk Road, much as Persian was in the Middle Ages. So, as we progress east through various dialects, we'll be able to communicate with people all the way into China." It wasn't until a half hour later that one of them finally asked, "What can we do for you?"

"Marko Polo nun Ipek Yolu Yolculugu" (Marco Polo traveled the Silk Road), we began, and then filled them in on our plans.

A couple of days later the piece was out, a full page with a color photo of us sporting our backpacks. By getting in the papers we had become quasi-celebrities and the article opened

(opposite page) "On the sea coast lies the town of Ayas, a busy emporium. For you must know that all the spices and cloths from the interior are brought to this town."

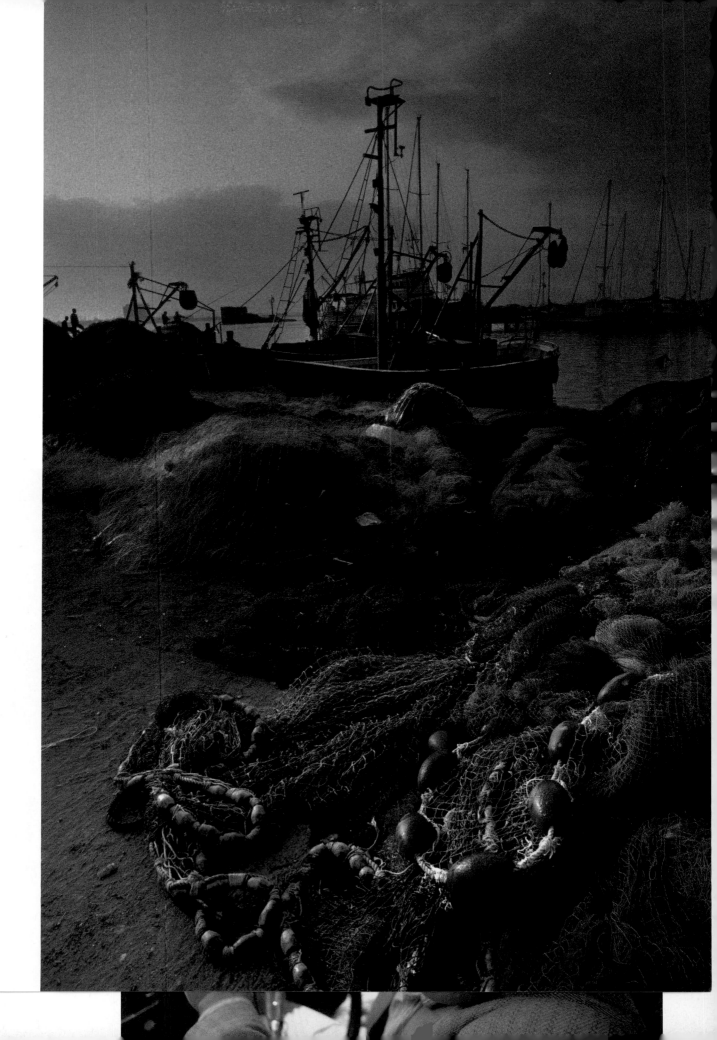

"Um, no . . . I haven't, but we're retracing Marco—"

"It will be my honor to take you there then. The lineage of that king can be traced back through two legends, Greek and Persian, evidence that this land has always been the crossroads of civilization."

"That's fascinating," I said. "And you obviously know your stuff. . . . Are you a professor? A PhD? A doctor? . . . Dr. No!" I laughed. "I was wondering if you've ever heard of—"

"Marco Polo? Yes, I heard you the first time. Polo mentioned the legends of Alexander often in his book."

"He must be a rich widower, with too much time on his hands," Fran said to me after we'd convinced him to stop at an Armenian castle from Polo's time period. "He's in his fifties, well educated, probably spent some time in the States. I like him but we should ditch him tomorrow after breakfast and move on. We still have a lot of work to do."

"C'mon," I said. "He was put in our path for a reason! We're 'Asia's guests' and he's

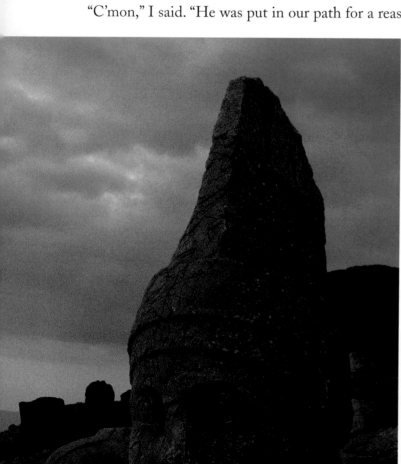

'Dr. No.' I say we stick with him and see where it leads."

We spent the next few days touring ancient sites in southeastern Turkey in his vintage 1950s American car. He wouldn't let us pay for a thing, even refused money for fuel, and he seemed to be known and respected wherever we went. As he had

The mausoleum, or tumulus, of Antiochus (69–34 B.C.) is a UNESCO world heritage site and one of the most ambitious constructions of the Hellenistic period.

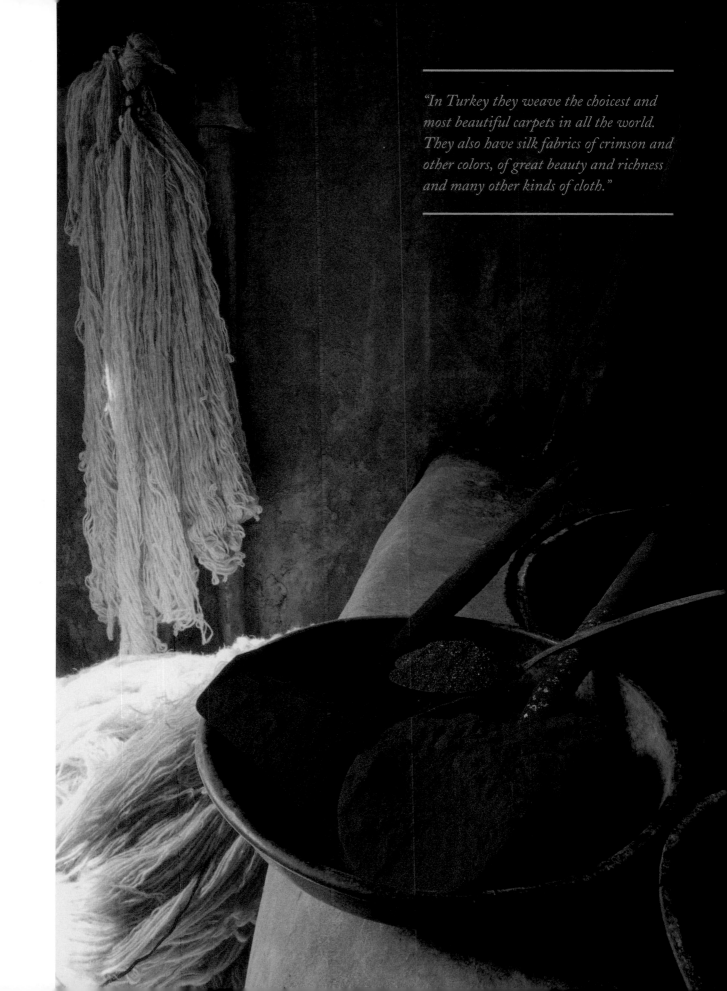

"In Turkey they weave the choicest and most beautiful carpets in all the world. They also have silk fabrics of crimson and other colors, of great beauty and richness and many other kinds of cloth."

promised, he brought us not only to Antiochus's tumulus at Nemrut Dag but also to the forgotten ruins of a Byzantine church, far off the beaten path. Pointing to the ground, he told us to dig gently, and we unearthed a magnificent 1,500-year-old mosaic floor. He never told us who he was or gave us his name.

"Cok sagol, abi" (Much thanks, big brother), we said when we finally parted. "By the way, do you know any carpet dealers in Konya?"

馬哥孛羅

Handwoven carpets were among the most sought-after trade goods in Polo's time. As the son of a merchant of Venice, the young Marco was being educated by his father on how to recognize quality goods that would turn a handsome profit.

In the town of Konya, a center of carpet-weaving, the great Sufi poet Mevlana Rumi lived and is buried. A contemporary of Polo's, Rumi and his poems of brotherly love and spiritual ecstasy are greatly admired today and represent some of the most mystical writings in Islamic thought. That such a teacher was preaching interfaith tolerance during a period of extreme conflict between religions is a great lesson for us all today, when it appears a handful of extremists have hijacked the whole of Islam.

Like all religious fanatics, like the Crusaders of Polo's era, Islamic fundamentalist groups today strip away all their legacies, except theology. Because they enlighten and educate, Islam's long traditions of mysticism, philosophy, science, and the arts are completely ignored. Though Polo's book reflects the

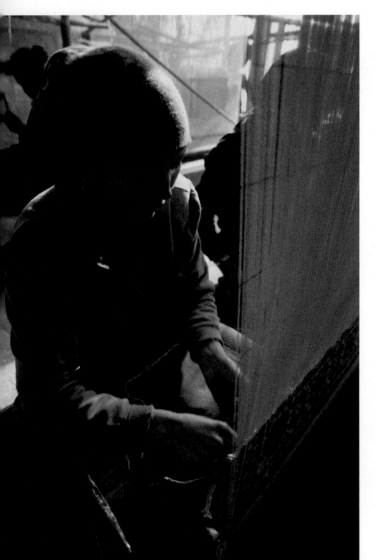

A carpet weaver in Sivas plies her trade. Young women and children are believed to have more nimble fingers to work the looms—employing designs and techniques that have changed little since Polo's time.

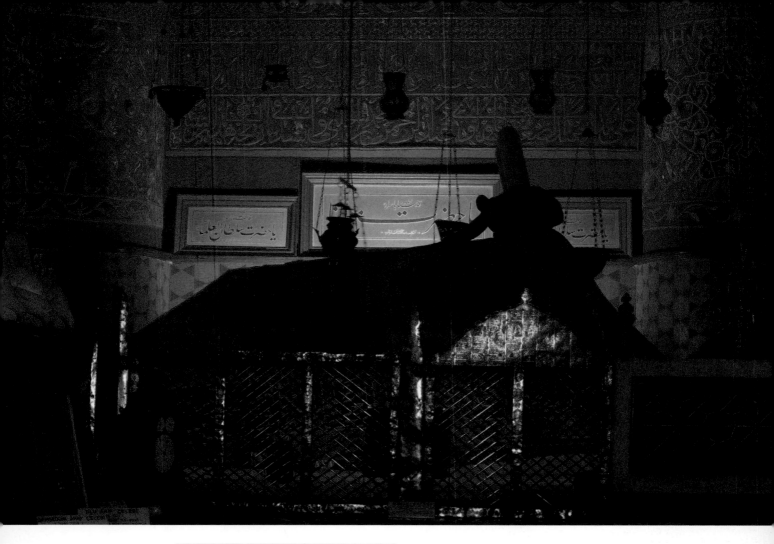

The tomb of the great Sufi poet Mevlana Rumi in Konya, Turkey. Rumi was a contemporary of Polo's, and his poems of brotherly love and spiritual ecstasy represent some of the most mystical writings in Islamic thought.

prejudice of his time and has little good to say regarding Muslims, Marco courageously admitted that he'd made friends with a man of great intelligence—a certain Turk named Zurficar.

Of course, prejudice is not the only source of conflict among men, as Fran and I discovered early on. Friends or not, our nerves were frayed after yet another fruitless day at the Iranian embassy, and Fran and I lost it in the posh lobby of the Ankara Hilton, just next door.

We hadn't agreed on the affordability of eating the hotel's breakfast buffet, and so a full-on, knock-down, drag-out fight ensued. Fists were flying, legs a-scrambling, as we rolled around on the lush carpet to the horror of the staff and guests.

"What difference does it make now!" I said, pulling myself away from him and referring to the real reason we were fighting. "The project's over."

"They were just screwing with us, purposely torturing us over these visas 'cause we're Americans!" Fran said, helping me to my feet in the busy lobby before engulfing me in a bear hug.

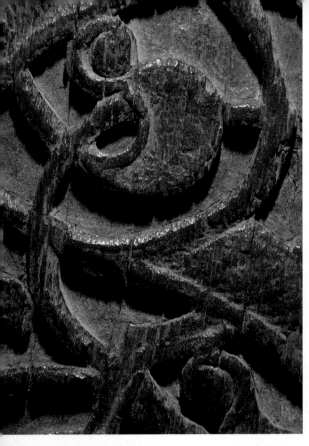

With the arrival of the Seljuk Turks (1055–1256), the center of the Muslim world shifted from Arabia to Turkey and Iran, and with it a distinctive style of architecture was formed. Its most striking feature is a profusion of finely carved details, as shown in the photo below, taken at the caravanserai in Sultanhani. Another characteristic feature of the buildings from this period is the decorative use of unglazed bricks arranged in eye-pleasing geometric patterns, which can be seen at right in the minarets of the Çifte Minaret Madrasa in Sivas. At left is a detail from an intricately carved wooden door found in Konya. The style of the Seljuks would go on to shape the art and architecture in the Persian world for centuries to come.

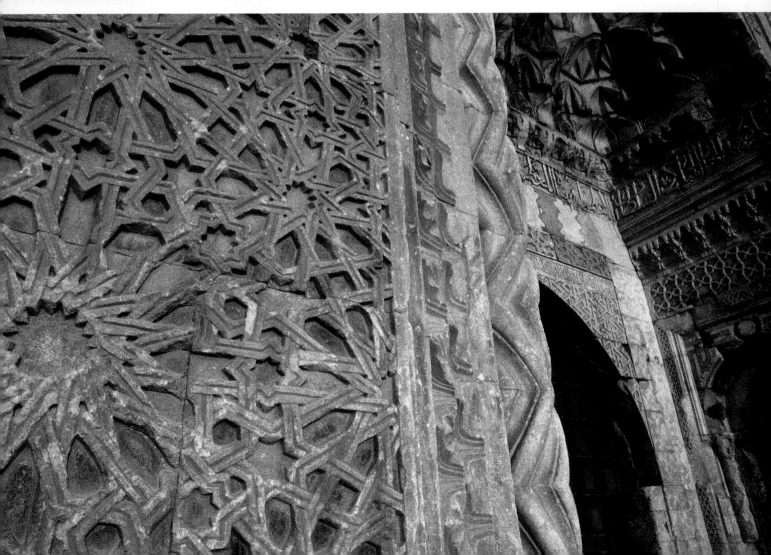

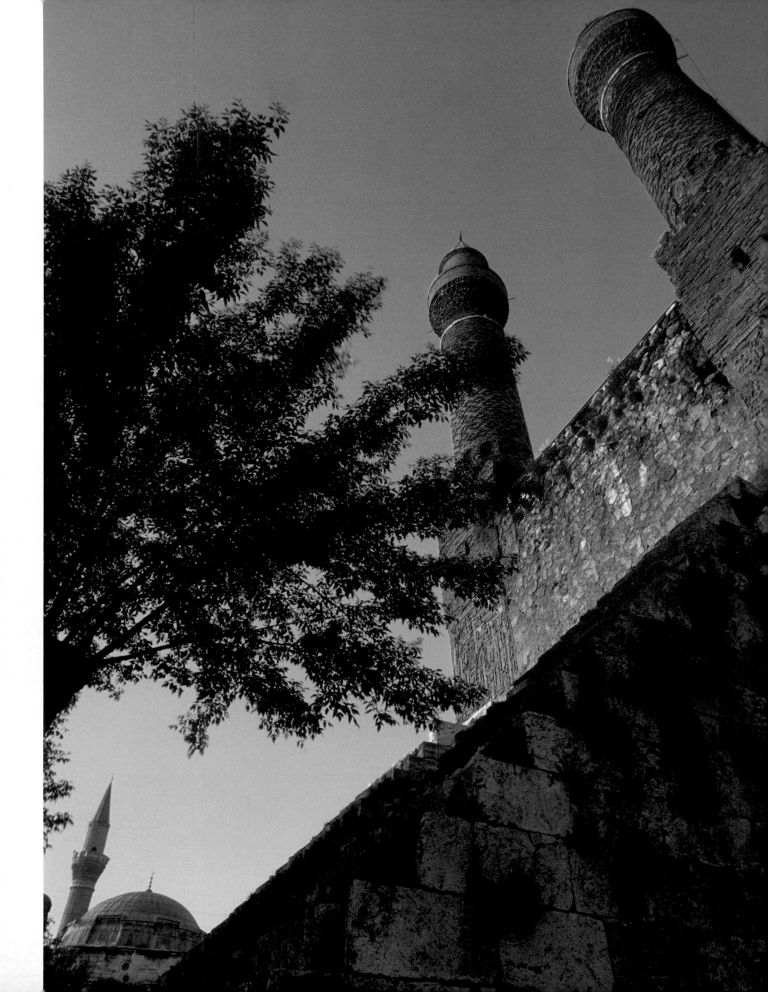

Incredibly, no one tried to stop us as we made our way to the buffet. "What were we thinking?" I said, wiping blood from my mouth while we stood in line for pancakes.

"I know . . . did you see the concierge's face?"

"No, no . . . I'm talking about the Iranians. They don't just let Americans in. Why did we think we'd be any exception?"

Fran shook his head. "He gave us his word and we believed him."

Since there were no diplomatic relations between our countries, we had gone to see the only person back in the United States who could help us get a visa to Iran, Ambassador Kharrazi, Iran's envoy to the United Nations. Somehow, we arranged a meeting at his office high above Third Avenue, which seemed—had it not been for the goons who frisked us at the door—more like an apartment. He was very friendly and open, even strangely at one point inviting himself out to Queens to have dinner with my family. We spoke of history and art, and he was clearly well versed on Marco Polo's travels through his country.

"I believe your project is a fine one and I will give you all the assistance I can." He gave us a book on Persian miniatures along with his promise that our visas would be waiting for us in Turkey. "You have my word."

But every day in Ankara, for six aggravating weeks, we'd enter the embassy only to be told another story. At first they didn't understand why the ambassador would tell us that we could get our visas here. Then after a flurry of calls to the UN, his secretary assured us he was in Tehran working on it. Then we were told it was approved but stuck in the Ministry of Culture and Islamic Guidance. Then it was definitely approved . . . and then, finally, after all the effort and wasted time, they said no—a definite no. We were denied visas to enter the Islamic Republic of Iran. It was over.

"How can I go home and look everybody in the eye who believed in us?" I sighed. "Let's just hide here in Turkey for a few years and say we retraced it, like What's-Her-Name says Polo did in the first place! Just think, we could rent a place down by the beach and get some girlfrien—"

"We're not giving in!" Fran shouted, perhaps a little too aggressively because I was ready to clock him again. "Polo went through Persia twice, coming and going. Do we really need to? If we do the rest of the journey as accurately as possible, the Iranians will have to believe we're not spies and let us in on the way back. Then we could pick up the few hundred miles we missed."

"Are you nuts?" I asked, pouring us some more strong coffee. "Why would they? If they turned us down once, they could again and then what? Go through all this? Putting ourselves at risk and all, only to turn around and *not* get into Iran on the back end? That would mean we had failed. We would have done most of it, I grant you—a kick-ass journey no doubt—but without getting into Iran, at least once, we couldn't say we had retraced the route of Marco Polo."

PERSIA

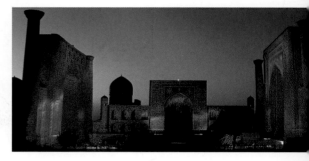

The Genesis of the Story

WE MADE LEMONADE FROM THE LEMONS WE'D BEEN DEALT, for Marco Polo's book doesn't really hold a set itinerary. It is, in fact, what he originally claimed it to be, *A Description of the World.*

The account deviates from the accepted route to places we know he didn't go, such as Siberia and Africa, but in the Persian city of Bukhara he recounts the tale of his father and uncle's own historic journey years before. This gave us a Plan B and brightened our moods. As long as we get into Iran on the way back we could cover more places described in the book. We had always planned to go to Bukhara, whether taking a side trip from Afghanistan on the way to China or from Iran on the way back; we felt it was that important to the story.

Besides, Marco Polo himself had to change his plans in Persia. The three clansmen had wanted to sail from the gulf to China, but after seeing the poor quality of the ships in Hormuz, they decided to continue overland through Afghanistan. By cutting north through Central Asia and on to Bukhara like his father and uncle, we remain historically correct. After all, it is the genesis of the whole Polo story.

馬哥孛羅

For thousands of years, the peoples of the Middle East had acted as middlemen in the trade between Europe and the Far East, eventually spreading their culture and religion as far as Indonesia. It was only after the whirlwind of destruction left by Genghis Khan's Mongol hordes, who swept down from the steppes of Central Asia, that the Muslim stranglehold on trade was finally broken. The sacking of Baghdad, then one of the most brilliant intellectual centers in the world, may have robbed humanity of precious knowledge, but it ended the caliphate, a blow the Islamic world would find hard to overcome.

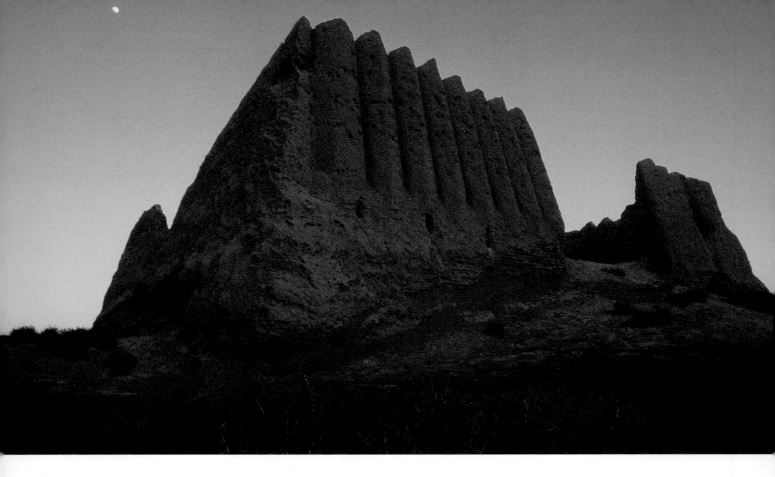

The Kiz Kala fortress in Merv, Turkmenistan, built in the sixth century. Merv was called the "Pearl of the East," and its extensive libraries were legendary. The city's refusal to open its gates to the Mongols in 1221 assured its ultimate ruin; hundreds of thousands were put to death in retaliation.

As terrifying as the onslaught of the ferocious Mongol hordesmen was, their control of most of Asia and so-called Pax Mongolica did create an environment of cultural exchange. For it is during this window of opportunity that Marco Polo's father and uncle were able to venture east on the Silk Road during their previous trading mission from 1260 to 1269.

After 17 days' journey through a desert wherein they found neither town nor village . . . they came to Bukhara, which was the most splendid city in all of Persia.

馬哥孛羅

The heat was oppressive and we were feeling cocky. "Go ahead, you first," I offered to Fran as he cupped his hands under the spout of a public fountain in the back alleyways of Bukhara and threw water over his baking head, literally letting off steam. He then

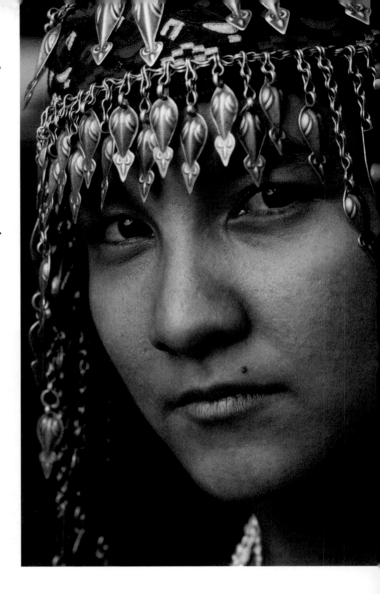

A Turkoman girl from one of tribes in the region Polo called "the dry tree" on the Iranian border. "They are a good looking race and the women in particular are of out-standing beauty."

went under the spigot and took a big gulp. "You know we are going down for this," he said before moving aside.

"I don't care," I replied as I took a long, revitalizing drink in turn.

It took a few days, but when it hit, I'd never felt worse. When not losing fluids from all orifices simultaneously, I was doubled over in pain. Fran escaped fairly lightly, and at my insistence left me in the care of a kindly innkeeper to go explore more of the town.

"We must take care you do not dehydrate," said Mobinjan, a Persian in an historic Persian town now surrounded by Uzbek Turks. He practically force-fed me liquids I could hardly keep down.

"My ancestor built this house," he had told us when we had first found lodgings with him, "229 years ago when Bukhara was still Persia and he was a caravan merchant, free to move from one place to the next. When the Bolsheviks came in the early twenties my great-grandfather painted over all the decorations so we would not look so wealthy. I promised my mother on her deathbed that if the Russians ever left and we had independence, I would restore the house, just as her father had asked of her and just as I would have my son. But *mashallah*, by the grace of God, we are free now and I am restoring the house."

He put us in a stunning room with fifteen-foot ceilings and built-in arched niches, cut out in the shapes of genie bottles, but I recuperated for the most part outside on a raised divan padded with rich carpets and cushions in the local style, where it was cooler but still more than a hundred degrees in the shade, and Mobinjan nursed me back to health with yogurt, rice, and salted chai.

馬哥孛羅

After Bukhara's destruction by the Mongols, its inhabitants rebuilt, and the city reached its zenith in the fifteenth, sixteenth, and seventeenth centuries. In fact, many believe that the mosques and madrasahs of Samarqand and Bukhara represent the height of artistic expression in Persian Islamic architecture. These academies of learning were places where one could gain the wisdom of astronomy, mathematics, geography, as well as religion, the likes of which Europe and the West wouldn't see for centuries to come.

The Polo brothers found themselves stranded here for years, unable to go further or turn back because a civil war had broken out between rival Mongol clans. Finally, they encountered an envoy of Kublai traveling back to China.

The tomb of the Samanids in Bukhara, constructed circa 900, is the oldest building in Central Asia. Its design was inspired by pre-Islamic Sogdian architecture.

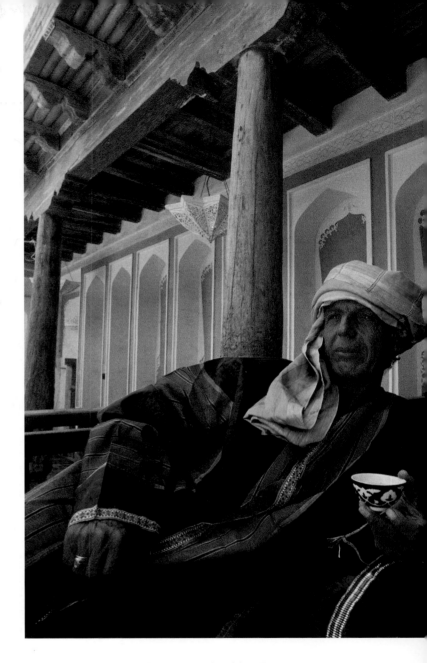

Mobinjan relaxing on a divan in the courtyard of his 229-year-old house in Bukhara, Uzbekistan. Honoring a promise he made to his mother on her deathbed, he was in the midst of restoring the home to its former splendor.

When the envoy saw them, he was surprised and said; Sirs, I assure you that the Great Khan of the Tartars has never seen a Latin and is desirous to meet one, if you accompany me to him, he will treat you with great honor, and you will be able to travel with me in safety and without hindrance.

If not for this fortuitous meeting we would have never heard of Marco Polo, for only a few Westerners had dared to venture beyond this point since Alexander the Great. In fact, most people do not realize that Niccolo and Maffeo Polo helped pave the way on the Silk Road for all Europeans who followed in their footsteps, including Marco. To venture into this unknown world took enormous courage.

It's hard for us today to grasp what the Mongols represented in the minds of thirteenth-century Europeans. Their meteoric rise was believed by some to be the onset of the end of days. They were the very horsemen of the apocalypse. So, just what motivated the Polos? Surely it wasn't just turning a good profit. They must have possessed that certain innate sense of wonder and curiosity that spurs all true explorers to risk everything . . . only to find bliss in what they feared most.

馬哥孛羅

"If you would have told me a year ago that I'd be in a highly restricted area of the former Soviet Union with an invalid visa in my passport and pissed off because what used to be the KGB wouldn't let me cross a river into the chaos of a civil war, I would have said you were crazy," I said to Fran one day, as we sought relief from the sweltering August heat in a pomegranate orchard. "Now I'm questioning my own sanity." Beyond the checkpoints and the guard towers, overlooking the Amu Darya River and bridge, we could see Afghanistan.

In what was becoming a habit, we'd been stuck for weeks, waiting for permission to move on. Just how we finagled visas through two of the most repressive regimes in the former USSR is a whole other tale deserving its own chapter, but I must go on. As Marco would say, *What need to make a long story of it?*

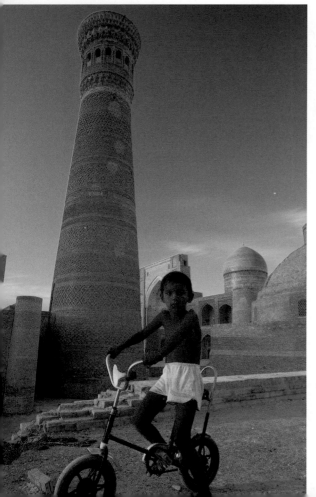

The Kalon Minaret, built in 1127. For centuries the enemies and criminals of Bukhara were thrown off this 155-foot minaret, known as the tower of death. Legend holds that Genghis Khan himself spared it because of its beauty.

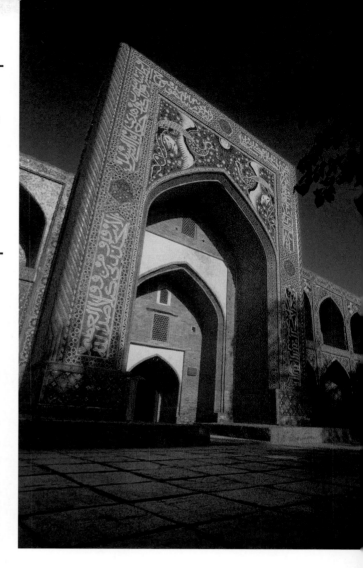

The Nadir Divan-Beghi madrasah, built in 1622. Initially constructed as a caravanserai, this madrasah's majestic façade is embellished by phoenixes, representing Bukhara's rise from the ashes left after the firestorm of the Mongol invasion.

It is necessary in Uzbekistan's police state to have visas to visit individual cities and towns. With dogged persistence, flattery, baksheesh, and by way of an angel, we miraculously obtained them for Termiz, the most strategically sensitive and militarized town in the whole country. But still the border guards stopped us cold. They said we needed to get visas just to cross the bridge. We were trapped now in the former Soviet Republic, our Termiz visas expired.

"We've been personas non gratas with valid visas and now we don't even have those. What the hell are we going to do?" I asked Fran over the hiss of cicadas in the dry yellow field.

"Forge ourselves a new date and give ourselves more time," he answered. "What the hell, we've tried everything else, including bribery." That night I carefully changed the number "one" in seventeen to a "two," buying us an additional ten days until the end of the month.

But still we got nowhere. Day after day, a KGB agent masquerading as a bureaucrat questioned us. He held our passports in his skeletal hands while he repeated his monotonous questions: What were we doing in Uzbekistan? How had we obtained these visas? Why did an ex-Marine and a photographer want to go to Afghanistan?

"How many times do we need to go over this?" I asked in exasperation, trying to grab back the passports before my forgery could be detected.

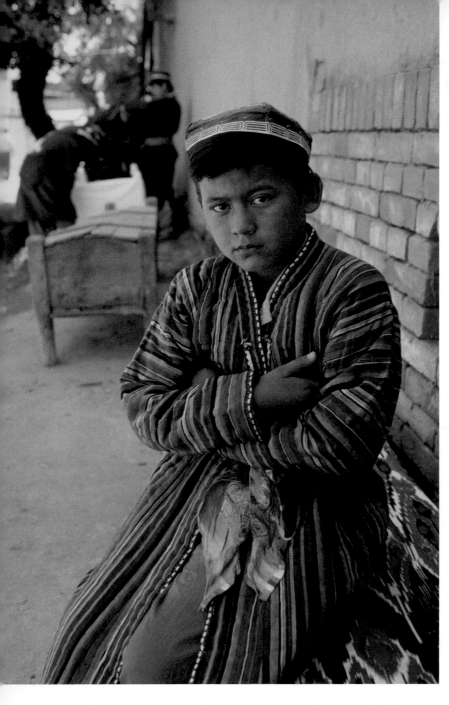

As his father is being prepared for burial, a Jewish boy sits in mourning, dressed in a coat of many colors. After being cut off from the rest of the Jewish world for more than 2,000 years, the Jews of Bukhara have recently fled Uzbekistan in an exodus.

"We have to get the American embassy in Tashkent involved," Fran said as we walked back to the United Nations High Commission for Refugees (UNHCR) compound we had talked ourselves into.

"Who knows how long that will take? We've lost too much time; the mountain passes will be snowed in," I said.

"We might have to wade across the river on one of those ancient, air-filled goatskin rafts we saw the other day," he suggested.

"The banks on either side are heavily mined," I reminded him. "Besides, they're looking for smugglers doing that; we'd get shot."

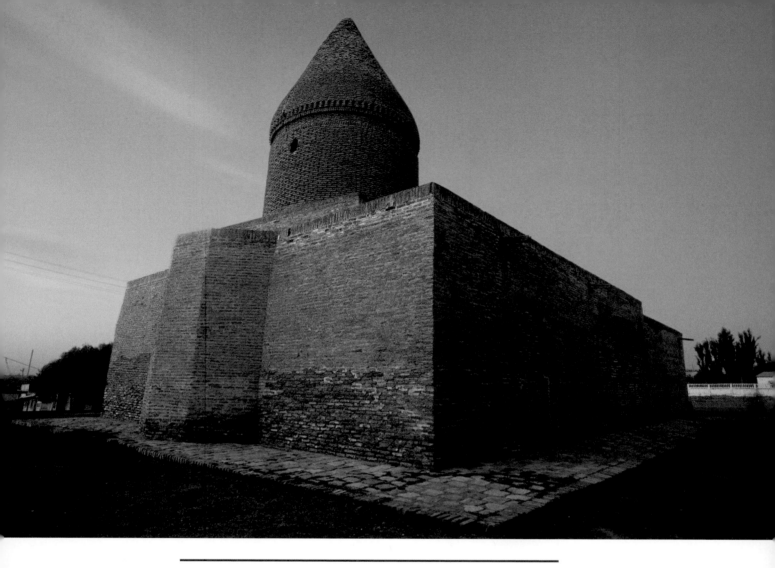

*The Chasma Ayub Mausoleum, or Job's Well, built in 1160.
Bukhara is the most complete and unspoiled example of a
medieval Central Asian town. It is said that the Chasma
Ayub was built over a natural spring, which the biblical
prophet Job created by striking his staff in the desert sand.*

Finally even our forgeries expired. Out of blind frustration, Fran rebelled. "We're going," he said out loud, two or three times, as if trying to convince himself. By the time we saw the KGB agent again he was cold and controlled. "We're American citizens being held here against our will," he said. "Our visas for your country have expired. Do you want an international incident? We're crossing into Afghanistan tomorrow. Are you going to let us go or are you going to shoot us?"

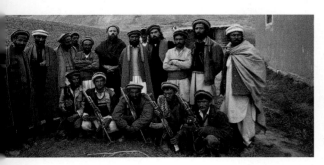

AFGHANISTAN

The Word of a Warlord

JUST AFTER DAWN, WE CROSSED THE IRONICALLY NAMED Friendship Bridge, which the Russians had built to transport war supplies into Afghanistan. I remembered the footage of withdrawing Soviet tanks bumping along this steel expanse in 1989, slinking away from ten years of futile fighting. For us, the fear and uncertainty of crossing the Amu Darya River in the opposite direction was a rush of pure adrenaline, and though it was only a few hundred feet, felt much longer.

Marco Polo never needed to forge a visa. Documents we'd found impossible to get in order to cross the troubled borders of today were of little worry for the young Venetian.

> The Great Khan gave the brothers a tablet of gold, on which was inscribed that the ambassadors should be supplied with everything needful in all the countries through which they should pass—with horses, with escorts and, in short, with whatever they should require.

Our golden tablets were the letters we had secured from Mr. K addressed to various warlords along Polo's route. After sewing them into our clothes, we guarded them carefully, for without them we literally wouldn't survive.

As we entered northern Afghanistan, a soldier in unlaced high-top sneakers and mismatched camouflage fatigues waved us casually through the checkpoint. His Kalashnikov leaned unattended against a dilapidated brick post topped with barbed wire. He did not check our documents, assuming correctly that the guys in the sharply pressed uniforms on the other side of the border in Uzbekistan—the Russian troops with their spit-polished boots and shiny hammer-and-sickle insignias still in place—had done a good job of it.

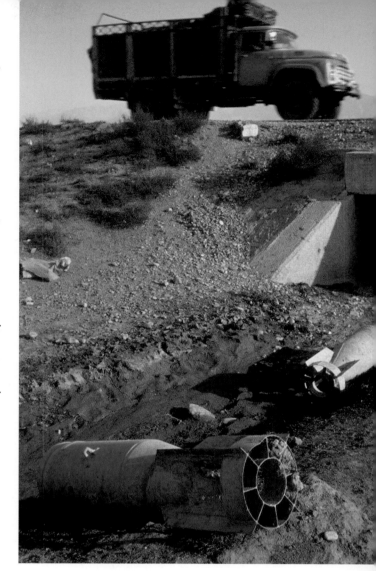

Undetonated Soviet bombs littered the road to Mazar-e Sharif and were a sobering reminder of the myriad dangers we would face in the coming months.

The road to Mazar-e Sharif lay flat and straight before us, like a pale gray ribbon stretched across the Kara-Kum Desert to the foothills of the Hindu Kush Mountains.

Lavender and yellow desert flowers grew around the burned-out tanks and armored personnel carriers that dotted the landscape, enduring monuments to the devastating war that had killed a million Afghans and left countless thousands maimed. Undetonated bombs bearing Soviet markings littered the verges of the pockmarked road.

The sky was gray and overcast, but in the distance the sun was breaking through, streaking "God-rays" down on highlighted hills. We passed a few military garrisons with anti-aircraft cannons poised on the roofs and camouflaged tanks parked outside and ready. Every couple of miles we saw crude shacks housing two or three sentries. War was an everyday fact of the life in this ravaged land. The tribes who had united to fight the invader had turned their weapons on one another, and now every day was a bloody struggle for land and control.

As we approached Mazar-e Sharif, adobe structures, some with tall towers and castlelike fortifications, seemed to spring from the surrounding sand. Traffic began to build as cars, trucks, motorcycles, brick-laden horse and donkey carts, slow-moving sheep, and camels carrying heaps of straw shared one of the last paved roads in Afghanistan. Everyone was carrying weapons, including the kids.

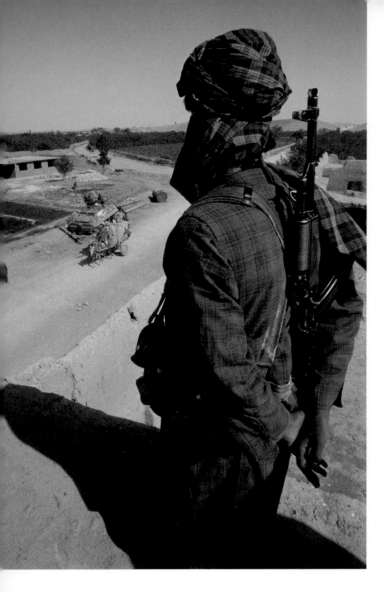

Checkpoints were always tense for us. The tribes who had united to defeat the Russians were now fighting one another in what historians are calling the "warlord period."

A looming billboard portrait of the ruthless Uzbek warlord, General Abdul Rashid Dostum, was a forbidding welcome. We wanted to make contact with Commander Ustad Atta Mohammad, the Tajik warlord and Dostum's rival for control of the region.

Atta, the leader of Jamiat-i-Islami (Islamic Society) forces, was our key contact and the only person who could guarantee our safety.

"How can we find him?" I asked Fran. "We can't just pick up a phone and call, because there are no phones, and we can't just choose someone at random off the street and ask directions—not without knowing what side he was on."

"Yeah. The friend of my enemy is my enemy," he acknowledged, repeating the well-worn adage of the region.

Once again, we would have to approach our goal in a Byzantine way, going through layers of people and hoping we'd end up in the right place. Meanwhile, we wandered around taking pictures—and getting noticed. Between two tractors stopped in the center of the road, an old man struggled with his stubborn mule, trying to get him moving again. We gave him a hand and were rewarded with a smile and a blessing: "May you never be tired."

Under the stern and watchful gaze of Dostum's portrait, young boys hawked gasoline out of jerry cans. In a small open bazaar, a cluster of women, veiled from head to toe in the traditional pleated burqa, their faces covered with mesh masks, rummaged through boxes of used clothing. Next to a string of kebab houses stood a butcher shop,

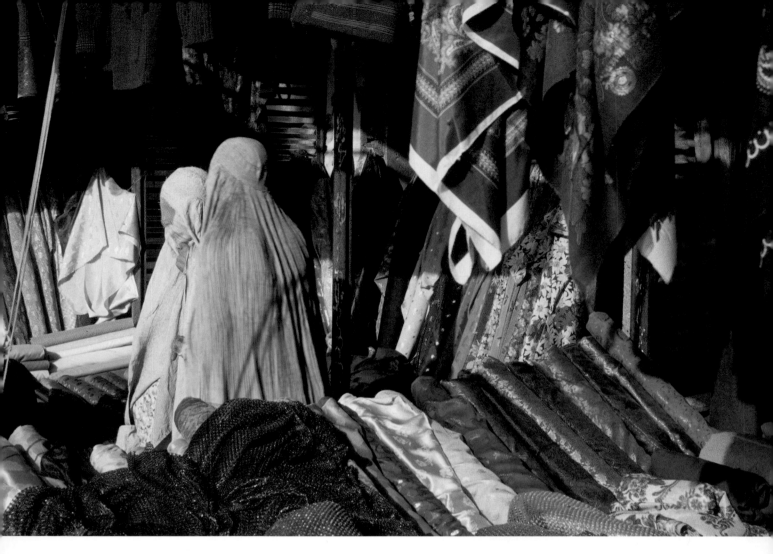

Seemingly camouflaged, two women in burqas shop in a colorful market in the center of Mazar-e Sharif.

its owner swatting flies from the unrefrigerated meat that hung from metal hooks. A sheep was being bled by the neck according to the Islamic law of halal. Blood mixed with the sawdust from the carpentry shop next door where craftsmen fashioned doorjambs and window frames. The sounds of trade and commerce joined with the sounds of hammer on steel and saw through wood. Mazar was in the midst of a construction boom.

In one of the metalworking stalls, a little boy in thick metal goggles was welding the frame of a donkey cart. We learned that his name was Najibullah and that he had been orphaned in the war. He was only ten years old, but it soon became clear that childhood was brief or nonexistent here.

As we meandered around the corner people called out "chai, chai," beckoning us to their shops. We stopped, once, twice, three or four times, sharing cups of the local heavily sugared version, communicating with phrases in Turkish and English and Dari, with friendly gestures and shared cigarettes. No one would let us pay.

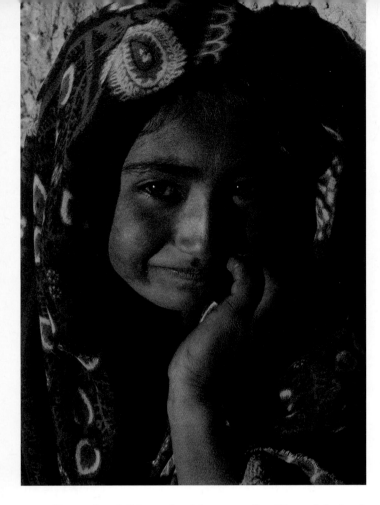

The Afghans have been afflicted by one of the greatest tragedies of modern times—nearly thirty years of warfare, which have left untold dead and maimed. As is usual in such dire circumstances it is the children who suffer the most.

Since the Afghans had become familiar with foreign reporters during the war, we told people we were journalists. It was easier than trying to explain Marco Polo. As we roamed back streets and alleyways, stopping for bits of conversation whenever a friendly face beckoned, something became clear to us. Years of fighting and bloodshed had left the people weary, and many now viewed the mujahideen as outlaws and thugs. We heard over and over again how the people wanted peace, to get on with life, to have what—by accident of birth—we took for granted.

In the heart of the town, thousands of white doves circled the majestic blue dome of the great mosque, the Shrine of Hazrat Ali. Perhaps the holiest site in Afghanistan, it is the presumed resting place of the son-in-law of the Prophet Muhammad. So sacred is the tomb to the Afghans, they covered it with earth to hide it during the Mongol invasion.

In search of temporary lodging, we sought out Raja Wickremasinghe, a UNHCR official we'd been told might help us while we searched for Commander Atta. We found Raja in a yurt, a domed felt tent, in the Sakhi refugee camp set up for the thousands fleeing the civil war over the border in Tajikistan. A tall Sri Lankan ex–Air Force colonel with short-cropped salt-and-pepper hair, Raja was a formidable figure who reminded us of Colin Powell. He was not intimidated by the warlords who were constantly ripping off his supply trucks. "I got in one guy's face once," he said, "and he put a gun to my head. I pushed it away, then thought, 'It's not worth losing it over a bunch of firewood.'"

When we said we'd like to meet Commander Atta, Raja seemed concerned. "We get more assistance out of Dostum and the Uzbeks," he said. "Getting to Atta is not easy, but let me see what I can do."

Armed with one of Mr. K's precious letters of introduction, we were picked up and driven to Jamiat-i-Islami headquarters, a villa-turned-fortress on the outskirts of town. An iron gate was set into high adobe walls surrounded by sandbags and dozens of heavily armed warriors. A tank was moved to let us enter. Once inside, we passed a high-tech communications center and climbed a flight of stairs. The rooms and corridors were packed with soldiers, cleaning and readying their weapons. We were ushered into a spacious office and told to wait.

On the wall, above a poster of Islam's holiest site—the Kaaba in Mecca—were several framed portraits: charismatic leader Ahmad Shah Massoud; Commander Ishmael Khan, the lord of the western city of Herat; and Professor Burhanuddin Rabbani, the contested president of Afghanistan and head of the Jamiat party. We sat down with a group of commanders and advisers, sipping tea and making small talk in English. "You are Americans," said a slender young soldier, a smile on his face. He told us of his war injuries and his evacuation by the CIA through Pakistan for treatment. "Very good doctors in California," he said, "very good hospitals. Thank you very much."

Suddenly the door swung open. The room was filled with the powerful presence of Ustad Atta Muhammad in full battle fatigues and a black leather jacket. Thick eyebrows shaded dark, expressive eyes, and a perfectly groomed beard cascaded down his chest in tight black curls like an Assyrian king's. He held a walkie-talkie, much as an executive might hold a BlackBerry. Atta's elite guard and security personnel followed, and the room became crowded. Everyone stood up to give the standard Afghan litany of greetings: *As-salaam alaikum*, *Khūbasti*, *Chitorasti*, *Jonjorasti* (Peace be with you, How is your health? Your family? Your well-being?), punctuated by placing the right hand over the heart.

Commander Atta gave us an expansive two-handed handshake and sat down. We all followed suit. We handed over the letter we'd been carrying for several months and watched intently as he read. How would he react? We desperately needed his approval and help. If he blew us off, we'd be finished.

He put down the letter, smiled, and leaned back into his chair. We exhaled. "First, I want to welcome you to Afghanistan," he said. "The man who entrusted you with this letter is a brother to me. I will give you any assistance within my power."

Atta listened to us attentively and though it was clear he had no idea of what we were after or who Marco Polo was, he said he would help. "The territories between Mazar and Taloqan are extremely dangerous," he said. "For your own safety, I will give you a helicopter that will take you directly to the Badakshan region. Then if you wish you can go visit our great hero Ahmad Shah Massoud."

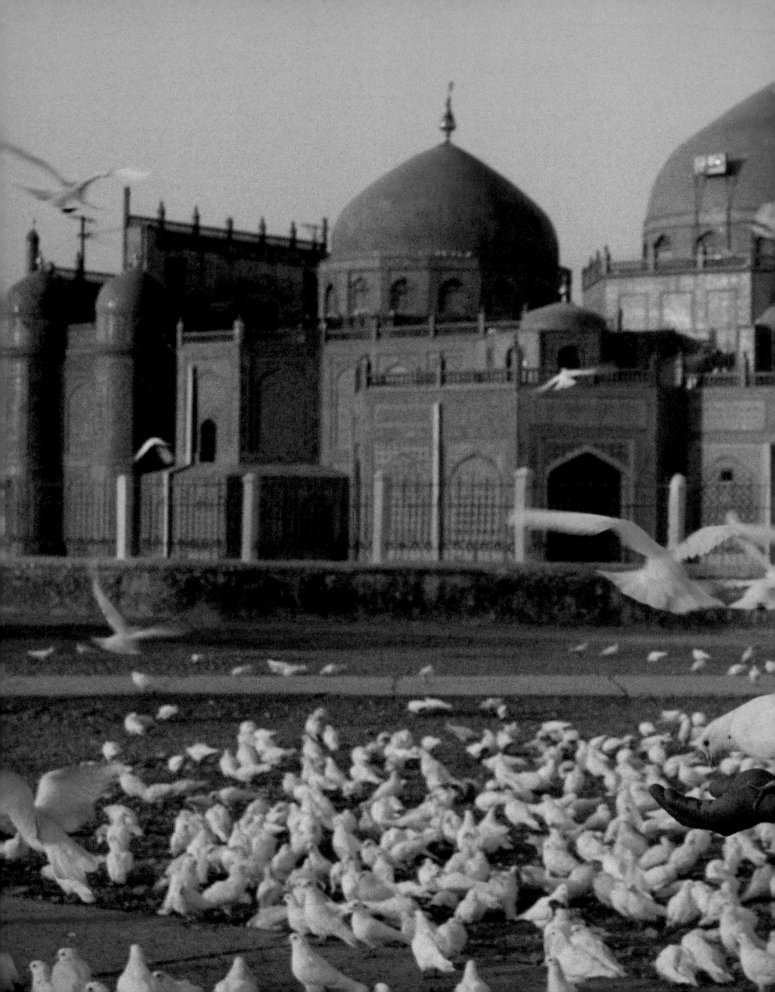

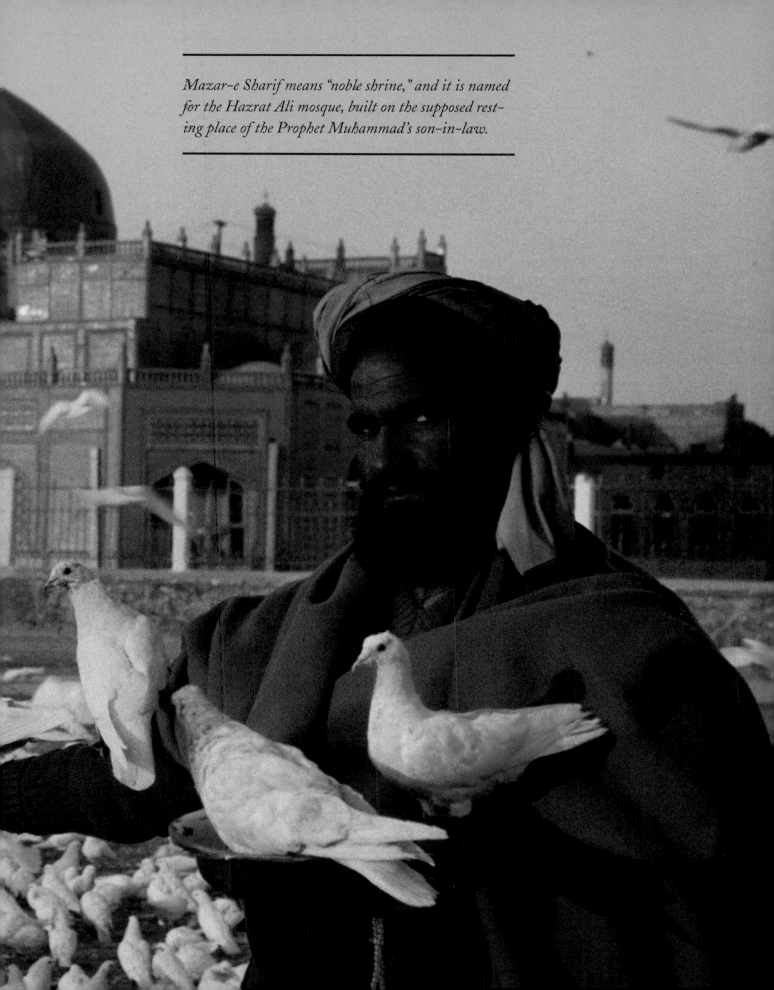

Mazar–e Sharif means "noble shrine," and it is named for the Hazrat Ali mosque, built on the supposed resting place of the Prophet Muhammad's son-in-law.

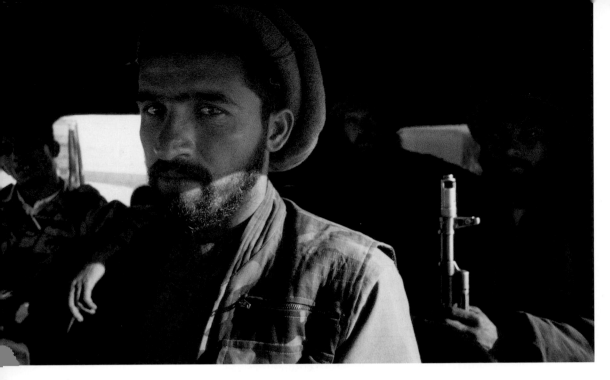

Waseq in the passenger seat, Mustafa at the wheel, and Fran in the backseat with a bodyguard on the day we went to Balkh.

Uh oh, I thought. The man had just made an incredibly generous offer and we'd love to meet Massoud, but how do we decline without offending? We thanked him for his kindness. "But we can't take the helicopter, we need to travel as Polo did—overland. No flying."

"I see." He nodded. If he thought we were crazy, he was too polite to show it. As he began to discuss our route with his generals, the slender young soldier with a wispy attempt of a beard on his chin whispered into my ear. "I am called Waseq," he said. "The man who wrote your letter is my uncle. Since you are friends of his, I would be honored to accompany you. Will you ask Commander Atta if I may go?"

It was more luck than we could have hoped for. Waseq was Mr. K's nephew. If the friend of your enemy is your enemy in this part of the world, then the friend of your friend is your ally—a truth that instantly bridges oceans of difference.

Waseq was Atta's chief of security, so we made the request diffidently, not knowing how Atta would feel about giving him up. To our surprise he nodded approvingly. He seemed to feel it would be fitting for Waseq to safeguard us, just as Waseq had watched over him. "I'll give you men and jeeps, as many as necessary. When will you be ready?" We thanked him profusely, amazed that in the midst of his own private war, Atta was ready to commit men and much-needed resources to a project he did not understand simply on the request of an honored friend.

In the months to come, we would see the power of such requests demonstrated again and again. Wherever we showed our letters, we were given food, shelter, horses, and supplies—in short, the same kind of assistance Polo received when he displayed the golden tablet of the Great Khan.

BALKH

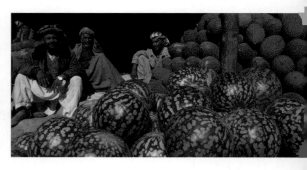

The Mother of All Cities

WE AWOKE AFTER YET ANOTHER MORNING in the villa to the sound of shooting. After weeks in the war-torn country, we had grown accustomed to automatic weapons fire. We had learned to go to sleep to it, watching the red glare of tracer fire light up the dark skies, and were awakened by it, like an alarm clock we couldn't shut off. We knew how to distinguish between exuberant shots that celebrated a wedding or birth or a true firefight, simply by the rhythm of the blasts.

"We want to go to Balkh," we had told Atta the night before. A lift of his bushy eyebrows told us what he thought of the idea. But in his matter-of-fact way, he assigned us a jeep. Waseq would escort us.

The gunfire that morning seemed to be more widespread than usual, but when we mentioned this to Waseq and our driver Mustafa, they seemed unconcerned. We piled into the jeep. As we rode, Fran read aloud from *The Travels*:

> *Balkh is a splendid city of great size. It used to be much greater and more splendid, but the Tartars and other invaders have sacked and ravaged it. For I tell you that there used to be many fine palaces and mansions of marble, which are still to be seen, but shattered now and in ruins.*

Balkh was a name that stirred the imagination, a place that seduced archaeologists with promises of magnificent artifacts yet unseen. More important for us, the ancient capital of the great Bactrian Empire had been a prime stop on Polo's route.

We drove about two miles toward the center of Mazar, then turned onto a street that normally would be bustling with activity. It was empty. Shops were boarded up, fruit stands deserted. A car stood abandoned in the middle of the street, the driver's door ajar. "Maybe we should turn back," I said aloud, as the sound of gunfire was getting

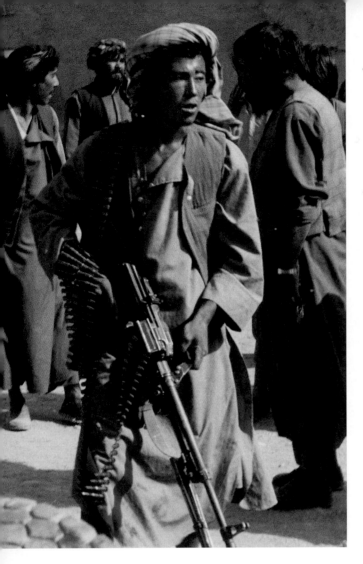

closer. But being professional soldiers, Mustafa and Waseq wanted to investigate and gather intelligence. Mustafa reported our location on his walkie-talkie, and it seemed our trip had turned into a reconnaissance operation.

At the far end of the dirt street, we suddenly saw the crouched figures of armed men carrying a fallen comrade. We heard warning shouts, but it was too late. Our jeep slowed to a stop as a terrified boy, maybe fifteen years old, crept in front of us, his assault rifle trained on my face. A second later, ever so slowly relinquishing his cover, a second combatant emerged, his rocket launcher pointed at our windshield. *This is it*, I thought. *My life's over, done, I'm dead*. I envisioned the jeep going up in a fireball and turned to Fran in the backseat. He looked grim.

Shouting in Dari, the guy with the rocket launcher motioned our jeep to follow. The fifteen-year-old ran alongside us, banging directions on the passenger side window with the muzzle of his gun. I stared at his finger, fixed on the trigger, at the sweat that beaded his brow, fearing that at any moment he would empty his clip into our vehicle, into us. He waved us onto a side street, where we were instantly swarmed by armed fighters and dragged from the jeep.

"Journalist!" I shouted, pointing to my cameras. "BBC! Journalist!" I didn't know if the name of the BBC would keep them from shooting us, but I prayed that something would.

Mustafa and Waseq were stripped of their weapons but even as his bayonet was yanked from the sheath of his cartridge belt, Mustafa kept speaking into his walkie-talkie, giving our location and situation. His message was clear: Others know where we are. Kill us and there will be reprisals.

We were pushed up against a wall at gunpoint while they dragged Waseq and Mustafa off to one side. We looked at each other, fully aware this might well be our last moment on earth. The gunfire around us grew even louder, the smell of smoking gunpowder filling the air. We heard the splats of bullets, the ping of ricochets. Standing on an oil drum next to us, a machine gunner returned fire over the wall. His empty, still hot cartridges rained down and bounced all over us, forcing my eyes downward on his filthy feet in blue plastic flip-flops as he shouted for more ammo between bursts.

Standing against that wall, I wished I were an orphan. My life didn't flash before my eyes, but the rest of my parents' lives did as an image of them receiving the news of my death made me shudder. Fran turned to me. "If we get out of this alive, we're out of this country."

"No doubt!" I replied. "No friggin' doubt!"

We watched as Mustafa and Waseq were pushed and pulled by the gauntlet of soldiers that had formed around them. I strained to decipher the chorus of angry, guttural sounds. Whatever was going on, Mustafa and Waseq showed no fear or agitation, even as they were forced to their knees—execution-style. My heart was racing and my mouth was dry. Everything seemed to be happening in slow motion. "Stay calm, stay calm, they despise fear. They might kill our boys, but they'll probably keep us as hostages," I whispered to Fran.

I turned my camera on the gunman who held us, looking through the lens at fierce eyes glowering at me. It was a strange feeling, framing the image but never taking my eyes off the face of a man who was holding a gun to my head. He lowered the weapon. I took the picture, the lens separating me from the reality of the situation, as if I was viewing it from afar.

Suddenly a white car came careening down the street, rifles out the windows firing furiously into the sky. We fell to the ground. The car disappeared among the cheers of our captors. The firing ceased, voices that had been raised in anger dissipated. Dramatically, guns were lowered. Grim expressions changed into smiles.

"What the hell is going on?" I asked Fran.

Mustafa came over to us and explained: These men belonged to the Hezbe Wahdat faction and were under attack by the Uzbek forces of General Dostum, who wanted to disarm them. Not about to surrender their weapons without a fight, they had just pushed the Uzbeks back. Realizing we were with Tajiks (who this particular day were not the enemy), they let us go.

The relief that swept over me was as powerful as the fear. I was incredibly happy to be alive. Waseq told us to get back in the jeep. We were not their enemies, but in this fierce and tragic country, lives could be cheap in the heat of confrontation.

The boy who'd shoved his gun into our faces now smiled and ran ahead to see if it was safe to cross the road. When he gave the all-clear sign, we drove away, snaking through side streets and back alleys, heading for a Jamiat-i-Islami stronghold across the street from the Hazrat Ali mosque.

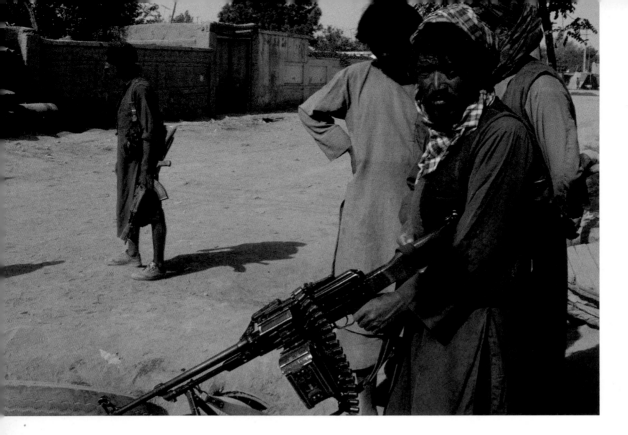

This fierce warrior had his machine gun pointed at us just seconds before this photo was taken. Another fighter looks on as our bodyguards are forced to their knees in the street.

While we were against the wall we had studied our captors' faces. Their Mongoloid features marked them as Hazaras, a minority ethnic group of Shi'a Muslims believed to be the descendants of Genghis Khan's hordes.

> *They are banditti . . . the sons of Indian mothers by Tartar fathers. . . .*
> *Man, woman or beast, nothing can escape them! . . . The old men*
> *whom they take . . . they butcher; the young men and women they*
> *sell for slaves. . . . I must add the fact that Messer Marco himself was*
> *all but caught. . . . Howbeit he lost his whole company except seven*
> *persons who escaped with him. The rest were caught, some were sold,*
> *some put to death.*

It seemed that for us, there were no coincidences. This very same tribe ambushed Marco Polo himself. Despite hundreds of years of persecution, the Hazaras have retained their sense of bravery, determination, and will to survive. Certainly their Mongol characteristics set them apart from other Afghan tribes and are a living testament to the scope and breadth of the Great Khan's empire.

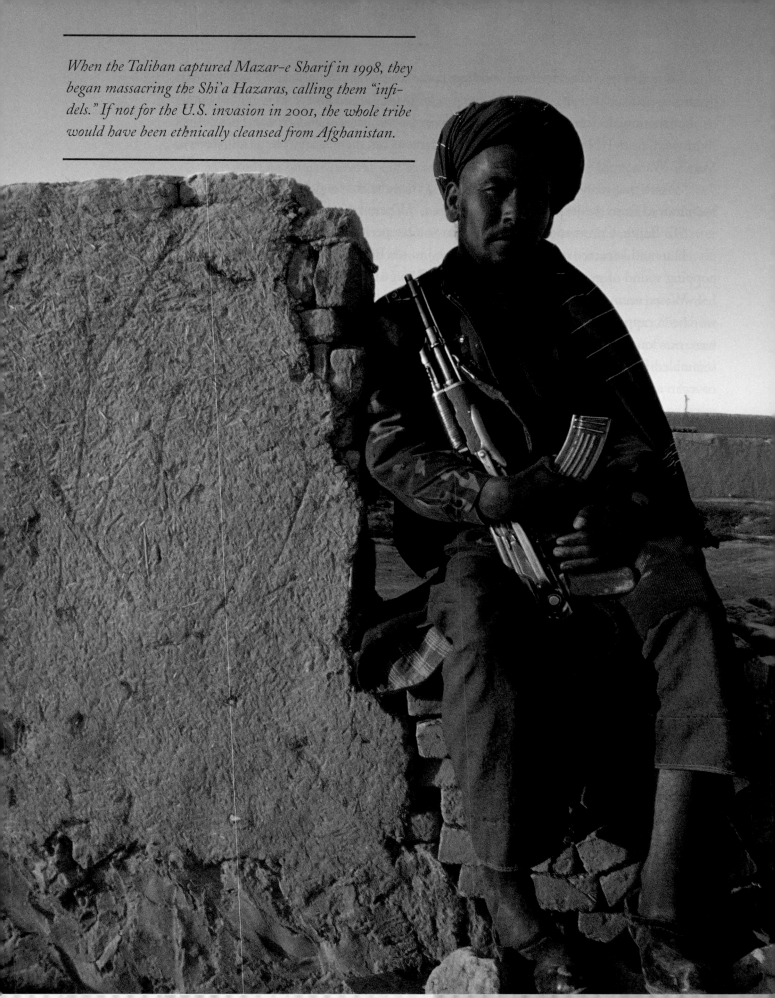

When the Taliban captured Mazar-e Sharif in 1998, they began massacring the Shi'a Hazaras, calling them "infidels." If not for the U.S. invasion in 2001, the whole tribe would have been ethnically cleansed from Afghanistan.

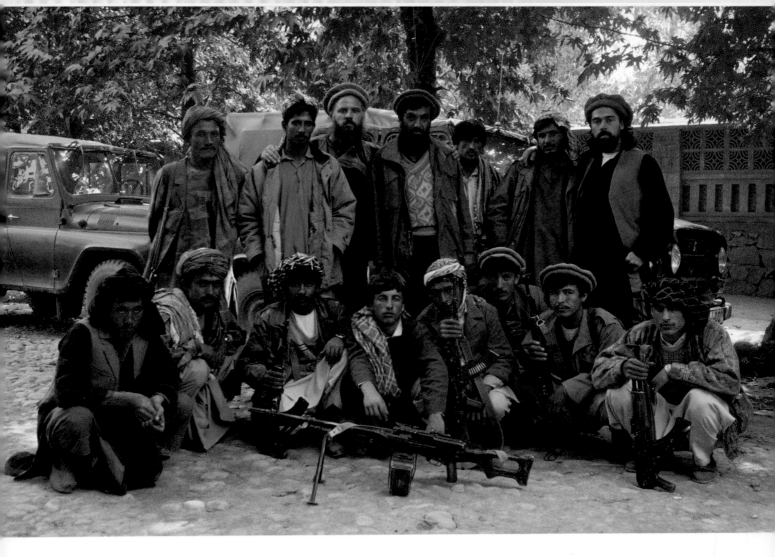

Fran (third from left) stands between Waseq and General Wahab (center); I'm on the far right, along with some of our bodyguards in Talikhan.

people are among the most extraordinary on earth. The Afghans have also been affected by one of the greatest tragedies of this century—the longest running civil war in this era, which has brought untold misery. . . . Their story and their character invoke immense contradictions. Brave, magnificent, honorable, generous, hospitable, gracious, handsome, Afghan men and women can also be devious, mean, and bloody-minded.

馬哥孛羅

The night before we left to cross the country, Atta gave a feast in our honor. Heaping platters of kebabs and rice studded with raisins and nuts, towers of bread, potatoes and dumplings, melons and pomegranates covered a massive carpet. In this poor country, our feast was as lavish and sumptuous in scale as anything Polo might have received at the court of Kublai Khan.

So after traveling for six days . . . you come to a city called Sapur-gan. It has great plenty of everything, but especially the very best melons in the world. . . . When dry they are sweeter than honey and carried off for sale all over the country.

Tempted though we were by so much bounty after weeks of Spartan meals, we ate sparingly, knowing there were scores of soldiers waiting to be fed. The mood was festive, the atmosphere light. We risked a personal question. Atta's men called him *Ustad*, or teacher. "What did you teach?" we asked, thinking that he may have led an academic life before the war.

"Warfare," he said bluntly. "I teach war."

Oh. "Of course, of course, you're a great warrior, a great commander, a great teacher of war," we rambled, trying to cover whatever blunder we might have committed.

"Afghanistan has never been defeated by foreigners, they can't capture our land, our hearts, or our souls," he said, more to his surrounding soldiers than to us.

After we'd eaten and toasted the health of our hosts with cans of soda, Atta took us with Waseq into another room. "Do you know Mr. Thompson?" he asked. "Did Mr. Thompson send you? Will you be seeing him? Are you here to buy back Stinger missiles?" We shook our heads, bewildered by the queries. Atta obviously believed, despite our protests to the contrary, that we had a CIA connection. Had he worked with Mr. Thompson in the past and believed we could help revive their relationship? Was this a test of some kind, with a right and wrong answer? Did Mr. Thompson even exist?

With some experience with the logic of the East, we had come to understand that there were often hidden meanings in simple statements and questions.

"No," we said emphatically. "We don't know Mr. Thompson. Really, we don't."

He nodded philosophically. "Never mind. It's not important."

The following morning, Atta entered our room with General Abdul Wahab, his second-in-command. As tall and bearded as Atta, they could have been brothers. He gave us letters addressed to all the regional commanders along our route and said Waseq would go with us and act as interpreter.

Atta embraced and kissed us. "You are always welcome here, my brothers," he said. "We hope to see you again, inshallah." He gave Francis a fur-lined buzkashi hat. "For the Pamir," he said. He handed me a Russian bayonet because a few days earlier I had given him my buck knife after he'd admired it.

Filing down to the courtyard and our waiting vehicles, some of the soldiers we had befriended over the past few weeks came to see us off, practicing the English we had

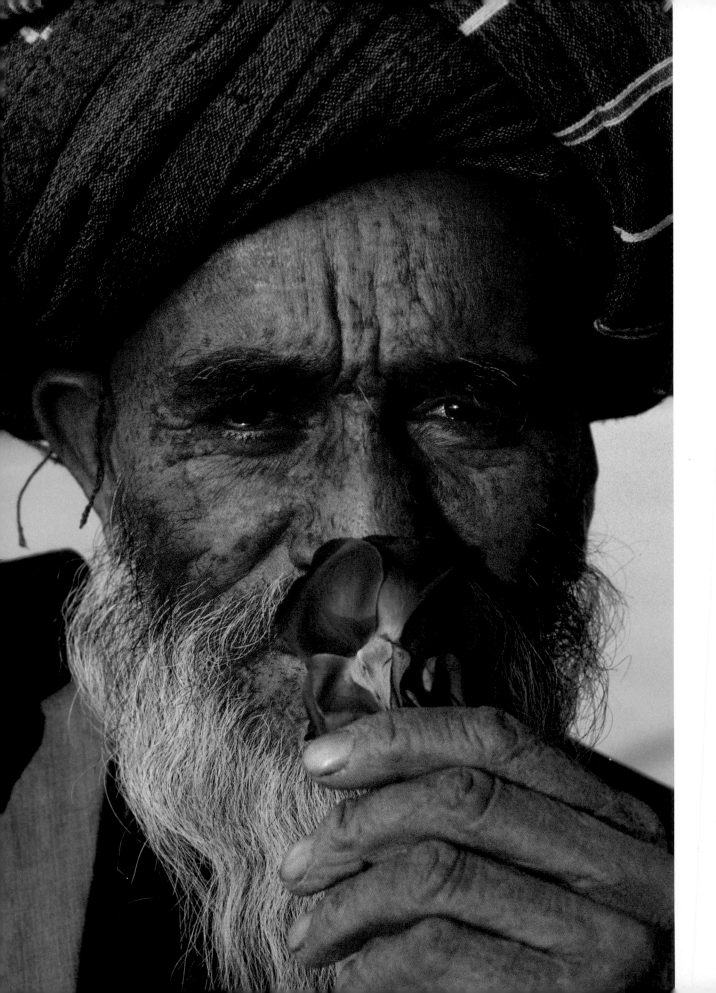

taught them. "Bye, bye," they called out. "Thank you every much!" "Hello, hello!" they shouted. As we left the villa, we wondered how many of these young men would ever reach our age.

Taking up the whole road in a scattered formation, our convoy of eight Russian jeeps, one truck, and twenty-five heavily armed bodyguards sped to Sakhi refugee camp. "Waseq, please tell General Wahab we'd like to enter the camp alone; we don't want to scare anyone, just say good-bye to a friend."

We found Raja and said our good-byes. "You guys have a lot of gall, I'll give you that," he said. "Be careful and if you make it, look me up next year when you get to Sri Lanka, my contract is up in a few months, and I'll be there."

We left him as we had found him, helping the Tajiks, who had begun to dig bunkerlike dwellings into the hard desert earth for winter. Men, women, and children were working quickly to pack mud over the beams issued to them for

(opposite page) What the Afghans all had in common was bereavement and loss, losses so terrible that we had stopped asking questions about family or spouses or children. The answers, we had learned, were painful to give and painful to hear.

The Tajik refugee graveyard in Sakhi camp on the outskirts of Mazar-e Sharif.

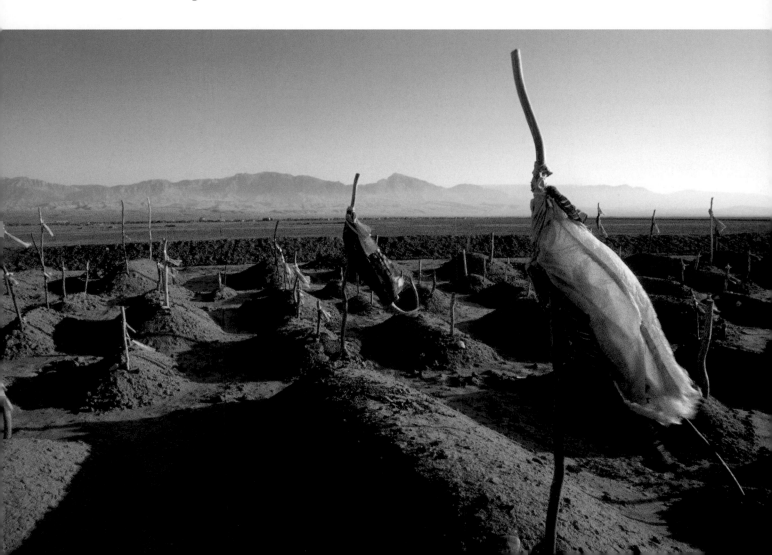

roofing. Wells were being dug, schools built, plans for a mosque considered. When we had first visited the camp we'd been struck by the size of the graveyard. "Eight hundred and eighty-five people, mostly kids under the age of five, and most died from dysentery," Raja had said. "What a shame."

Driving eastward for about three hours, we came to the mountain fortress town of Tashqurghan, where the local mujahideen had based their resistance against the Russians.

After Hafiz, the fortress commander, welcomed us, we were given chai and invited to rest. In most places, the first question people ask is what country you're from. Not in Afghanistan. The first thing they wanted to know was our religion. "We are Christians," we replied. Though we weren't very observant, in this part of the world it's inconceivable and highly suspicious for anyone to be godless. "Issa (Jesus), peace be upon him, was a great prophet," said Hafiz. He did not add, though others sometimes did, "but Muhammad is the last, greatest, and truest prophet."

The next question: were we in the military? When Francis said he'd been, Hafiz beamed and started handing us guns and Chinese-made RPGs, insisting we try them out. Before we could take advantage of this "professional courtesy," Hafiz had his men radio the next outpost and let them know that the firing they would soon hear was not for real.

Later, while sharing a meal with Hafiz and his troops, one of the soldiers—a man with a friendly face who looked more like a kind cleric than a warrior—pulled up his shirt, revealing a vivid pink scar running from his hip across his chest and onto his back. Three bullets had hit Hamza just a few short weeks before, in the midst of a forty-day siege, and his face still twisted with pain when he moved. He spoke calmly and dispassionately of being shelled and bombarded day after day by opposition troops. We listened, knowing only what history books had told us of sieges—Troy, Masada, or Stalingrad—the two sides, the outcomes, and the heroes.

In a corner of the room sat Amir, a boy of twelve. His father, Nazim, the former commander of the post, had been killed during the siege. Amir watched silently as we were shown a painting of his father holding an AK-47 and floating in clouds. A martyr guaranteed entrance to Paradise.

Amir had been given honorary command of twenty men, many old enough to be his grandfather. The little lieutenant was shown much respect, and the soldiers spoke of his valor in combat, saying he would become a great commander if he survived.

After the meal, however, Amir was expected to do cleanup duty, as befitted his tender age. But there was nothing childlike about this boy.

The next day, crossing the desert, our jeeps split out to span the width of the plain so as not to become easy targets. This maneuver had the added benefit of minimizing the sand kicked up by the vehicle in front. We'd been eating the fine baby-powder dust

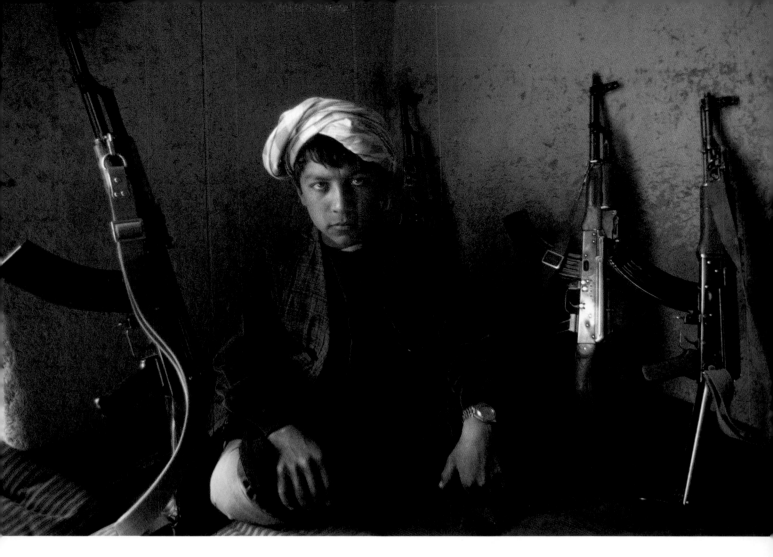

With his father killed just weeks before, twelve-year-old Amir was given honorary command of the fortress at Tashqurghan.

for days, and our hair, beards, and eyebrows—indeed everything inside the jeep—was covered with it.

Though one of our jeeps was having engine problems, General Wahab said we would have to push on. We'd have to clear this heavily disputed area as quickly as possible to arrive at the terrorist-infested town of Kunduz by night-fall. The only signs of life we passed were a few villages, whose domed roofs grew organically from the monochromatic dunes, taking on the sensuous curves of surrounding foothills. Of his trip across this desert, Polo wrote: *The traveler rides fully twelve days' journey toward the east-north-east without finding any habitation because the people have fled to mountain fastnesses for fear of the bandits and invaders who used to molest them.*

Once again his words proved prophetic. As we were funneled single file again, into a hilly pass, our driver spotted a lookout atop a golden mound. He quickly disappeared behind the dune. It was a perfect place for an ambush.

Quietly, quickly, efficiently, we were smuggled out of Kunduz. "Who betrayed us?" I asked Waseq. "Was it one of our guys?" He shook his head. "The Arabs came here to help us fight jihad against the Russians," he finally said. "Now, they think it is their country. They treat Afghans like dogs and would pay a lot for your heads."

We fell silent as Waseq lit a hashish joint, illuminating his face. "No, it was not one of our guys, but maybe someone from near the safe house . . . don't worry," he paused. "When we find him, we will kill him." His words hung in the air for a long time, refusing to mix with the sweet smoke billowing up from his spliff.

The warm glow of the rising sun made the terrain a feast of colors. Pastel shades of yellow, green, pink, and red tinted the edge of an enormous crevice. An old fort, abandoned centuries ago, clung timelessly to the opposite bank. The crevice was like an earthquake's fault line, weaving its way toward a green plain, a place where, Polo said, *the traveler finds a town called Talikhan.*

Shepherd Khalil Ali Daoud in his field.

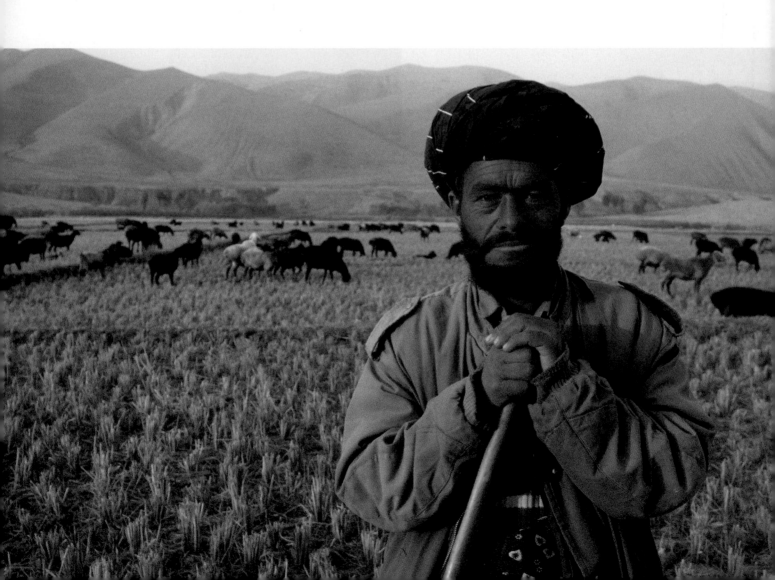

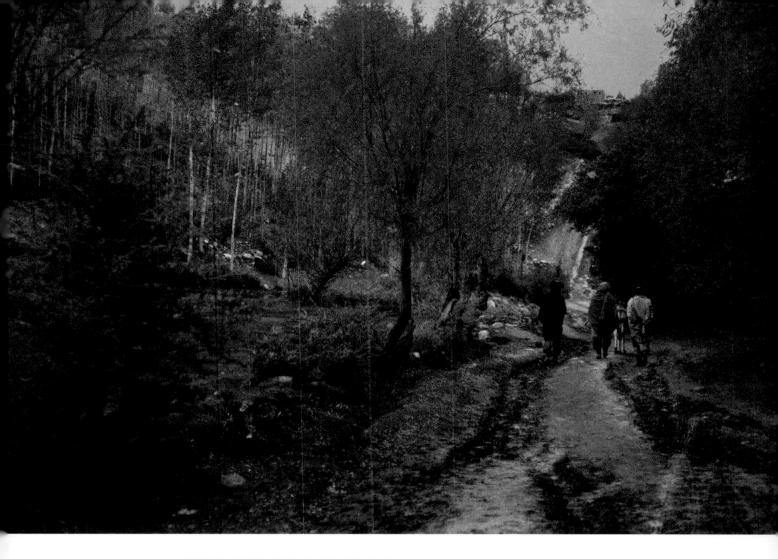

Talikhan also known as Taloqan, has huge deposits of salt under its rich soil. Something not unnoticed by Polo, "For it is esteemed the purest that is found in the world."

He remembered the fertility of the land: *It stands in very fine country.* We noticed the trees in full autumn bloom at once. There were more trees than we'd seen since home. Talikhan was indeed fertile ground. We explored the area on foot, braced by the crisp air that cascaded down from the mountains and gave us a taste of the cold that lay ahead.

*The peasants who keep cattle abide in the mountains, in caves . . .
beasts and birds for the chase there are in great abundance. Good
wheat is grown, and also barley without husk; they have no olive
oil, but make oil from sesame and also from walnuts.*

When we could, we spoke with the people who worked the land; people who, in the face of adversity, were still trying to eke out a normal life. Once, not long ago, Afghanistan was able to feed itself from the fruits of its shepherds and farmers. But years of

*When the traveler leaves Badakhshan, he goes twelve days' journey
east–north–east up a river valley.*

We found our driver trying to drum up new passenger business in the picturesque alpine town. When none appeared, we pushed on with the old man, the young woman, the four children, a goat, and a few less melons. The old guy was glad to see us. We had become friendly, sharing the camaraderie that comes with mutual discomfort.

Hajji (an honorific used by Muslims who have made a pilgrimage to Mecca) explained that the woman was not his daughter but his fourth wife; the children were theirs. Subtracting fifteen years from his appearance, we guessed that Hajji was about seventy. By her hands, we could tell his wife was young and, we imagined, pretty. With no access to over half of the population, we found ourselves enticed by a glimpse of an ankle, the delicacy of her slender fingers, or the way the wind swept the robin's-egg-colored burqa against her feminine form.

For two more days, she sat in the back of the jeep like a shrouded ghost, never uttering a word. Though she had married a wealthy man, her choices were limited to a degree we could not comprehend. In public, she must always wear a burqa. She cannot leave her home unescorted and when she does, she can go only to her father's home, her brother's house, or to the market. How strange, I thought, here you could be the closest of friends with a man for life and yet never see his wife's face. How different, then, when Polo was able to observe: *There are some ladies who in one pair of trousers or breeches put anything up to a hundred ells of cotton cloth, folded in pleats. This is to give the impression that they have plump hips, because their men folk delight in plumpness.*

This obvious hint at feminine sensuality and fertility, celebrated seven hundred years ago, is now completely covered up.

It's unfathomable how harsh women's lives are here. Some are sold by their fathers for bride-prices, others stolen and forced into slavery. Robbed of a voice, they face rape and injustice. They are an invisible gender living inside a veiled prison.

We delivered Hajji, his family, fruit, and goat to their hamlet. As he and the driver untied a sack from the roof, we caught a glimpse of his wife as she lifted her burqa and hustled the kids into their compound. She stood and stared back for a brief second, more beautiful than either of us could have imagined.

We spent the next few jarring days riding through forbidding valleys of red sandstone streaked with iron ore and imagining the wealth of lapis lazuli and rubies Polo explained were now surrounding us.

(opposite page) Sentries man the walls of the fortress in the divided river town of Ishkashim, gateway to the Wakhan Corridor.

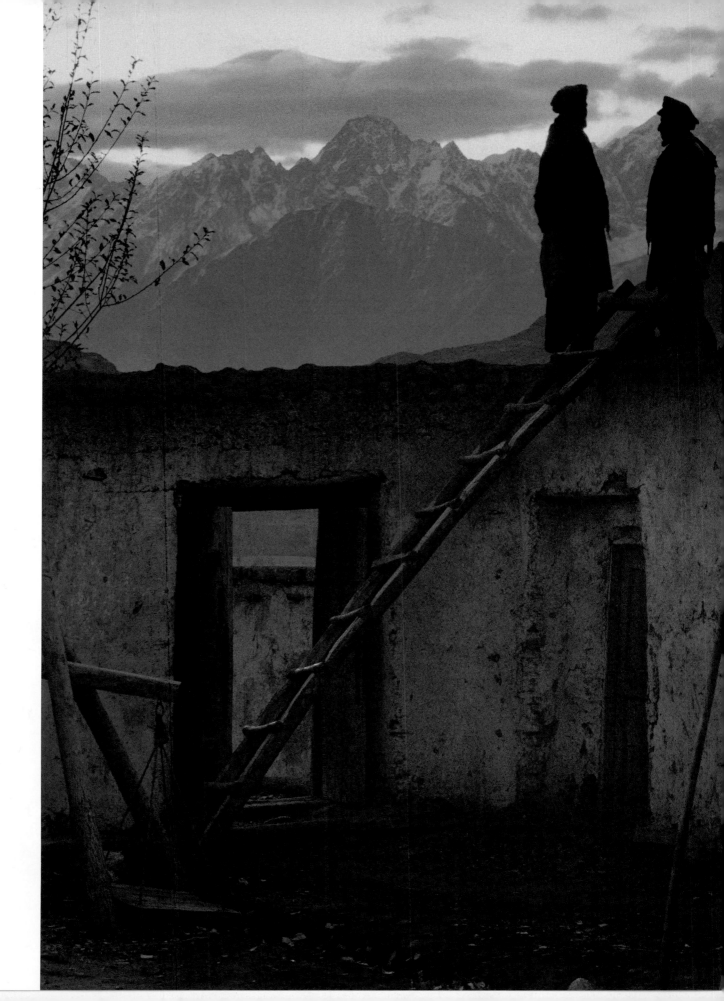

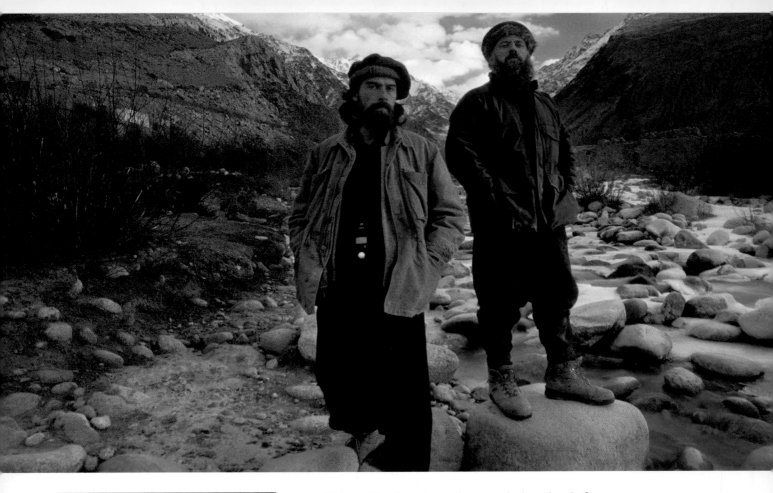

To paraphrase Peter Hopkirk in
The Great Game: *Because it is so
remote, few westerners have seen the
Oxus even today, and most of those
who have done so have viewed it
from the air.*

to China. Bordered to the north by the lofty Pamir mountain range with its dizzying peaks, hanging glaciers, and snow-capped spires and to the south by the impregnable heights of the Hindu Kush (which means "Hindu Killers"), the Wakhan Corridor takes the traveler from 9,000 feet all the way up to the Bam-i-Dunya, "The Roof of the World."

Our chance came on a crisp, golden morning. The terrain ahead of us was wild and rugged and perilous, but we were as excited as kids at Christmas. In the past seven hundred years, few outsiders had come this far, and the thrill of being the first to retrace Polo's correct route was intoxicating.

Following the Oxus, the mountains soared heavenward, flanking us with their high white walls, awing us with their terrible, timeless beauty. But this land of natural grandeur and serenity could also be hard and cold, and there were ugly reminders that danger was never far away, the first being the high, stilted guard towers that sat ominously on the Tajikistan banks of the river. The possibility of shots being fired and the ever-present risk of detonating a land mine made us carefully measure each step forward through the fields of frost-laden, yellowing grass.

The last and most remote mujahideen outpost was in Khandud, a muddy one-lane town. As we hitched our horses to a wooden post outside the fort, the villagers stopped their work and gazed at us. There were no electrical wires, no television antennas, no telephones, cars, trucks, or motorcycles—none of the noises of modern life. We heard only the sounds of rushing water, a blacksmith's hammer, and the snorting of the horses.

Abdullah, an ethnic Uzbek with high cheekbones, a strong nose, chiseled jaw, and straight black hair, reminded us of a Navajo scout. A son of the Wakhan, Abdullah knew every stone in the corridor and was greatly respected in the villages. He would be our guide for the remainder of our time in Afghanistan.

His clothes were hand-made and trimmed with the fur of an animal unknown to us, and his helmetlike gray karakul hat was the traditional headpiece of a buzkashi player. We had read about the ancient game of buzkashi, which had probably been introduced

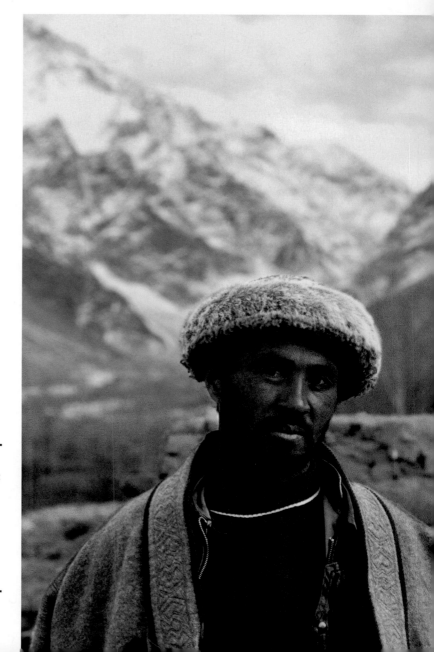

His eye still blackened from the buzkashi match played in our honor, Abdullah poses with the mighty Pamirs as a backdrop.

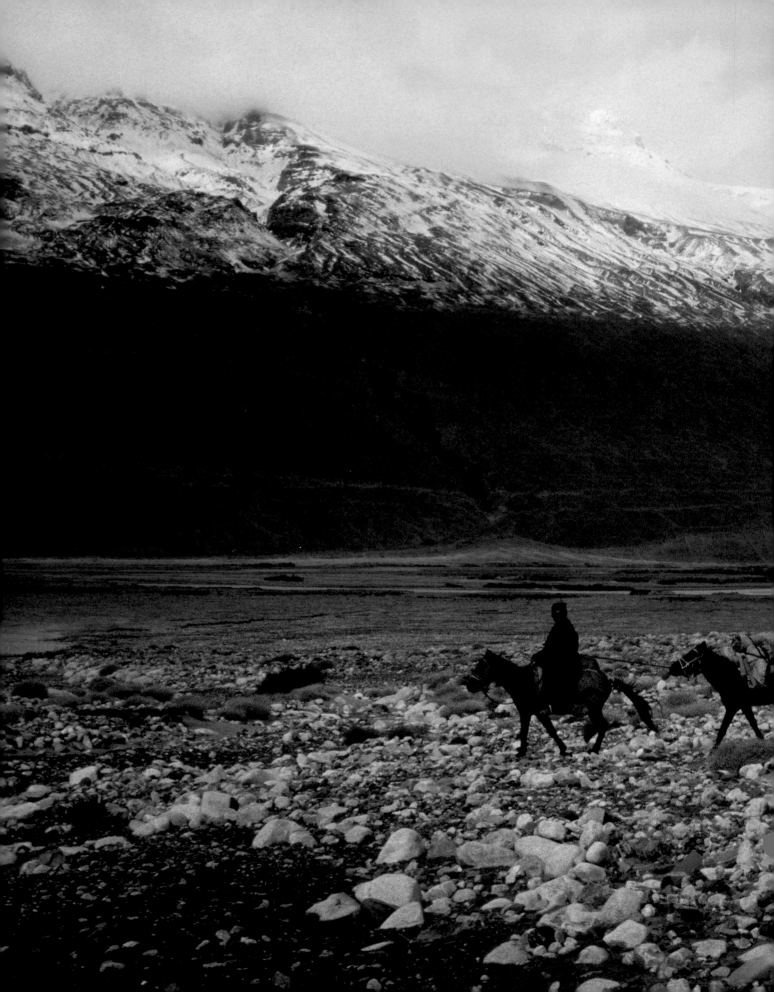

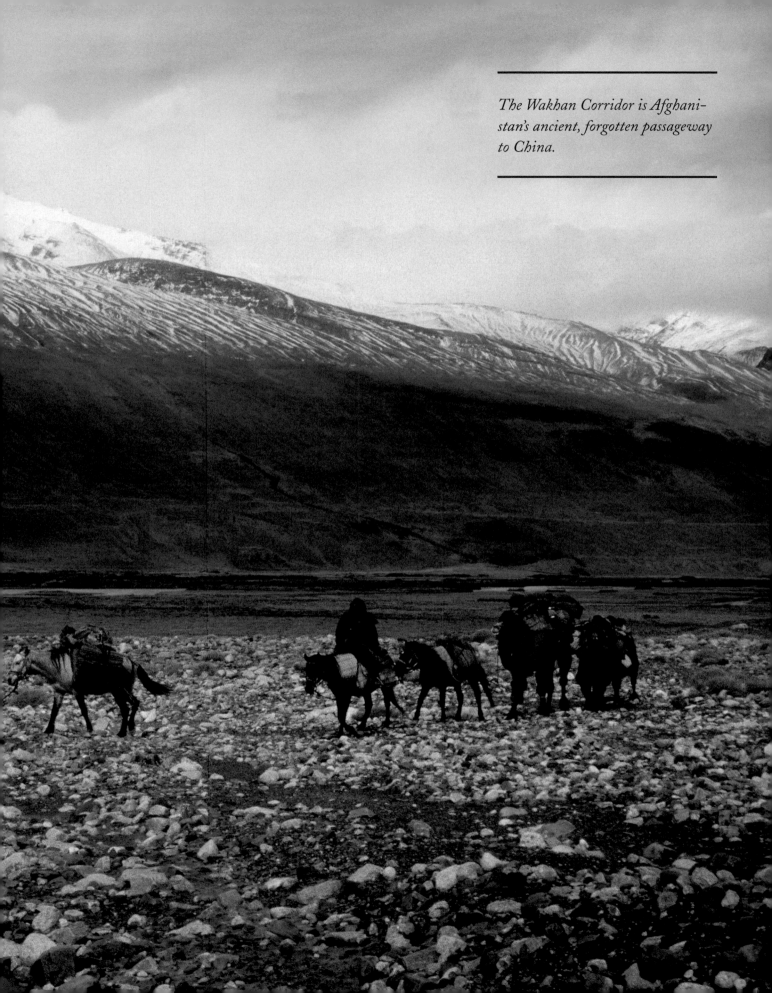

The Wakhan Corridor is Afghanistan's ancient, forgotten passageway to China.

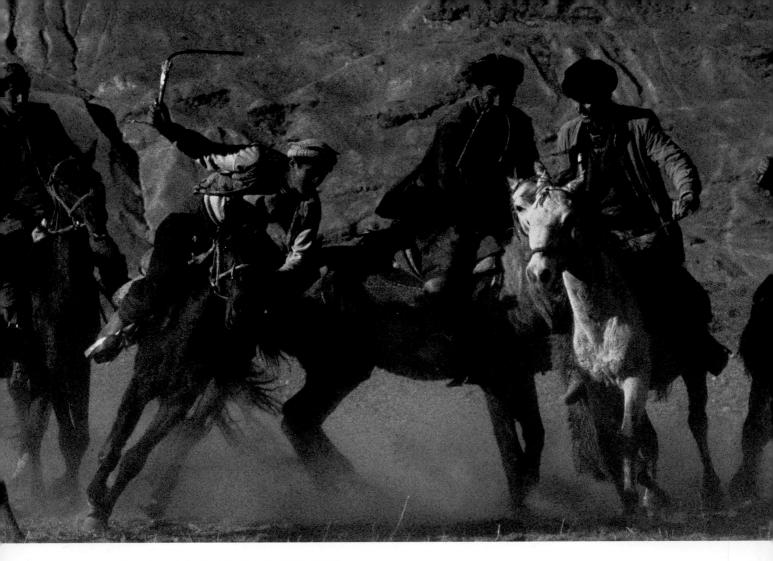

by the Mongols in the thirteenth century. Since we knew it was still popular in isolated pockets throughout Central Asia, we asked Abdullah if it was played here. He said it was and promised to organize a game in our honor.

This country . . . produces numbers of excellent horses, remarkable for their speed. They are not shod . . . although [used] in mountainous country [and] go at great pace even down deep descents, where other horses neither would nor could do like.

With the pyramid-shaped Pamirs as a backdrop, forty horsemen gathered on an open field under the bright sun. Some mounts were festively adorned, with silver-studded, hand-tooled saddles, colorful felt blankets, and embossed leather reins and bridles. Our friend Abdullah was riding a white stallion.

A sheep—the "ball" in this contest—was killed and beheaded and held up for all of us to see. The villagers shouted and cheered in anticipation of the action ahead. A circle was etched into the earth and the sheep dropped inside it. About a hundred yards away, a wooden post was driven into the ground. The object of the game was to grab the headless carcass (which weighed about seventy pounds), ride around the wooden boundary marker, return to the circle, and throw the sheep into it.

There was no starting whistle. Slowly, cagily, the riders began to move like prizefighters, each waiting for the right moment. Suddenly Abdullah broke away from the pack, swinging out in a wide, looping maneuver. Holding his reins in his teeth, hanging from his stirrups, he scooped up the sheep and thundered away, a few dozen riders in close pursuit. No sooner had he rounded the goal post than a younger man, a teenager, caught up with him and attempted to wrestle the sheep away. Without a moment's hesitation, Abdullah gave the youth's horse a savage kick, causing the animal to rear up. Advantage gained, our friend charged toward victory, kicking, flailing, battering anyone who got in the way and hurling the sheep into the ring with a mighty throw. The crowd roared their approval, rewarding him with small tokens of money and a red ribbon for his stallion.

When a rider was knocked off his horse and nearly trampled, no great fuss was made. The injured rider was simply dragged off the field and given first aid by his family. The horses continued their foamy pace and the riders became bolder and more aggressive. When a grizzled old-timer, a clear favorite with the crowd, "stole" the ball from a much younger player, everyone cheered. The youth chased the old man's horse, whacking its flank ferociously, attempting to unbalance the rider. Another player moved in and snatched the sheep. In the frenzy, the horsemen stormed into the crowd, wreaking havoc among the spectators, and destroying Fran's video camera as it hit the ground and was trampled under pounding hooves. The melee only seemed to heighten the crowd's enjoyment.

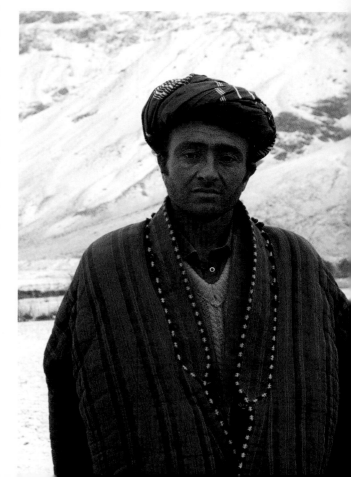

A throwback to the days of feudal lords, Shah Sayid Muhammad Ishmael is revered by the Wakhi people.

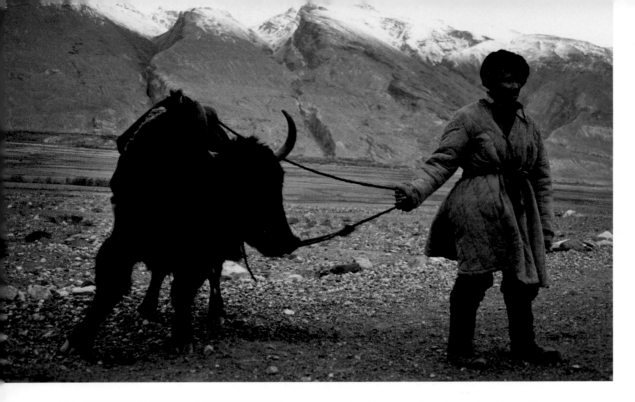

It had been a dazzling display of horsemanship and only when the sheep carcass was beyond recognition did they stop play. At the close of day, Abdullah brandished a fistful of red ribbons and seemed indifferent to his broken fingers and swollen black eye. In this country, courage and honor were constantly being tested in almost every aspect of day-to-day existence—even in the games the people played. The gladiatorial sport of buzkashi seemed to mirror another aspect of life here as well: there were no sides and no rules.

馬哥孛羅

We joined the commander of the Wakhan, Hajji Abdul Samad, together with Abdullah and two bodyguards, Jalal and Askha Khan, and left Khandud following a trail over fields of stone and small streams until we reached the heart of the corridor. "We should stop in Qala Panja," said Samad, "to pay respect to a very important person," he explained. Abdullah agreed. We protested. It was already dangerously late in the year and we couldn't afford to waste any precious days. "We must stop," Samad insisted. "The Shah of the Wakhan will be offended if we do not."

"The Shah of the Wakhan?" We turned to each other and began to laugh. "True serendipity."

> *The people, who worship Mahomet . . . are doughty warriors. They have no ruler except one whom they call Nona, that is to say in our language, Count.*

A feudal lord as his ancestors were in Polo's time, Shah Sayid Muhammad Ishmael had a residence that reflected his status. His rambling adobe farmhouse had two stories, a real wooden staircase, and glass windows rather than the usual crude openings cut into the mud and covered with plastic. A great many people appeared to live in the house: workers, bodyguards, and, isolated from everyone else, the women of the family.

The shah was thirty-eight years old, a slightly built man with unprepossessing features. But his manner was regal, as was his elegant *chapan*, or kaftan—an ankle-length, purple-and-green coat of fine silk embroidery with classic Asiatic oversized long sleeves to protect his hands from the cold. His turban was green silk laced with fine threads of gold. He was a true Oriental potentate harking back to another age.

Afghans display their wealth on the floor, and we were received in a large room richly decorated with kilim carpets and embroidered cushions that ran the length of the room. The usual picture of the Kaaba hung on the wall and the horns of a Marco Polo sheep adorned the doorway.

Life here seems as unaffected by the fall of the Mongol empire as by astronauts landing on the moon.

In the Afghan tradition, a servant brought us an elaborately engraved, swan-necked ewer of warm water. As honored guests, we were invited

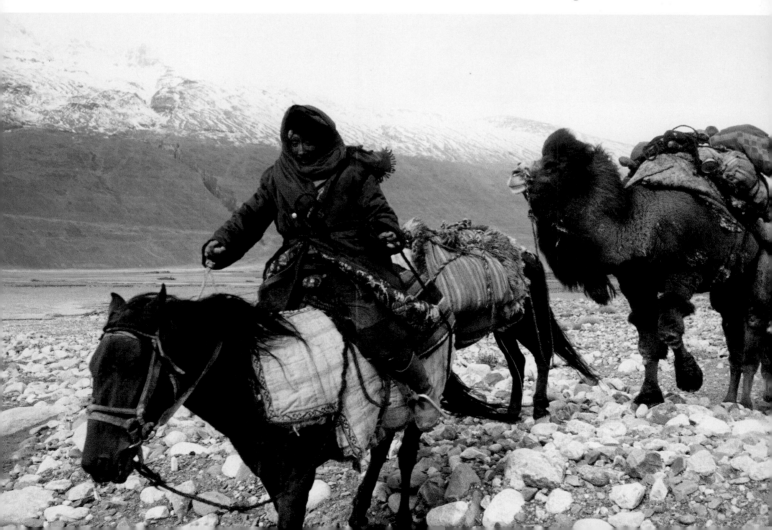

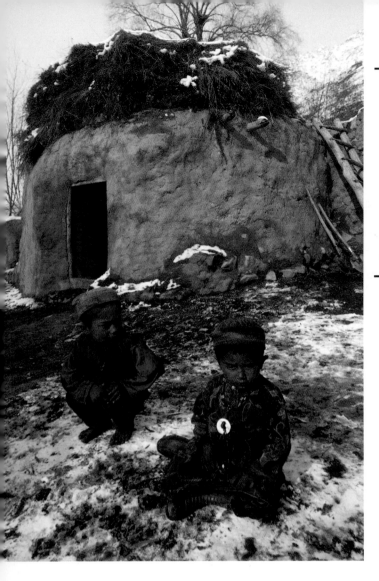

The children always got to us; their enthusiasm, their eagerness to learn was remarkable; their lack of supplies and medicine was heartbreaking, especially since billions of U.S. taxpayer dollars had been poured into this country to buy guns to fight the Russians.

to wash first. In accordance with custom we declined three times, insisting that our host precede us. We compromised; Samad washed first, the servant pouring water over his hands into the waiting basin. When our turn came, we squeezed our hands dry, as shaking was taboo.

A large cloth was rolled out over the carpet and the first of many rounds of chai arrived. We gathered in a circle as our host broke the round, flat bread into pieces, sharing it among us as if we'd entered a Last Supper scene. A large platter of fragrant rice and mutton was then set before us. Eating with our right hands, in communal fashion, we felt comfortable and very much at home. "This is the most delicious meat I've ever tasted," Fran said ravenously.

"Yeah, right," I joked. "After surviving on one onion and a bowl of rice a day, I'd eat the wings off a low-flying duck."

The shah began his story. He came from a long line of noble ancestors and had managed to retain his family's large landholdings. "You are the first foreigners I have seen in thirty years," he said. "Except for the Russians," he added bitterly.

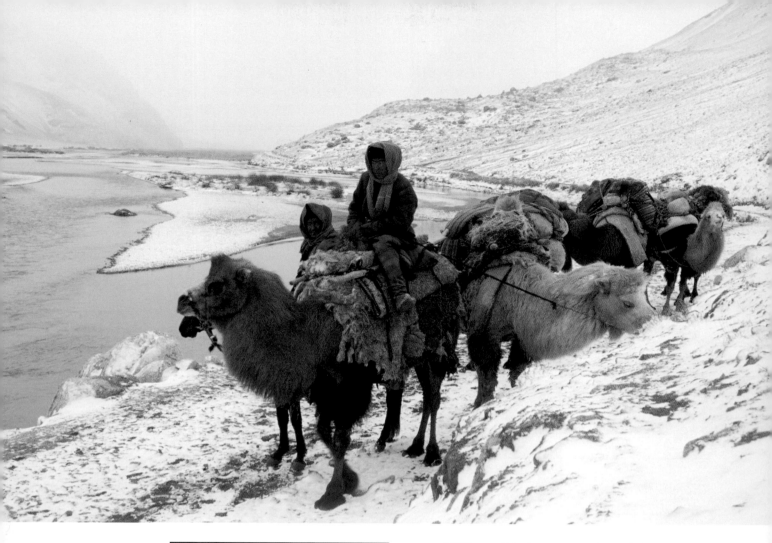

The Bactrian camel was domesticated at least 4,500 years ago in, appropriately, Bactria or Balkh. Its ability to withstand freezing winter cold and searing summer heat made it the preferred pack animal on the Silk Road.

"Where did they come from? The foreigners you'd seen before?" I asked and he smiled, as if remembering better times.

"I was only a boy then and my father was shah. Many foreign dignitaries came to visit."

We were puzzled. "Why?" we wondered out loud, as tactfully as possible, "would foreign dignitaries come to visit such a remote place?"

The shah smiled again. "Why . . . to hunt that which I have served you tonight, of course."

"Of course." We had just eaten Marco Polo.

馬哥孛羅

The next morning we awoke to find that a considerable amount of snow had fallen. "Rest a while longer," the shah implored us. "This is not a very good day for travel."

"Tashakur (thank you), your Excellency, but we must move on if there is any chance for us to cross the Pamir."

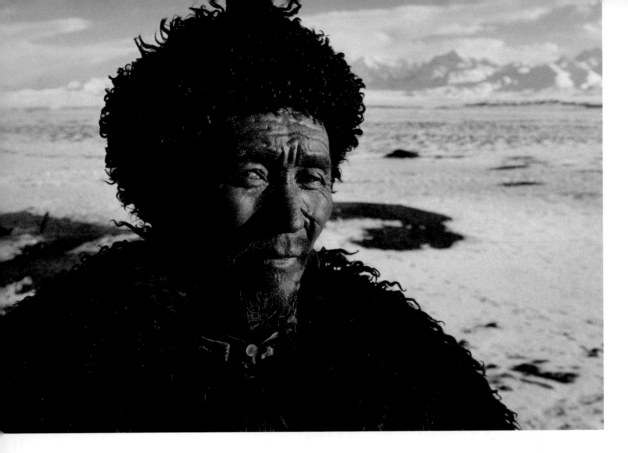

We did exchange a mule and a few horses that weren't keeping the pace we needed. And we did accept, with heartfelt thanks and grateful feet, the colorful thick wool socks the shah bestowed upon us.

We trekked steadily upward for days, ascending steep precipices that jutted from the stone cliffs. The trail was so tight that a misplaced hoof would have sent us, and our animals, hurtling down into an icy abyss. More than once, we blessed Abdullah's knowledge and skills, his silent strength, his hawklike eyes.

As the terrain finally leveled out, we crossed a frozen stream and came upon a foreboding pile of stones with ibex skulls, bones, and the horns of Marco Polo sheep pushing up through the snow. At first I thought it was a warning, like the entrance to sacred old Indian burial grounds. Then I remembered Polo's words: *The horns and bones of sheep are found in such numbers that men build cairns of them besides the tracks to serve as landmarks in the snowy season.*

It was mind-boggling. Here we were, seven hundred snowy seasons later and trails were still marked the same way.

But my feeling of unease returned when the clouds began to billow in from the surrounding peaks and the weather took a dramatic shift. Stinging wet snow blinded us and chapped our exposed skin. Soon our beards were covered with icicles. We struggled

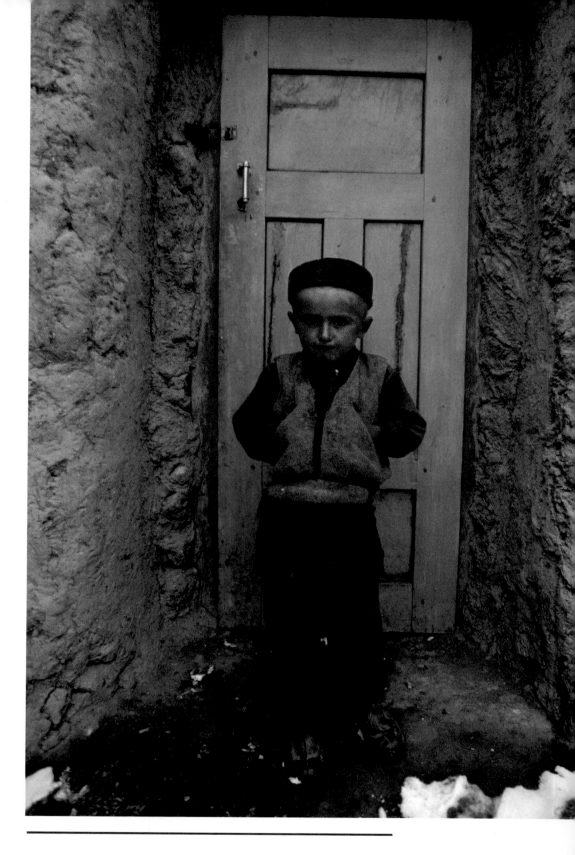

A boy of the Wakhi tribe. There are only ten thousand or so speakers of the Wakhi language. Vakhan (Wakhan) is based on the local Waxšu, the old name of the Oxus River.

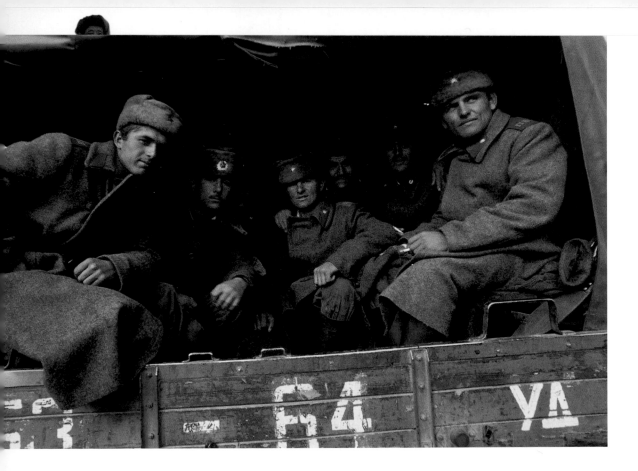

We had no choice. They piled us into the back of a truck filled with soldiers. Breaking out my cigarettes, I soon realized none of them spoke English. I turned to Fran. "They've got to let us in, our papers are in order."

Pulling into an armed compound, we were taken to a dimly lit room. After a while, Anatoli returned with four stern-faced goons. He explained that no foreigner had ever crossed this border post in seventy-five years. They needed to send somebody to get a stamp for our passports. Embarrassed, he said we needed to be strip searched, as were our possessions. They scrutinized every inch of skin, along with every roll of film, checking our camera lenses, tripods, and Walkmans, even our first-aid kit.

The only contraband they found was my bayonet but I was quick to lie that I had purchased it from a Russian in Uzbekistan. They motioned us to dress and left the room. Standing in the cold, we huddled by the stove. It was hours since we had crossed and night had fallen, along with the temperature. "Do you think we're under arrest?" I asked Fran.

"No, this is just a formality. Besides, it's a militarized zone. How else could we get through?"

Finally Anatoli returned. A more highly decorated officer, clearly the base commander, was behind him. He explained it was now too late in the day for the stamps to be issued. We were to be his guests for the night. He reassured us that everything was in order and that we would be processed the following morning. Yet it soon became clear we were his captive audience. He began with innocent questions: "What state are you from?" he asked. "Oh, I'd love to see New York," he exclaimed. "What do you do there? "You are photographers, journalists, UN?"

We dazzled him with Marco Polo and he feigned belief, all the while his questions becoming more insidious. "Coming from Afghanistan you must have met Commander Naj Madeen Wasik. Tell me, how many men does he have?"

We answered evasively. "We never met any Commander Naj Madeen."

"But how did you cross through Afghanistan?" he asked.

"By horse and camelback," we quipped sarcastically, determined not to give any Afghans up to a Russian.

Keeping his cool, he changed tactics, but his flushed neck revealed the truth. "Please join me for dinner; you must be hungry, and your journey sounds fascinating. I want to hear more . . ."

Embroiled in a brutal civil war, the border guards in Tajikistan were on full alert and gave us a thorough interrogation.

Despite our worries, we were allowed to leave the next day. Stamped passports in hand, we walked in the bright morning sun to the only town nearby. Because of the civil war there was a strict embargo on gasoline in the rebellious southern mountain region, and the town was our one chance of getting a ride north. We spotted a restaurant in the small square, sparsely dotted

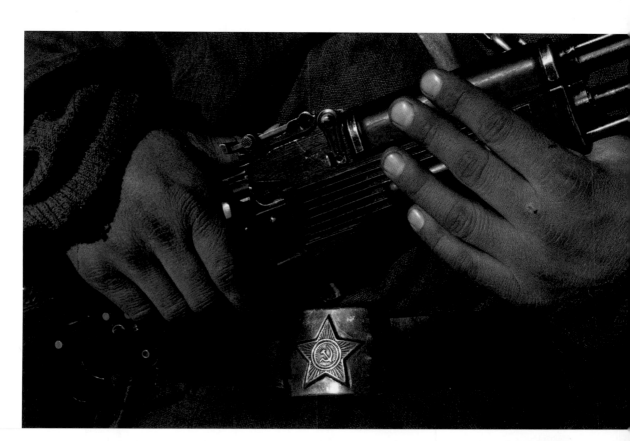

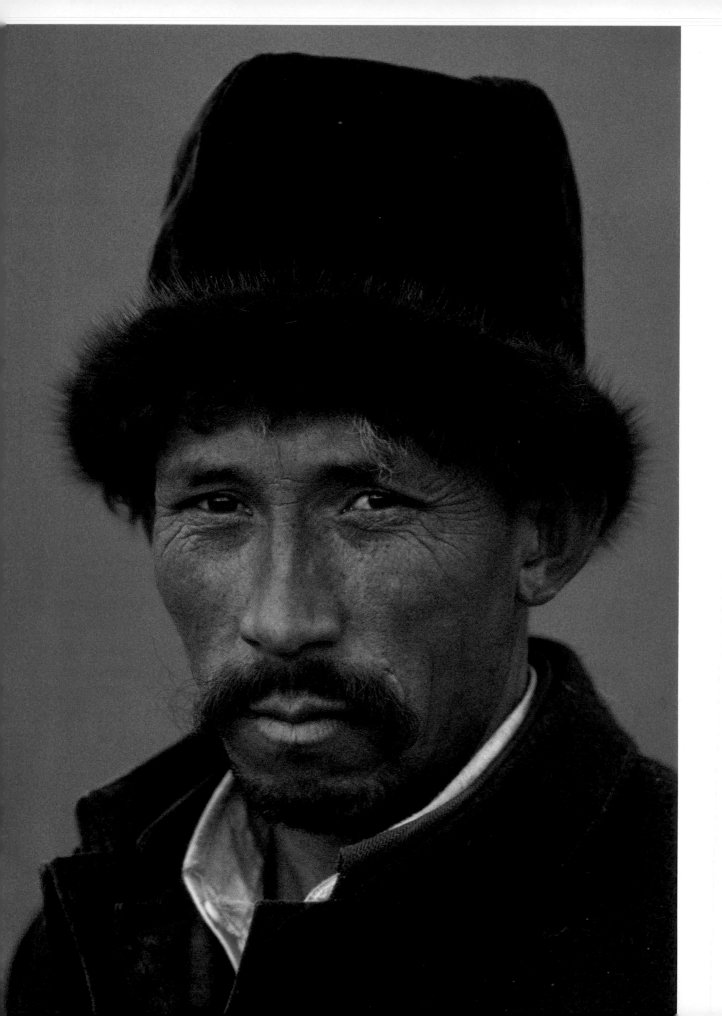

(opposite page) The Uighurs had a profound influence on Mongolian culture; among other things, their written script was used extensively at the Great Khan's court.

That evening we decided to have dinner in the beautiful nineteenth-century Russian baroque dining room of our hotel. Our nerves a little frayed and tense, our mood perhaps darkened by worrying over our China visas, we tried to look on the bright side: this would be our first proper meal in a while, and there was no chance of getting shot while we ate it. We let out a mutual sigh as we sat down. After months of shared group meals on Persian carpets, of being a curiosity and needing to keep our guards up, we just wanted to be left alone to decompress. We sat quietly gazing in a kind of reverse culture shock at the detailed plasterwork on the twenty-foot ceilings and the tables with silverware and glasses.

The cavernous room was empty but for a table of Russian men drinking and a four-man, eighties-style hair band on stage playing Abba songs. As I started to eat my soup, a drunken Russian in black leather stumbled through the door, looking like trouble. He proceeded to invite himself to sit down by pulling out the chair next to mine. "Wodka," he called slurrily to our waitress, but we were in no mood. I pushed the chair back in and said, "Nyet spasiba" (No thanks) and went on eating.

Furious, he threw a sucker punch to the back of my head, but he'd picked on the wrong guys at the wrong time. A full-scale brawl ensued when his buddies from the other table jumped in. A whirlwind of destruction tore through the imperial dining room, as tables were overturned, glasses shattered, food flew through the air. We fought all of them off until the band jumped in and they scattered away. I had a swollen eye and Fran a bloody lip, but we smiled at each other, relishing our battle wounds and feeling our spirits lift with the release of our pent-up tensions.

The waitresses, waiters, and the band apologized profusely as they reset the tables, telling us they were local wiseguys. "Please don't think bad of our country because of those bad boys," said a sweet Russian lady with clownish orange hair and flashing gold teeth. She had secured my ever-present camera bag during the scuffle and her calm voice and demeanor helped my adrenaline to ebb away. "They drink too much." She sighed, as if they were her own sons.

Russia is a very great province, lying to the north. . . . Both men and women are very handsome, being very white and tall with long fair hair. . . . Let me tell you of one of their customs. They make an excellent wine out of honey and panic, which they call mead, and with this they hold great drinking bouts.

The next morning the hotel director woke us, requesting we come to his office. We entered sheepishly, sure we would have to pay for damages, only to have our fears allayed by his sincere apologies. We left him with smiles and handshakes, not believing our luck.

We roamed the empty stalls of a Bishkek market, trying to buy something to bring to Thanksgiving dinner and getting into the holiday mood, and were prompt in arriving at Pam's apartment, starving for some American food and company. Pam was working for USAID (the United States Agency for International Development), and her accent made us feel at home right away. There was Shawn, a nice Jewish girl from Baltimore, whose job was to procure all things for the minuscule embassy staff. "If you need a dishwasher, I'm the source." She giggled. Mike was the third embassy secretary and we never found out what exactly he did. "Probably a spook," Fran whispered. Julie was the second embassy secretary who probably did the same job as Mike but had a better number. Snobbish and cool, she was our least favorite. "You'll never get a visa for China," she said snidely.

"If we believed everyone who's told us 'you'll never,' we'd be having Thanksgiving at home," I informed her.

"Ja, people told me I could never ride my bike across the world," said Heinz Stücke, the only non-American there, and the world's most traveled man, according to the *Guinness Book of World Records*. "I left Germany in 1962 on a bicycle I bought from a catalog and haven't stopped pedaling it since."

"I think that dude's been on the road way too long," Fran said, nodding in his direction as the German greedily scraped burnt brownie crumbs with dirty fingers into his mouth from the bottom of a tin tray.

Then there was Leroi, a Trumanesque sixty-eight-year-old in the Foreign Service most of his adult life. He loved our project. "That's right, boys, don't listen to those stuffed shirts," he said encouragingly. "Keep at it and never give up on your dreams."

Like a long-lost uncle, he enthralled us with his dry, witty stories as he kept us entertained over martinis.

They had flown in a Butterball turkey with all the trimmings, including cranberry sauce. There were mashed potatoes, yams, and Pam even made apple pie topped off with vanilla ice cream and fresh coffee. Thanksgiving in Bishkek with our surrogate family was all we could have dreamed of and we stayed late talking and laughing. If not for the eccentric German and the CIA, it would have been a real taste of home; then again, whose family is perfect?

In a scene out of *Doctor Zhivago*, we walked back in the moonlight through the snowy urban landscape. The broad tree-lined streets were blanketed in white, emanating that special hush that only comes with heavy snow. Dazzling icicles hung from the eaves

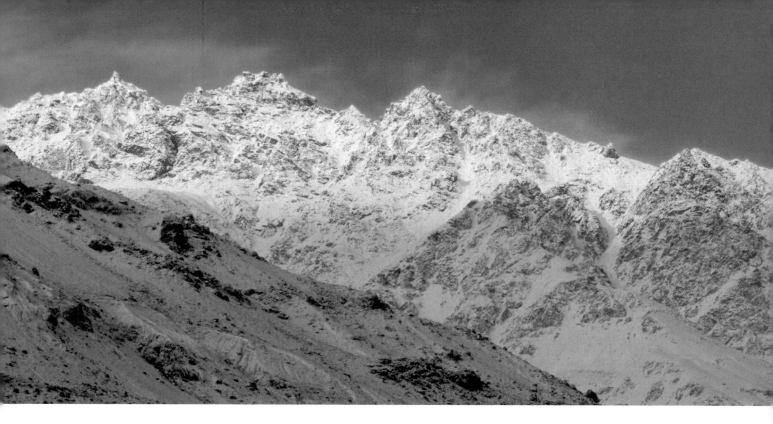

Known as Tangri Tagh (mountains of the spirits) to the Uighurs, this Central Asian range is more commonly known by the Chinese translation, Tien Shan (celestial mountains).

of onion-domed churches as we crunched along, sliding across frozen puddles like children.

Arriving to find the hotel's door locked, we were relieved to see a woman tallying receipts behind the counter and knocked on the glass. She ignored us. When our knocking became more emphatic, a guard approached saying we had missed the curfew and waved us away. My ungloved hands started to freeze so I resorted to kicking the brass footplate at the base of the huge glass doors. *Pazhalusta*, please, we begged.

Perhaps the cold had made the glass brittle or I kicked too enthusiastically, but it cracked violently and came down in a thundering crash. Stunned, we booted out the jagged debris and sauntered over the shattered glass, passed nonchalantly through the lobby as the two hotel workers sat in shock, and fled up to our room and beds.

馬哥孛羅

"We're going to be late, wash them later," I shouted to Fran through the bathroom door the next morning as we headed out for the Chinese embassy. He had just turned on the tub taps to wash his T-shirts and nothing but air had come out. We slunk out past the workmen replacing the glass door, ducking the hotel manager.

The Chinese International Tourist Service (CITS) wanted to talk, but a state-controlled bureaucracy was exactly what we wanted to avoid, preferring to travel

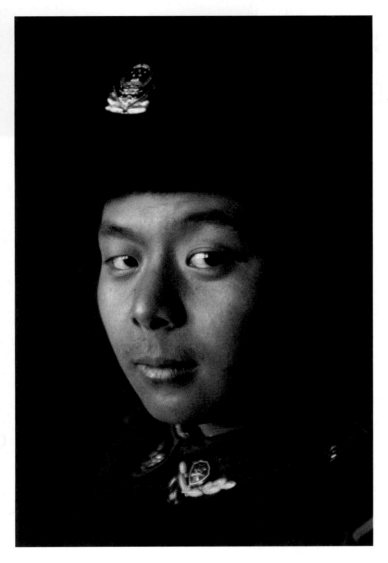

In one of the most remote outposts in the world, as far from the sea as you can get on this planet, we met this kind border guard who happened to have a brother living in New York.

here to rest up, get a warm bath, and enjoy a hot meal before resupplying for the next leg of the journey. But like all frontier towns it was a dangerous place that demanded constant vigilance. There were always political intrigues, thieves, and murderers lurking in the shadows—in short, Silk Road highwaymen looking to exploit the weaknesses of the many caravans passing through.

As the exchange rate in banks was never favorable, we set out to look for the black market to change money. We didn't have to go far; a crowd of Uighurs stood in back of the hotel circling like vultures as we approached. With guttural grunts they called out the going rates. Bargaining well, we snatched up our new Chinese money and left to explore the town.

We passed a street of billiards tables set out in the cold, where men were playing pool in the freezing air, their breath visible as they cued up. We saw fur stalls with the sickening sight of endangered snow-leopard pelts, wolves, foxes, even the skin of a Siberian tiger for sale. Sidewalk barbershops stood across from kebab houses spew-

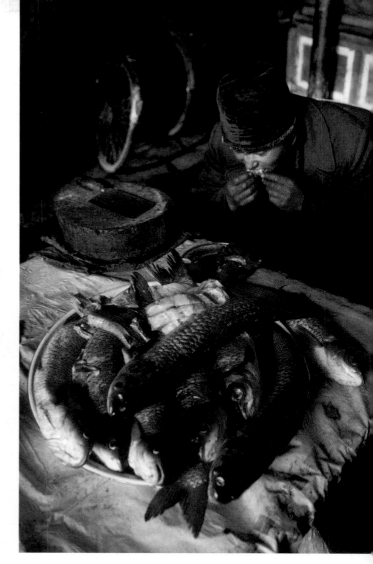

A Uighur enjoys his breakfast in the Kashgar market. "Kashgar was once a kingdom, but is now subject to the Great Khan."

ing acrid smoke from the burning rumps of fat-tailed sheep. Old men with skin that showed the creases and deep character lines of a harsh life walked with their wives, faces covered in brown shawls.

We came to realize there are two Kashgars. The Chinese city was dominated by a large statue of Mao, his arm raised and pointing east as a reminder of occupation. It had broad avenues and ugly, modern, blue-mirrored glass buildings. The old city was built along a maze of muddy streets, twisting and turning into little alleyways and dead ends overhung with festively painted balconies. To the chagrin of the Chinese communists, there seemed to stand a mosque on every corner, a testament to the Uighurs' strong Islamic traditions.

This division was echoed in the simple act of keeping time. Since the communists took over in 1949, all of China was supposed to run on Beijing time. This bizarre policy would be akin to forcing Los Angeles into the same time zone as Washington, D.C. That would mean the sun wouldn't rise until 9:30 in the morning here. The Uighurs, in small acts of defiance, followed the natural rise of the sun instead. "If we follow Chinese time, our children would awake for school in darkness 365 days a year," a young shopkeeper told us. "We are Uighurs, we have our own time."

No matter how we set our watches, days turned to weeks awaiting special permission from the PSB to track Polo into the desert. Entangled in more red tape, we began to get on each other's nerves. We'd been together twenty-four hours a day for ten months. I was exhausted, the anniversary of Rob's murder had just passed, Christmas came and went without any fanfare, and I was homesick. Finally word came from Beijing. We

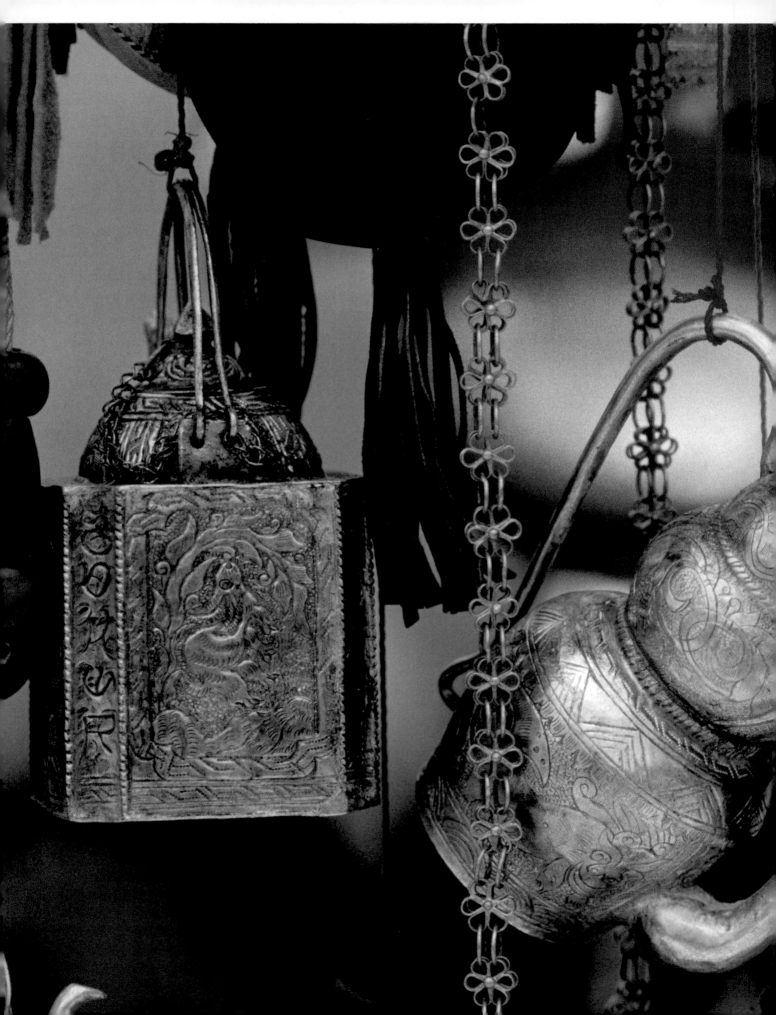

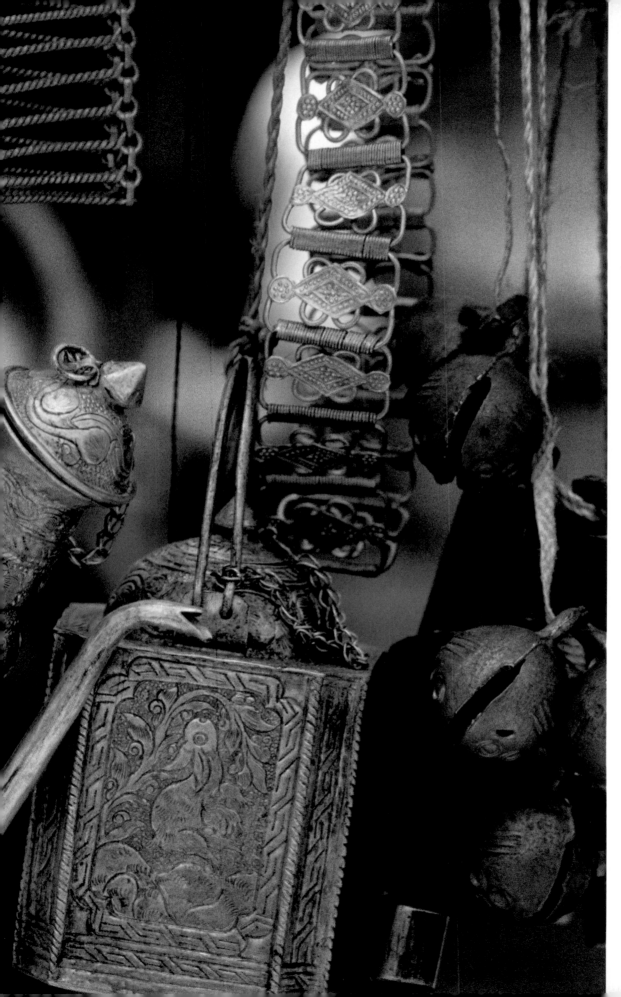

Metallurgy is a specialty of the Uighurs. Their handmade wares are much sought after by other ethnic groups of the region.

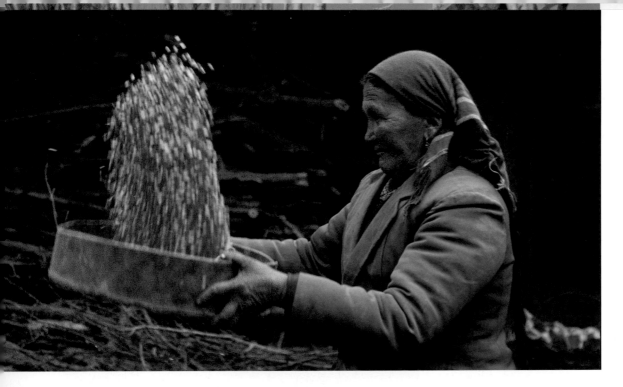

Though they were poor and could ill afford it, Jacop and his wife shared everything they had in their humble home.

We rode on for days, receiving similar hospitality each night. To our right, looming over the golden desert horizon were our constant companions, the purple Pamirs. I sat practically side-saddle, so I could gaze transfixed into their lofty summits, lost in the memory of crossing the roof of the world just a few short weeks before.

A strong gust of wind, stinging my face with sand, snapped me back. We were now in the world's second-lowest place, the Tarim Basin, home of the Taklamakan and Gobi deserts. The basin is just that, a huge bowl rimmed by the Himalayas, Pamirs, Tien Shan, Karakorams, Altun Shan, and Kunlun mountain ranges. Each range whipped down freezing blasts, making temperatures in the basin swing wildly, in some cases, sixty degrees in a few hours.

We came to a small town of low-slung adobe. As we rode down its only dusty street, people came out of their homes, blacksmiths quit their pounding, and butchers stopped their slicing. Life came to a standstill in the tiny town to stare.

We looked down to meet the bewildered gaze of an isolated people. We felt their suspicious eyes upon us as we relived the "stranger in town" scenario we've seen in dozens of cowboy movies but couldn't fully understand until this very second. We answered their looks with open and genuine smiles, placing our hands over our hearts in the Muslim manner. There is a special feeling you get when you're high in the saddle, I wouldn't say haughty, but commanding. You feel you are a presence, someone to be reckoned with.

Apprehensively, a group of town elders approached. "As-salaam-alaikum," we called down. "Wa alaikum as salaam," they mumbled in return. Luik asked where

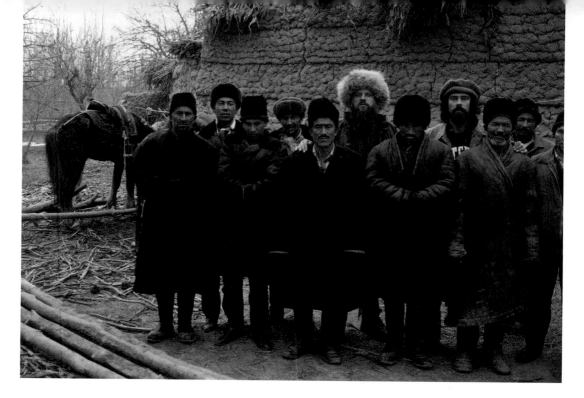

The Uighur villages skirting the desert were so isolated that—despite the fact that Pakistan was less than one hund-dred miles away—people often thought we were Pakistanis.

we could find lodging for the night and the answer came back: they were afraid of us. We should keep riding ten or so miles to the main road.

"There is a hotel for the truck drivers," one old man said through his straggly beard.

Luik vouched that we were honorable men, implying we were Muslims. He whispered conspiratorially, "We need to avoid the Chinese."

A hush came over the Uighurs who, nodding comprehension, whispered among themselves. "You are Pakistani?" they inquisitively assumed.

We did nothing to disillusion them. "Brothers," one of them said, "you will stay in my home tonight." Taking the reins of our horses, he said he was called Zunun. Behind his tall wooden doors was a typical Uighur home with an inward-facing cluster of rooms that lay hidden behind a façade of simple mud brick. Camel dung patties clung to the walls, waiting to be dried and used as fuel.

I give you my word that if a stranger comes to a house here to seek hospitality he receives a very warm welcome.

We tied up the animals in the courtyard and were taken to one of the rooms, as typical as the home itself. A large mud platform built off the cold ground took up a third of the space. It was covered with brightly colored geometric felt carpets. A stove

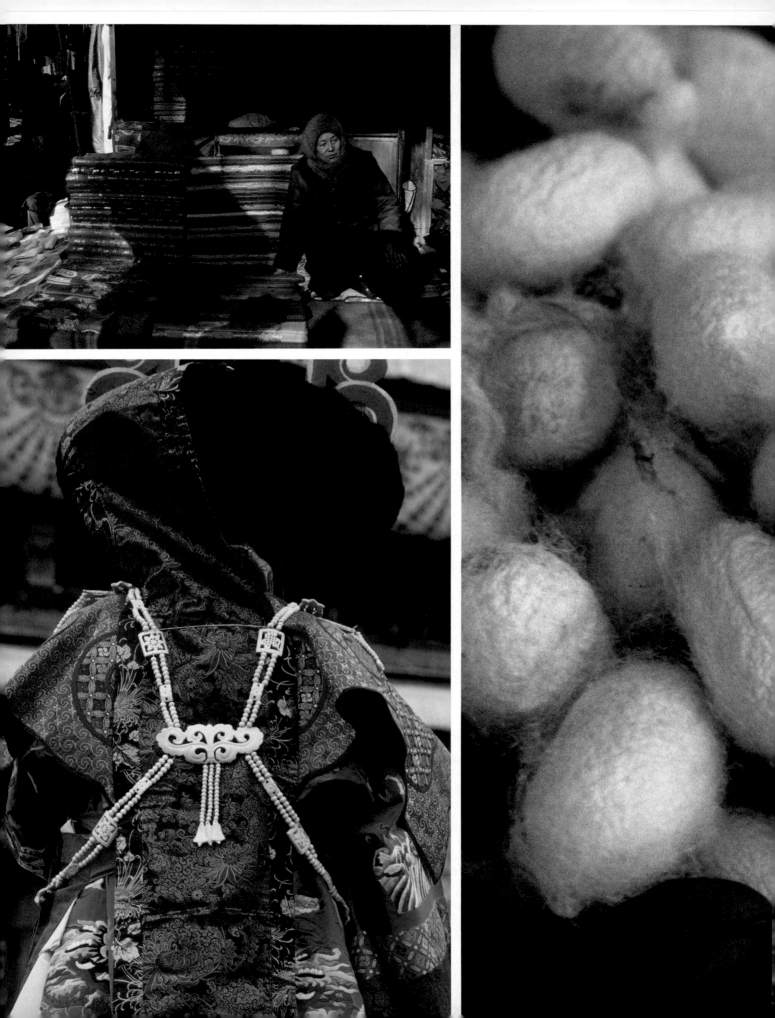

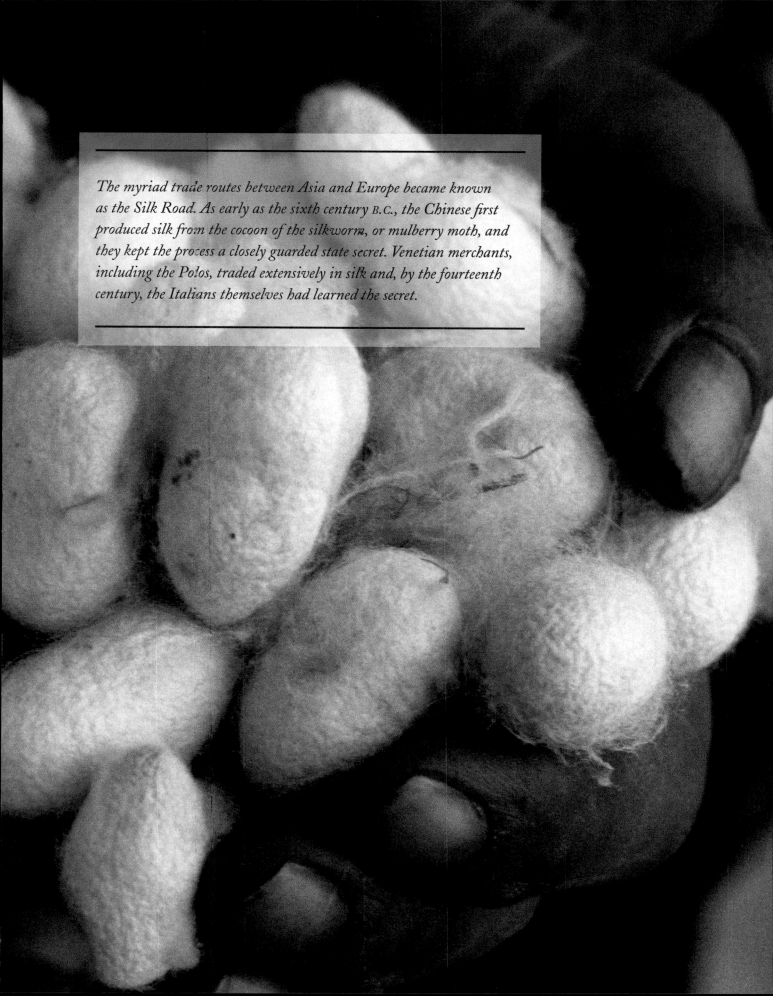

The myriad trade routes between Asia and Europe became known as the Silk Road. As early as the sixth century B.C., the Chinese first produced silk from the cocoon of the silkworm, or mulberry moth, and they kept the process a closely guarded state secret. Venetian merchants, including the Polos, traded extensively in silk and, by the fourteenth century, the Italians themselves had learned the secret.

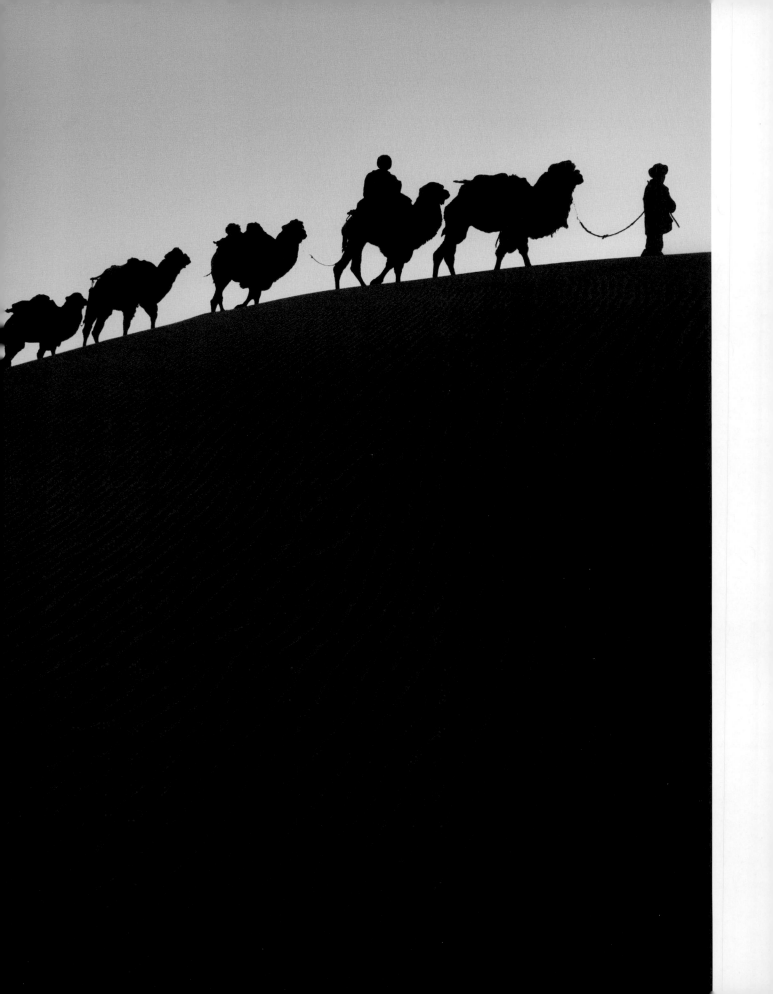

to the horse's pounding hooves. "Whoaahhh!!!!" I was dragged along the stony sand.

I finally fell into a rolling dust ball, my horse tumbling in front of me. I sat there checking for broken bones, the horse getting on its feet before I did. Fran and Luik came riding back, chuckling smugly from their horses. I dusted myself off.

"I hate when that happens," I said. "I want to cover Polo's trail, not have it cover me." We continued on but at a trot, my horse falling behind the others, occasionally stopping in his tracks.

"He must be injured," I shouted to the guys, who were calling for me to keep up.

"We have far to go until the next village," Luik warned.

But I was only able to get another five miles out of my horse. He quit just as it was getting dark, stopping dead in his tracks. Fran and I took turns at two-hour intervals riding his horse and dozing while the other walked ahead, holding the reins and pumping blood into frozen hands and feet. Now we blinked at old Hajji's warning; the temperature must have dropped fifty degrees as we pushed on in the punishing black night until we could take it no longer.

"It must be close," we implored a very quiet Luik. "We've been walking for eight hours, we should have gotten there an hour ago."

Whether he miscalculated or not, we'd had enough. "We have to make camp here," I said, pulling us into a depression in the sand. We tied the horses together to a boulder on top of the ridge, put on every article of clothing we had, and quickly got in our sleeping bags before the blood left our fingers. Huddling as close as heterosexually possible, the three of us fell into an exhausted frozen slumber.

A barking dog woke me as I lay still, trying to remember exactly where I was. My beard was frozen solid to the zipper of my mummy bag and only by hyperventilating hot breath on it was I able to free it and myself and sit up to get my bearings. I rubbed frozen tears and sand from my eyes and saw that we had been covered with a dusting of snow.

The horses had broken away from each other. Mine was alone, lying in the hard sand—not a good sign. The pack mules were nowhere in sight. The dog's incessant barks got me to my feet and I crunched up to the ridge toward my disabled horse and peeked over the edge. Through the morning haze I could see our mules standing under a strand of poplars; behind them were the tops of houses, their roofs spilling smoke into the gray sky. We had camped a half mile from a town!

"Luik," I shouted, kicking his sleeping bag. Fran sat up with a start, cursing as he struggled to work his beard free. Luik looked up with one eye open. "Don't quit your day job, 'cause you suck as a guide."

We hobbled into a town busy with people on a market day. Tired, hungry, thirsty, and disheveled, we must have seemed like aliens to the Uighurs. Their astonished faces

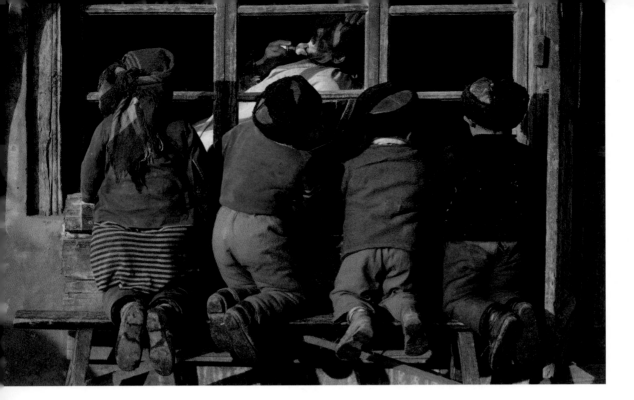

bore out their thoughts: foreigners sauntering out of the desert with horses, very strange. Luik confirmed this when a group of men finally asked. Loud and excited talk ensued, for Turks have a way of yelling at each other while conversing.

"These people have never seen a sleeping bag," Luik said, "and if we showed them one they'd never believe it would keep you warm." One of the Uighurs took us home, where we quickly gulped down a few large bowls of chai and passed out, utterly exhausted.

The afternoon was spent trying to trade my horse in at the market. Not an easy task given the fact he had a herniated muscle under his right foreleg. With a fistful of Chinese dollars, we were able to exchange for a good chestnut mare and gave the animals and ourselves a night of rest.

> *Khotan . . . is amply stocked with the means of life. . . . It has vineyards, estates and orchards in plenty.*

For two thousand years, prosperous agricultural communities have flourished on the southern Silk Road oases that skirt the Taklamakan. Fed by glacial rivers that flow into the basin from the Kunlun Mountains, these oases still produce *fruit in plenty.*

Providing 75 percent of China's grapes, the hibernating vines we now rode past became another toast to Marco. As an Italian he would have certainly taken special interest in a desert that could support vineyards.

TAKLAMAKAN

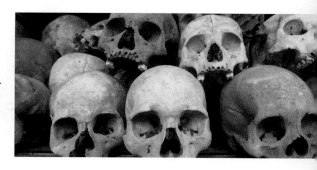

Sailing on a Sea of Sand

IN THE TENTS OF BROTHERS DERDINGIZ AND ALIM TURSAN we said our goodbyes to Luik. He'd had enough and didn't want to go along with our next plan. I took pity on him, for I was having second thoughts myself. He left with the horses and mules to sell in the markets of Khotan and catch the bus back to Kashgar. "Good luck, you crazy bastards," he called back, happy to be going home.

"I have two cousins in Khotan that could take you in," old Hajji had told us. "They supplement their winters by foraging for wood in the desert. Idle hands are the devil's work," he said, using one of his old-fashioned sayings and sounding like a stern ol' granpa.

Outside their camp the brothers had amassed the rewards of those hands. Cords of wood sat stockpiled as their sons split them with heavy axes. Whole tree stumps and twisted roots lay behind them, their smooth surfaces resembling driftwood, for indeed that's what they were. Thousands of years ago, the desert had encroached on a rich, fertile plain. Forests were taken over by the dunes and the trees were set adrift in the sea of sand, the sea of death—the Taklamakan. This wasteland has intimidated merchant caravans, explorers, and marching armies for centuries. We wanted to penetrate a realm whose very name translated to "the place where he who goes in does not come out." Taklamakan, I said again to myself, the land of no return.

> *This desert is reported to be so long that it would take a year to go from end to end. . . . It consists entirely of mountains and valleys of sand. There is nothing to eat.*

The size of Germany, the Taklamakan and its shifting sands have swamped whole towns and civilizations, leaving archaeologists able only to guess where they once stood. A lucky few have been discovered, along with mummies naturally preserved in the salty, arid sands. Carbon-14 dating has placed some of these finds as far back as the early

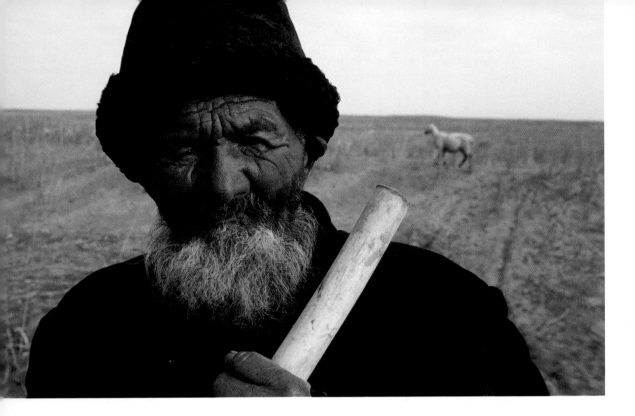

Bronze Age, 4,000 years ago. Remarkably, the mummies have proven to be of European descent, giving silent testament to the antiquity of the Silk Road. The ruins of two such sites, Rawak and Niya, were our next goal.

Besides goiters, the Uighurs have another particular physical deformity. It begins when they're young, getting more pronounced with age, and only affects men. They have a habit of pulling their thick felt hats down so far on their heads as to bend the tops of their ear cartilages horizontally. Years of this abuse leaves the hat wearer permanently disfigured, with the distinct look of one of the Seven Dwarfs.

Derdingiz and Alim were no exception, their ears jutting out from under their hats. The brothers stood barely five feet tall, with identical white beards. They wore the standard Uighur uniform—black karakul coats and hats, covered in dung and desert dust, over knee-high boots and suspenders—which only enhanced their fairy-tale appearance. They looked so similar that the only way we could distinguish them was by their dispositions. Alim was miserable, sour, and hard, and didn't want much to do with us. Derdingiz was as sweet as they come and very hospitable. We started calling them Grumpy and Happy.

With a caravan of camels carrying tents, food, and enough water to last a month, we left the camp with them and a few of their sons, descending a rocky escarpment that had been carved out annually from melting snow in the Kunluns. Rushing headwaters had created a wide floodplain, depositing boulders and stones carried down from the mountains. Polo, with his merchant's gaze, observed, *There are rivers here with stones of Jasper and Chalcedony . . . which are exported for sale in Cathay and bring a good profit.*

To this day, the Karakash (Black Jade) and the Yurungkash (White Jade) rivers meet in Khotan, making it China's richest source of a mineral most precious to them, jade, or as they say in old Persian, jasper.

We followed the confluence of the rivers until it meandered into smaller streams and creeks, the water disappearing under their stones. We were now in a rock-strewn path, sunken and carved among the small dunes, its high banks flanked with dried vegetation. Hours later the stony passage gave way to sand, as the banks came down to meet us in the great desert. Happy explained that the line of dried brush entering the wasteland in a crooked line toward the horizon was the river running underneath the sand. "If we ever get lost," he said, "we follow the vegetation out of the desert."

That night Hajji's cousins showed us how they can survive winters in the land of no return. They dug pits and filled them with the embers of our fire. A layer of sand was thrown on top, with a carpet rolled over that. On this we made our beds and stayed toasty through the freezing night.

In the morning we followed the underground river for a few hours before veering off into the dunes. I really enjoyed travel by camel, their easy gaits a stark contrast to the spine-jolting shocks the horses had been giving me. They're strange creatures, with large soulful eyes and big flat feet helping them cross the sand. They grunt, burp, spit, and regurgitate their stomachs, producing an awful smell, but I was very happy to be riding into one of the world's most inhospitable places on an animal designed by nature to survive the harshest of conditions. Their nickname, "ships of the desert," never meant anything to me until we crested a wave of sand a hundred feet tall, and I could see nothing but an ocean of dunes spread out before us like a turbulent, yellow Pacific. We came sailing down a swell, into a hole, and up the next wave, on and on all day, surfing the sea of death.

Coming upon a shattered tree that had drifted these waves for eons, I brought my camel to its knees and ran my hand over the wood's finely sanded grain. Maybe a child climbed this tree thousands of years ago when it was alive, I mused. Maybe a monk meditated under its leaves when it stood in the courtyard of a Buddhist monastery or perhaps a mad Tibetan marauder was put to death and hung from its limbs. Grumpy barked for his boys to start hacking at the bleached trunk, and I reflected on the tree's final demise. Tonight it would heat my bed and cook my food, completing its journey as it helped me on mine.

I joined Happy and Fran conversing by the camels. "How do you think they can navigate without a compass?" Fran asked as I approached.

"Beats me, maybe they read the dunes, like a Polynesian sailor reads the waves." When the boys had finished tying up their cache, we pushed on, making camp and bed before dusk brought a vicious drop in temperature.

The next morning brought a bright sun as we rode the mounds deeper in. Up we'd scale a massive dune as if climbing the blocks of a golden pyramid, its breadth filling our peripheral vision. The higher we went, the more we could see, until the vista opened before us upon reaching the summit, and we were rewarded with the sweeping panorama of peaks and valleys running to the horizon. The sun's warm embrace briefly beat upon our faces before the camels led us down into the cold shadowy abyss of the next dune. It could take half an hour until we saw the sun again, now a bit higher in the sky. Our shadows got shorter then disappeared as we plunged down into the freezing bowls of sand again.

The Taklamakan in January was no joke. Surrounded by high mountains in the heartland of Asia, hundreds of miles from any open body of water, the desert temperature at night dropped well below zero.

The high midday sun equally lighted the peaks and valleys and still we sailed on. There were no signs of life, not even a bird dared fly over this wasteland, but we did pass the sun-bleached remains of a wild camel jutting out from the sand, its ribcage half buried.

When our shadows started getting long again with the sun's descent and day's end, we crested yet another summit. Like a mirage, we

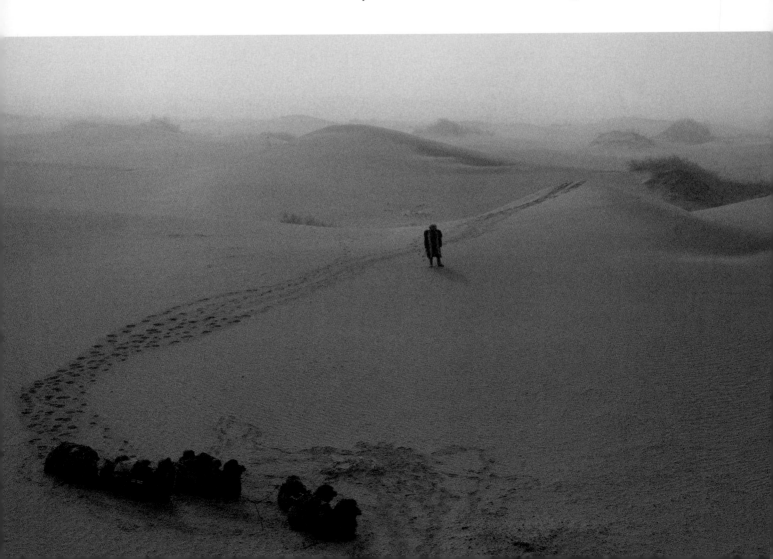

saw the ruins of Rawak, glowing pink in the sweet light, its mud brick stupa standing apart from the yellow sand. As it grew closer with each summited dune, we were teased with its fleeting vision. Finally we turned a wall of sand and came to the ancient site. Ten-foot-high walls half consumed by the shifting sands enclosed a large circular stupa ninety feet high. A towering dune rose behind its back, like a tsunami wave perched to swallow it whole.

I threw my legs over and jumped down from my beast, kicking my feet out karate style, trying to return some blood to my toes. I wondered how many times the shifting sands had claimed this isolated site, only to reveal it again. I pondered how many wrecks lay below the surface waiting to be discovered, how many lost cities we rode over today, buried down deep, like a desert Pompeii.

Happy's and Grumpy's loud voices awoke me from my daydream. They stood around their sons in what seemed to be a confrontation with Fran. "What's up?" I asked.

"They don't want us to camp here, they want to continue in," Fran said testily. "No way! We traveled here to see this place."

After a confusing exchange, we compromised and made camp a few hundred yards away, but an uneasiness pervaded our party. With hardly a word now spoken, the Uighurs set up the heavy canvas tent. "At least we could explore the site in the morning," Fran said as we unloaded our camel bags. We all stood around a blazing bonfire of ancient wood, the flames bending in the wind, the tension seeming to lift with our body temperatures.

And then, a particularly strong gust howled ominously into the camp. It hung over us momentarily and then whispered off, dissipating over the dunes. The Uighurs panicked and ran to the camels and started pulling up the tent's stakes, visibly frightened. "What the hell's going on?"

We grabbed Happy as he was rolling up his bed mat. "Jinn, Jinn," he said excitedly, ignoring our pleas for further explanation. Fran lifted him off the sand. "There are spirits here, bad ghosts that drive people mad!" Happy wailed, trying to break free. "I've seen them with my own eyes," he insisted. "They come up from the sands, they don't want us here!"

We tried calming him down. "It's only the wind," we reassured him.

> *When a man is riding by night through this desert . . . he hears*
> *spirits talking. . . . Sometimes, they even hail him by name . . . these*
> *voices make him stray from the path, so he never finds it again . . .*
> *in this way many travelers have perished and been lost.*

"If you leave, we want our money back," we said as Happy quit struggling and Fran let him go. "And we will tell old Hajji you were afraid of the wind, like children."

We had chastised him, for the last thing we wanted to do was start riding in the desert at night. This got his attention, and he seemed momentarily to forget about the ghosts. Happy looked anything but, as he went out and spoke to the other men. In the morning we left the slightly embarrassed Uighurs safely in camp and set out to explore.

Sitting among fertile green fields when it was built, the now half-buried ruins of Rawak Vihara were established by Indian missionaries bringing to China a new religion: Buddhism.

The flow back and forth on the Silk Road included not just goods and commodities, but religious, philosophical, and artistic ideas. A stupa, traditionally, is a solid structure that houses a holy relic of the Buddha. Rawak's tower had openings and passageways, appearing more like a temple, its surrounding walls creating a courtyard. We noticed some painted polychrome stucco at the corner of the quadrangle and started to dig away the freezing sand. A life-size stucco figure slowly emerged. Out of breath, we sat back, blown away by the serene face of a bodhisattva staring back at us, a face from the ancient Silk Road, the same face that we had looked on for inspiration eleven months earlier in the Metropolitan Museum of Art. From the Gandhara period or school, the figure had Hellenistic features and flowing, pleated robes that reflected the merger 2,000 years ago of Greco-Roman naturalism with South Asian iconography. East meeting West, it was a perfect face for the Silk Road.

Gandhara Buddhism flourished in Central Asia, encompassing present-day Pakistan and Afghanistan until the rise of Islam in the eighth century. It was the intolerable act of destruction by the Taliban of the colossal Gandhara Buddhas in Bamian that first brought world outrage and attention to that backward regime.

The walls were once resplendent with these reliefs inside and outside the courtyard. We reburied the bodhisattva and wherever we found exposed plaster, covered it with sand to help preserve it from the harsh elements. "Not too many people get a chance to unearth something like that," Fran said, as we followed our tracks back to camp.

"This is what it's all about," I started to say. "To be here, doing what we love best . . ."

". . . erases the pain, hassles, and fatigue you put up with on the road," Fran said, finishing my sentence. Relinquishing Rawak, its faces and spirits, giving ourselves back into the hands of the capricious desert, we rode due east.

Now sensitive to their fears, we assured the Uighurs that in a few days when we came to Niya, we'd set camp a safe distance away and explore the ruins alone. The mood in the caravan was also helped by the discovery of driftwood. Helping them with their treasure trove, we taught the boys to sing, "Heigh-ho, heigh-ho, It's off to work we go. . . ." as we became a chorus for the catchy Disney tune, even eliciting a smile from Grumpy.

Laden with newfound wealth, the caravan moved slowly for days, collecting more until we crossed another underground river. Like a bushy great wall dividing the dunes, it wound its course as far as the eye could see in both directions.

"The spirit city you seek is four days' journey," Happy informed us that night over a bowl of noodles. "Tomorrow I will follow the underground river south to Keriya and sell the wood." We nodded quietly, cupping the bowls for warmth. "My brother Alim and his boys will take you to Niya," he said, to our regret.

"Grumpy's not so bad, he's been coming around. Besides he seemed less freaked out by the ghosts," Fran later said. "The only problem is, he doesn't have the patience to explain and listen like Happy." With basic Turkish spoken for months in all its original Central Asian dialects, we were able to comprehend a lot, but only with someone who was willing to go at our beginner's pace.

We left Happy and his fellows, wishing them Allah's continued grace, and followed Grumpy and his band into the wilderness. Two days passed uneventfully with only a few twisted branches retrieved. Fran and I talked of lost loves and past journeys, art and music and politics, breaking the hours of monotony from the backs of the plodding beasts. "Name every David Lean movie you know," it would start. "Did you ever see John Wayne as Genghis Khan? What's up with that?" We'd laugh.

"What's your favorite Kirk Douglas epic?" Fran asked, "*Spartacus* or *The Vikings*?"

I contemplated the thought silently as we rode on. "They're both great," I finally said. "But what has become epic for me is *Lust for Life*."

Our reverie was interrupted when we spied blanched wood lying at the bottom of a yellow bowl and slid down to collect it. Little rivers of pale sand followed us in gritty avalanches. The camels seemed restless, more vocal than usual. They cried an eerie moan, causing Grumpy to look around with concern. Then, the camels dropped to their knees and buried their mouths in the sand.

"Kara boran! Kara boran!" Grumpy shouted to the boys, springing into action. The winds picked up and I could feel something bad was going to happen. We mimicked the Uighurs who had tied bandannas over their faces to protect them from the now swirling sands. Two of the camels broke away as a few of the boys tried huddling them at the bottom of the bowl. Running after them and up the banks they either couldn't hear or intentionally ignored the concerned pleas of Grumpy, now struggling with the remaining beasts. I watched as they disappeared into a wall of sand spiraling around the edge of the ridge and helped Grumpy pull up a camel that had nudged its nose deeper in the sand. Getting together to form a protective barrier, we arranged the camels closely on their knees into a circle.

I looked up beyond the rim of our crater into the gray dome of sky above us. It grew darker with the approaching roar. Covering ourselves with the canvas tent, we huddled inside the wall of camels to ride out the storm. We held down the battered tent edges

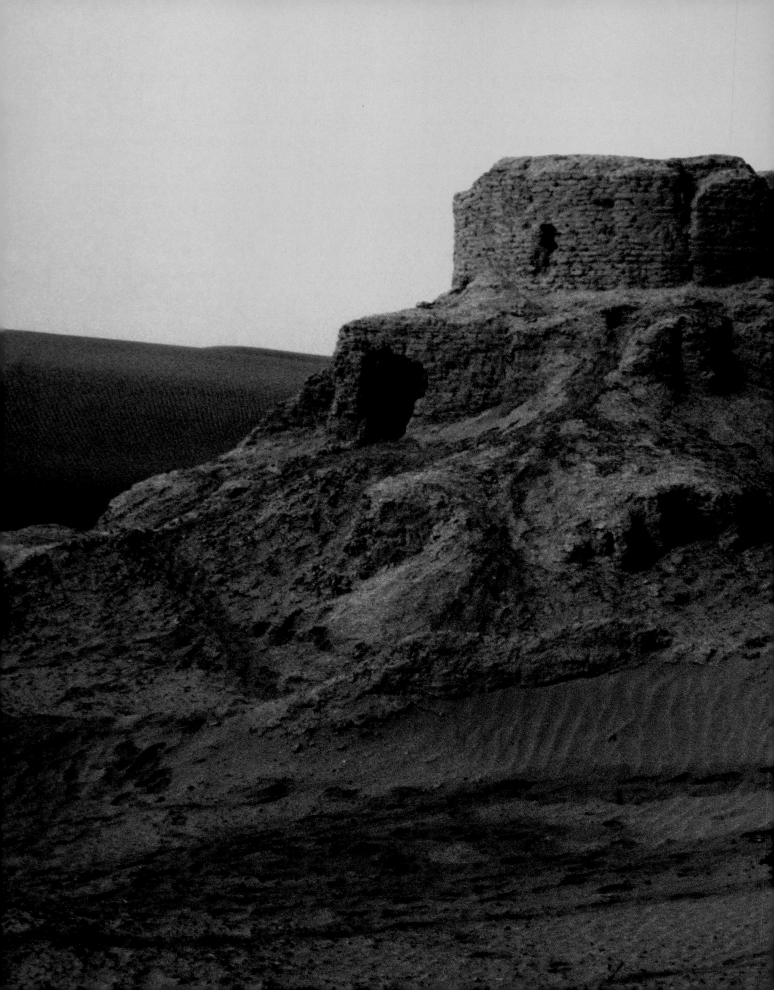

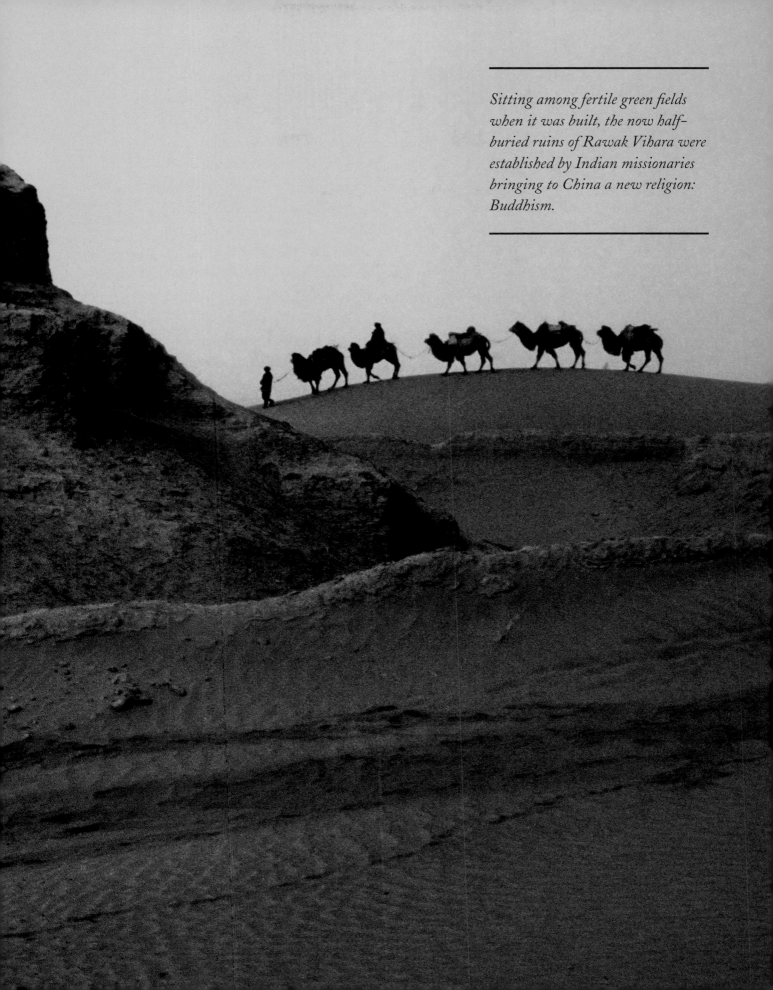

Sitting among fertile green fields when it was built, the now half–buried ruins of Rawak Vihara were established by Indian missionaries bringing to China a new religion: Buddhism.

that were flapping violently out of our hands. Hailing sand pounded the canvas, flying in from pulled-up corners. We were blinded and could hardly breathe, choked by the whipping, stinging grains.

And then the sky went black as night and the flapping stopped. It seemed the storm was abating; the wind had died down and was going away. All of a sudden, sand rained down in a torrent. We struggled to keep the tent from pushing down on us with the pressure of so much weight. Two of the boys couldn't hold a corner that had grown too heavy. Sand poured in from a collapsing dune threatening to drown us. "Why are we riding out this storm in a bowl?" I shouted to Fran, thinking we would have fared better escaping with the camels and boys. I was sure we were going to be buried alive, as if a giant hand was refilling a hole it had dug in the beach. And then as suddenly as it came upon us, it went.

We crawled out to see we'd been covered in inches of sand, clawing the fine dust from our eyes, coughing and blowing our nasal passages clear. Grumpy wiped off a camel bag and pulled up a plastic five-gallon jug of water. He turned to us with concern and kindness and perhaps respect he hadn't shown before. "Yahximusiz?" (Okay?) he asked, pouring the water for us to clear our mouths of grit. Fran returned the favor as I started to dig out the buried, barely visible tent.

To our relief all four boys were in the distance walking toward us with one less camel and we could see the swirling dark storm working its wrath deeper into the desert.

Grumpy berated his two sons for chasing the camels into the storm, but we could tell he was a relieved father. After we found the missing camel, he told us the Karaburunas (black veil or cape) have enveloped whole villages. "Up in the north," he told us. "A few months ago, forty people were killed by a Karaburuna. We are very lucky today; that was a small one." We didn't need much convincing from him to call off Niya and head south to the southern Silk Road. "It's not a Marco Polo site anyway," Fran reminded me.

Those last few days with Alim made us friends, and he proved to have more patience than his brother. One night, his face lit by the blazing stars, he told us of the Jinn. "Uighurs do not have windows in their homes for fear of these spirits," he said, taking his time telling us stories of ghost armies or caravans that roam the desert at night. Our disappointment over Niya was forgotten in his tales. "The spirits go for women," he said. "They torment them, driving them into the desert. This happened to our sister," he confided. "She came out many days later . . . mad, and was never the same."

Before we reached the road and our next town, Keriya, we said farewell to the boys and Alim, whose paternal kindness since the storm had made us realize we'd mislabeled him. We would now forever remember him as "Doc."

The Desert of Lop

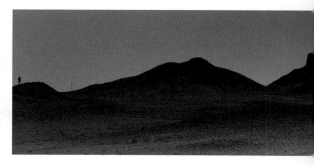

And the Road That Doesn't Exist

TRYING NOT TO BE NOTICED, we rented a grimy room attached to the Keriya bus station. The beds consisted of thin mats thrown over wooden planks stretched between four chairs. It was more comfortable in the desert, but we slept for a solid sixteen hours, hibernating in the noisy room. However, when the door burst open, we leaped instantly to our feet. A squad of green-uniformed public security officers poured in, demanding our documents. We needed to come to the station, they said, to explain how we had gotten here. They couldn't understand how we weren't spotted getting off the bus.

"But that's why we are staying in the station," we lied. "What do you think? We came riding out of the desert?"

We stuck to our stories and they asked us to sign a confession. "I'm not signing anything," Fran said.

"If you don't confess, I revoke your visa, you leave China tomorrow," the officer in charge threatened, handing us paper and pen. "You write."

With no choice, we wrote. "We are sorry that you didn't see us get off the bus, we promise to be more conspicuous in the future." We signed our names and passed it over. For some bizarre reason this satisfied them and we were released.

The bus to Charchan was a zoo. There were a half dozen sheep, cages of birds, and a calf in the aisle. The bus was crowded, unheated, and equipped with seats made only for tiny Asian bodies. I sat on the aisle, kicking a pile of dung out of the way and stretching my feet under the warm, fatty rump of an adult ewe. The lady next to me held two white doves in her hands for the entire fourteen-hour ride. This amazed me because at every stop the Uighurs would push, shove, argue, and climb over each other to get seats. She sat like an angel, never letting go of her birds, feeding them drinking water by taking a sip of hers and letting them stick their prying beaks into her open mouth.

We entertained the Uighurs with our Turkish and our experiences in the desert, and they shared their tea and food with us. Somewhere out there, after the desert had encroached over the road and every bump we hit meant nearly cracking our skulls on the ceiling, we came to a checkpoint. Two Han Chinese PSB officers got on and started making their way toward us, checking a few Uighurs for documents. We pulled our hats over our faces pretending to sleep but they spotted us and asked for our tickets, which they said were no good. We would have to pay them again. It was obvious extortion and we weren't going for it. "Meiyou" (No), we said, refusing to pay.

The Uighurs looked on in amazement, afraid to say anything in our defense. "We already paid the foreigner price (double) at the station and we're not paying again." They asked for our passports, we said "meiyou." They told us to get off the bus, we said "meiyou."

It was about to get even more physical when one of them grabbed my arm. Fran held me back by the scruff of my neck and said in rehearsed Chinese, "Wo fuqin pengyou Deng Xiaoping" (My father is a friend of Deng Xiaoping). The officer let go of my arm as Fran opened up a book we'd been carrying since we left the States. In it were letters to every governor of every province of China on very official stationery. Our friend and sponsor Robert Zincone, the former president of Sikorsky Aircraft, had had them written in Chinese. The clincher was a photo of Zinc shaking hands with Deng Xiaoping, the then Communist Party leader, upon the conclusion of a deal for helicopters. The cops looked at it dumbfounded as I got out a pen and arrogantly grabbed the officer's badge, writing down the numbers. They quickly turned and exited the bus. The driver started it up and we were off to the applause of the Uighurs, who were now slapping us on the backs.

About to take up our Uighur friends' offer and head home with them, we changed our minds when we saw the police waiting in the station and walked out alone, looking for a room.

> *All those who keep inns or provide lodgings for travelers write down the names and dates of their stay. . . . So the Great Khan can know who is coming and going through his domains.*

"Meiyou, meiyou," a man with thick glasses said, refusing our entry and slamming the door in our faces. We had a found a hotel, but with a rude clerk who wouldn't let us in. "Meiyou," he said once more after we knocked again.

We walked the cold, empty streets until we found another hotel, signed in, and quickly fell asleep. Awakened a short time later by the man with thick glasses from the first hotel, we were astonished.

"What do you want?" we asked groggily.

"You must come back and stay in my hotel," he demanded nervously. We slammed the door in his face, returning his earlier kindness, and went back to sleep to the protests of his banging and demands.

The next morning he returned with a tall English-speaking Han in plain clothes, claiming he was the police. He told us we had broken the law by not staying in the one hotel designated for foreigners. "The hotel run by this man," he said, pointing to a now-smiling Mr. Thick Glasses.

"We tried checking into that hotel," pointing back at the hotel clerk, "but that prick wouldn't let us in."

"Give me your passports," he demanded.

"I'm sorry," I said. "Do you have credentials? I mean, you're not in uniform and could be anyone." He looked stunned as I continued, "You understand we don't just hand our passports over to anyone." This made him very angry.

"I asking questions!" he stammered. Definitely a cop, I thought. He was used to being obeyed. We turned to each other.

"Don't you agree, Fran?"

"Oh yes, yes, we couldn't do that, no, no, that wouldn't be appropriate."

We continued babbling in English, totally ignoring them. "No, you should always keep your passport. . . ."

"Stop speaking!" he yelled. "I, I, I off duty, this man come my home, so there be no trouble." We played it dumb. "If you want I go back. Put on uniform," he offered.

Though it was tempting, we thought it better to let him save what little face we'd left him and handed over the passports. He checked the visas, writing down the numbers and our names, and said, "You have one hour to move other hotel, then I arrest you."

We procrastinated, getting there an hour and a half later. The hotel wasn't much different than the off-limits one we had just left, except Mr. Thick Glasses promised there would be hot water. Needless

Ubiquitous along the Silk Road, with its staple aromas of tea and kebob-infused smoky fires, a chai hana or teahouse is a place to eat, rest, and meet people.

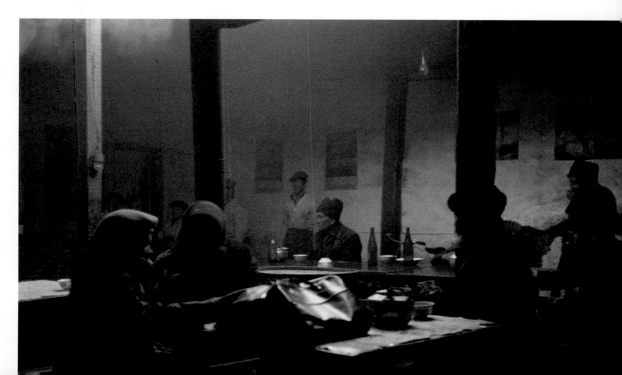

to say, when I had stripped down and was looking forward to my first bath in a while, nothing but dust and air came out of the showerhead.

"Meiyou," was all Mr. Thick Glasses had to say when confronted. "Meiyou." We were beginning to hate the first word we had learned in Chinese.

We woke up at 3:00 a.m. (Beijing time) to catch the nine o'clock bus (local time) leaving for Qarkilik at 5:00 a.m. (Beijing time). Walking the dark, cold streets to the station, we passed two young girls in white surgical masks playing netless badminton under a telephone pole. Loudspeakers crackled and blared, in high-pitched Mandarin, communist propaganda on the reform of agriculture, science, technology, and national defense. An old hunched-over woman passed us, walking backward. I turned to see her gaze transfixed to the ground, her Mao hat the same color as her suit. We passed a man squatting in the dirt over the human-like, pink face of a pig. He was blow-torching the hairs away, turning the flesh black.

It was nightmarish. As if when you have a dream, and in that dream you know you are dreaming, but in reverse, because I knew that I was conscious.

The station was obviously open. The lights were on, buses warming up, people milling about, but the gates were padlocked with a sign saying, "Open eight o'clock." Couples were handing their children and bundles over and climbing the gates. We followed suit, chucking our packs over, only to find the bus wasn't leaving till 10:30—local time.

We pulled into town in late afternoon and were met by two policemen, who had obviously been called ahead. "Where are you going?" they asked.

"To Beijing," we answered facetiously, as they walked with us to the ticket window.

"The road east of here is closed, you must go north to Korla," they warned.

"Yes, we know," assuring them, as we came to the counter. "Liangge piao Korla mingtian" (Two tickets to Korla, tomorrow), I said loudly in pidgin Chinese to the ticket agent, so they could hear. We bought the tickets and they followed us out of the station.

"Where is the foreigner hotel?" we asked them innocently.

"We take you." And off we went with our new shadows.

"We have to travel that road," Fran said as he laid out the NASA map showing the road clearly running east of here, the road that didn't exist on any Chinese map, the off-limits road—closed because it cuts through the desert of Lop, where the Chinese do their nuclear testing.

"If we get caught, it means the end of China, the end of the journey, and all this work," I said. But, we agreed, "It's our only choice. It's the way Polo went. We have to gamble and take the risk."

We waved hello to the uniformed cops out by their jeep, turned a corner, and walked briskly up the street, zigzagging the alleys and cutting into a covered bazaar to get lost in the crowds before finally exiting a side street and ducking into a chai house.

If someone was following us we were sure we had lost him. It was dark and smoky inside and we found a table in the corner and ordered up some laghman noodles. The boy who served us was besotted at the sight of two strange foreigners and couldn't wait to make friends with us.

When we had finished, we asked if he knew anyone we could hire to drive us to Dunhuang. He told us to wait and disappeared into the back room. "What if he's going to get a cop? You never know who is a collaborator," Fran worried. But I had a hunch about the kid, and a half hour later he showed up with his brother Vagar, who became equally enamored with us.

"You know that road is off-limits," he said, which we acknowledged with a lift of our brows and silence. "It would be dangerous, we'd have to drive at night and sleep in the desert." We nodded. "It would be very expensive," Vagar whispered, as if trying to talk himself and us out of it.

That night, we snuck out of the hotel through the communal toilets out back and climbed a wall. Vagar was waiting in an olive-green army jeep as we had agreed. There was another man with him and we threw our packs over the extra gas cans in the back.

We eased off, down the last street claimed from the wilderness before entering a secluded dark alley. The driver shut the lights off, and we left *a city which stands on the verge . . . It is here that men take in provisions for crossing the Great Desert.*

We bounced along in the moonlight to the sound of rocks and boulders hitting the bottom of the jeep. A few hours later the lights of the town had faded behind and the driver took us up a steep embankment to the paved asphalt road. We sped along in silence, expecting the Chinese military to come up behind us at any moment, but not one vehicle did we encounter as the miles rolled away. Without headlights, our eyes had fully adjusted to the illumination the crescent moon offered and it was amazing how much we could see. The purple road led on, raised above the blue dunes and toward the open night sky and horizon. We all stared ahead quietly, hoping the inevitable wouldn't happen. And then it did.

In the distance were the oncoming headlights of a fast-moving vehicle. We slowed down, descended the embankment and hid behind some dunes, shutting off the engine, and sat anxiously until we heard the truck pass and saw the red taillights glow down the road. Greatly relieved, I offered the Uighurs one of the prized Marlboros I'd received in my last care package. We lit up and waited before inching back to the road and continuing east toward dawn. When a thin band of color cut the horizon and the road was turning crimson, we left it and searched for a good hiding place far among the dunes.

> *When a hostile army passes through this country, the people take*
> *flight into the sandy wastes. . . . No one can tell which way they*
> *have gone because the wind covers their tracks with sand . . . so it*
> *seems as if the country has never been traversed by man or beast . . .*
> *this is how they escape their enemies.*

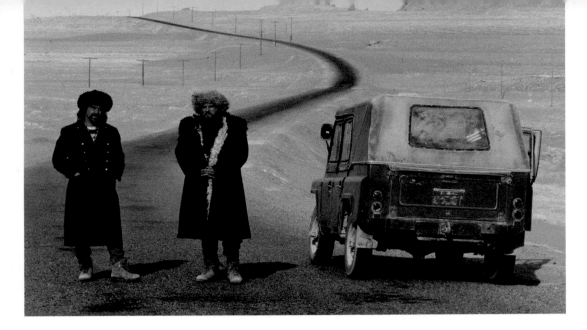

Fran and I on the road that doesn't exist on any Chinese map.

We hid the day away inside the freezing jeep, unable to waste the fuel for heat or build a fire in the dunes; the smoke would have given us away.

The two young Uighurs were classmates and the most anti-Chinese separatists we'd met. "When Kitai (China) is distracted, maybe by the death of Deng Xiaoping, or by some big disaster, we will rise up and revolt to gain our independence," Vagar told us, his breath smoky in the frigid jeep. "They banned all our literature, and our language is outlawed in the schools."

The driver piped up, "We have been here as long as the desert and will only give up our struggle the day a camel's tail reaches the ground."

Just three months before and a few miles away the Chinese had set off an above-ground nuclear test to the anger of the outside world. But I was less concerned about radiation than I was of getting caught out there, hiding with our cameras and lying to the PSB. I felt sure we'd be taken as spies.

"They'll probably just deport us," Fran tried reassuring me.

"Or, your family has to pay for the bullet to the back of your head, if they want your body returned," I said seriously, referring to the Chinese rules of execution.

In the indigo darkness we hit the road again, passing endless salt flats and luckily not seeing another vehicle all night.

As the southern and northern Silk Roads converge on the outskirts of the Taklamakan, there remain crumbling beacon towers that were once kept lit at night. Like lighthouses pointing ships to safety, caravans could see them from miles away and be guided out of the desert. Today there are no fires atop the ruined beacon at Yang Guan Pass, but just beyond its silhouette we could see glowing lights in the distance pointing us toward the ancient oasis city of Dunhuang.

THE MIDDLE KINGDOM

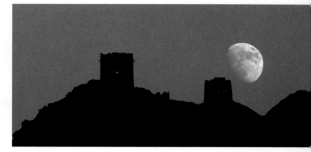

Marco Polo's Fabled Cathay

After you have traveled thirty days through the desert, as I have described, you come to a city called Su-chau, lying towards the east-north-east. . . . It is subject to the Great Khan and lies in a province called Tangut.

WE HAD MADE IT. We had traversed the entire southern Silk Road, one of our greatest obstacles in this quest. We coughed up twenty bucks for a fancy hotel in town and flipped a coin to see who got the shower first. Fran won and I sat waiting. We hadn't washed our bodies in over a month, just our hands and faces. It wouldn't have been fair to ask a poor Uighur family to waste precious fuel (either camel dung chips or ancient driftwood) to heat enough water, besides it would have meant taking off our clothes in the freezing desert. Out there the dirt was just another layer under our dusty long under-wear. Out there I'd gotten used to it. But now, hearing Fran in the shower, singing away, I could hardly contain myself.

"Sorry, dude," he said when he emerged after what felt like an eternity. "The tub's clogged up with water, you'll have to wait until it drains."

When it was still half full, I couldn't wait any longer and had the most religious shower experience of my life. When I had finished and was at the sink shaving, I saw my face in the mirror. It was a strange sensation that I always enjoy, seeing yourself for the first time after coming out of some mountain, jungle, or desert, where you don't care what you look or smell like. I was thinner, hairier, older in a way, but man did I feel exhilarated. I heard the drain of the tub finally emptying and looked to see the whole basin covered in a layer of sand. It had been in our hair, beards, in every pore and nook and cranny of our bodies. It was so thick I was able to write with my finger the word "Taklamakan" in the bottom of the tub.

We went out on the town like two sailors on shore leave. "Tonight we splurge," and sought out the best place in town for our first real Chinese meal.

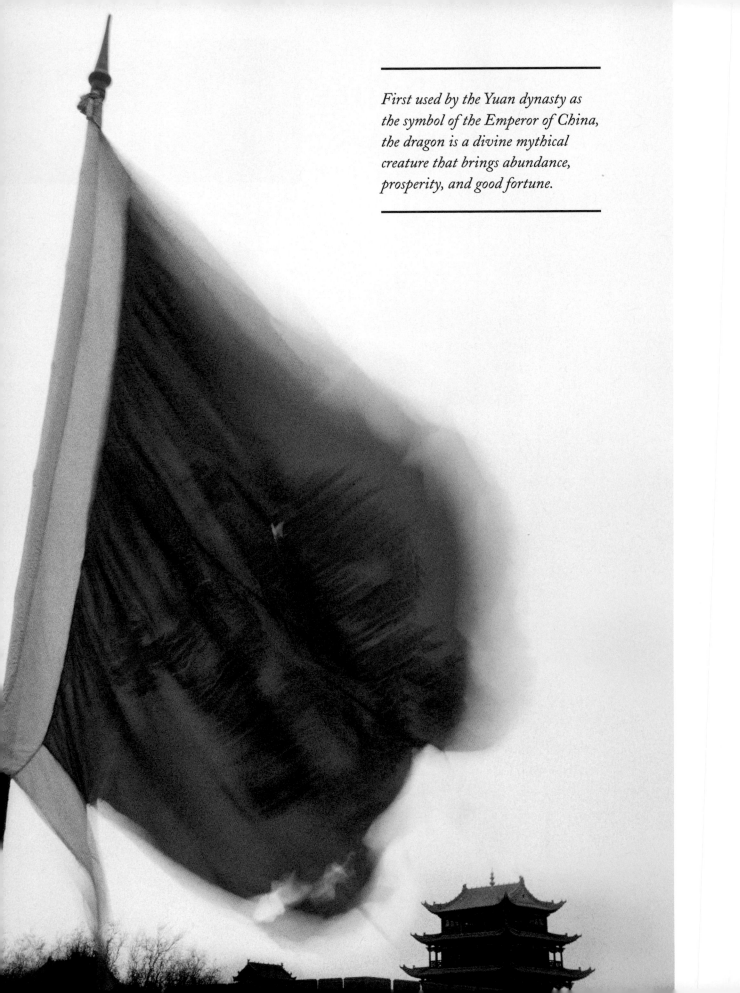

First used by the Yuan dynasty as the symbol of the Emperor of China, the dragon is a divine mythical creature that brings abundance, prosperity, and good fortune.

"If I never taste mutton, goat, or lamb again, it will be too soon," I told Fran as we ordered up a feast of roast pork, soups, fish, and dumplings.

"Some people say that American-style Chinese food is better than real Chinese food," Fran said, stuffing a dumpling in his mouth. "I'll tell you why Chinese food in China is better . . . because you're in China while you're eating it."

We found some nightlife in a string of karaoke bars and enjoyed the company of a table full of girls. They worked us for beers but we didn't mind, female companionship was a welcome change. Most of them were coquettish yet shy and girlish, covering their mouths when speaking.

These ladies are highly accomplished in the use of endearments and caresses, with words suited and adapted to every sort of man, so that foreigners who have once enjoyed them remain utterly besides themselves and so captivated by their sweetness and charm that they can never forget them.

Dunhuang's famous caves have made the town touristy, but not in February. There was only one other guest in our hotel, a lone Japanese tourist on his annual one-week vacation. We joined him for a breakfast of fish soup and went to see the Mogao Caves.

They have many abbeys and monasteries, all full of idols of various forms to which they make sacrifices and do great honor and reverence.

If Dunhuang was a place for caravans to recover after the desert, it was also the last big oasis before entering it from the opposite direction. For these reasons it became important to the fast-spreading religion of Buddhism. Wealthy merchants would sponsor monks and artisans to carve out caves in the Mingsha Hills and adorn them elaborately with Buddhist images. This patronage to the monasteries assured prayers and petitions to the divinities for a safe and profitable journey. For 1,500 years, through successive dynasties, the monasteries flourished here. Then a combination of disasters took place.

In an early case of industrial sabotage, the Persians stole the secret of silk, making it no longer necessary for them to play middlemen to the Chinese. With the crusading Europeans pushed out of the Near East and Holy Land, and the fall of the Mongol-Yuan Empire, there came an end to the Pax Mongolica that had permitted the Polos to travel here. A new dynasty calling themselves the Ming closed off China again. This forced sea routes to be explored, giving us Columbus and the Age of Discovery and leaving Dunhuang and the Silk Road virtually forgotten.

In 1907 a local Taoist monk stumbled upon the sealed caves, containing a mother lode of ancient manuscripts, including the world's oldest printed book. Within a few years, European and American archaeologists looted many of these priceless treasures for their museums, but even so, what was left behind was staggering.

The tower defending the west gate of Jiayuguan Fort has a plaque hanging with characters that read: THE GREATEST PASS UNDER HEAVEN.

Each cave has a brightly painted relief of Buddha seated in the lotus position, flanked by bodhisattvas, inert and undamaged in their multi-

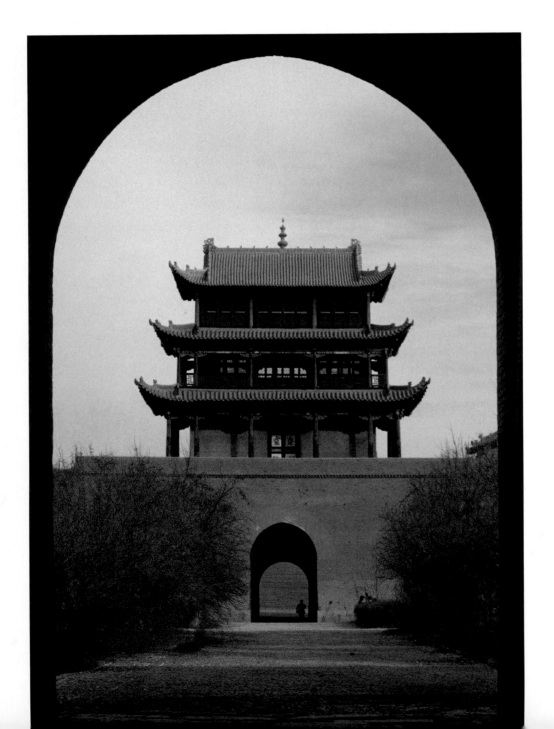

ringed halos. The surrounding frescoes echoed the dynasties that had produced them. There were flying angels, or Apsaras, showing early influences coming up from India. Some caves held hellish visions of a karmic underworld. There were repetitious depictions of the Buddha created during the Wei period, thousands of copycat images, their colors fading into vermillion outlines like old cartoon strips. Our favorites were the Tang dynasty murals. They reminded us of the art of the classic Maya (300–900), the Tang's contemporaries, halfway around the world. The delicate rendering of a bodhisattva's hand as it graced a musical instrument in the Western Heaven was strikingly similar to those in Mayan temple paintings we had seen in the Lacandon and Peten rainforests.

As we always did in such places, we tried to imagine what Dunhuang was like when Polo was here. In the caves the monks would be burning incense, its fragrant odor permeating the whole mountainside. Butter lamps would light the dark grottos from within, the sounds of hundreds, perhaps thousands, of voices would echo as the devoted chanted their prayers. This truly would have been an exotic place for young Marco, because like us, he had just brushed off the dust of Central Asia and was now about to enter the gateway to the Far East: Zhongguo (the Middle Kingdom)—Kitai, China proper, or Cathay, to Marco Polo.

The magnificent fortress at Jiayuguan became the threshold for us, our entrance to a new chapter. Though its forbidding walls had been built as a stoic guard against everything not Chinese, as a powerful symbol for barbarians to keep out, to go away, it meant for us that we'd arrived. Fran's words back in New York echoed in my head: "If we break it down to a bunch of smaller journeys . . ." Well here it was, China, laid out before us, and we were ready to turn the page.

After seven hours' journey to the east, the traveler comes to the large and splendid city of Zhangye, capital of Gansu Province. Polo recorded that he stayed here a year. We searched in vain for Marco's *three fine Christian churches in the city*, but did find China's largest reclining Buddha statue, just as Polo said we would, housed in a grand pagoda dating back a thousand years.

The temple custodians were adamant about policing a strict no-photography rule, so we decided to charm them. "We have come to document Polo's words on film, this is good for China," we explained, showing our letters and photos and lobbying why this statue was so important to us. "Marco Polo stood in this very temple," we told them, "it's one of the only times in his book that he mentions a specific work of art."

The keepers of the temple formed a party committee around our book of letters deciding what to do, only to reject us with a single dreaded *meiyou*. We went away blind with anger and determined to come back for as long as it took to get our jobs done.

Every day for a week, we'd ascend the stairs and entered the huge doors into a dark, secret world. Our eyes would need time to adjust and we'd stand still until the splendor of the sculpture would come into view. At first we viewed it just as superficially as Polo had.

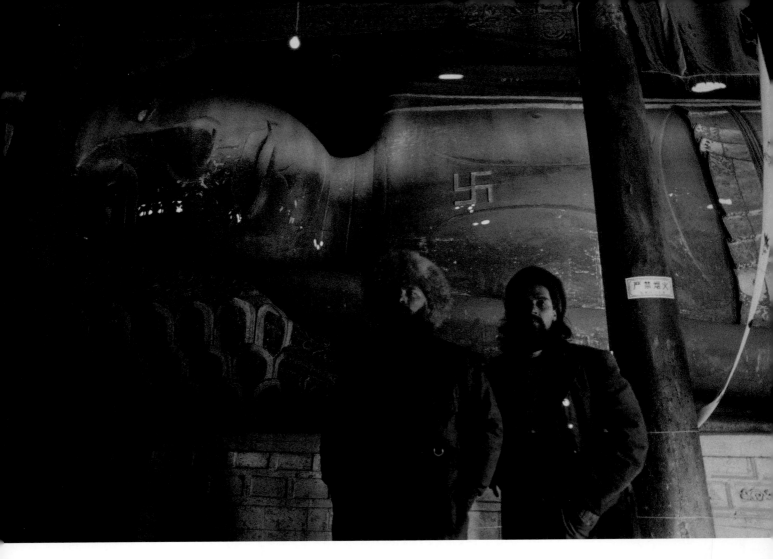

Svastika is a Sanskrit word meaning "all is well." In the Buddhist tradition of India, it means "seal on the Buddha's heart," and it is considered an auspicious talisman.

These huge idols are recumbent . . . all covered with excellently worked gold . . . and groups of lesser ones are set about them doing humble obedience.

But after sitting for days contemplating this great work, what began as a scheme to get the guards accustomed to us and open to a bribe turned into a sublime meditation. Perhaps we had, by the very nature of the project we'd undertaken, been concentrating too much on the past. The Buddha's peaceful expression as he enters nirvana made us reflect on what really matters. Right here, right now, this moment.

TIBET

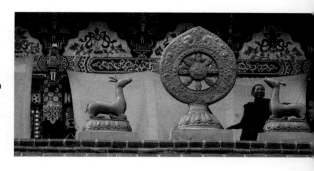

"The Greatest Illuminations the World Has Ever Seen"

THE BUS WOUND ITS WAY THROUGH A FOREST of tall pines dusted with snow. The clean-scented air wafting into the stinky bus awoke in me a great feeling of well-being—the smell of the trees back home, upstate in the woods, a smell I hadn't been expecting, a smell I hadn't experienced for what seemed a great while. It was like comfort food, a childhood memory, Christmas.

We came down out of the hills and into a picturesque valley where in the distance a golden roof glittered in the late-day sun. As we approached the lamasery, a complex of exquisite buildings rose out of the terra-cotta soil. They were painted white with wooden beams exposed and trapezoidal windows painted black, contrasting beautifully. They were all crowned with golden stupas, befitting their status as among the holiest temples in Tibetan Buddhism.

After the bus came to its final halt we clambered out into the road and started walking in the direction of a group of colorfully dressed women. Unable to keep our eyes off their crazy fox and silken hats; robes with lynx and snow leopard trimmings; and chunky silver, turquoise, and amber necklaces, we nearly stumbled over another group lying facedown in the middle of the lane.

The figures slowly rose up, their faces covered in dust, their yellow eyes and moist lips jumping out at—and into you—like that old film footage of Bob Dylan onstage in whiteface singing "Tangled Up in Blue." They took a big step forward, bringing their hands together in prayer above their heads, then slowly down to their chests. Dropping to heavily padded knees they lay facedown in the road again, kissing the dirt and extending their arms straight in front of them. Some clutched wooden hand protectors as they went.

We passed more Tibetan pilgrims fully prostrating themselves this way, in a self-enforced march of pain, encircling the monastery dozens of times. Spinning their prayer

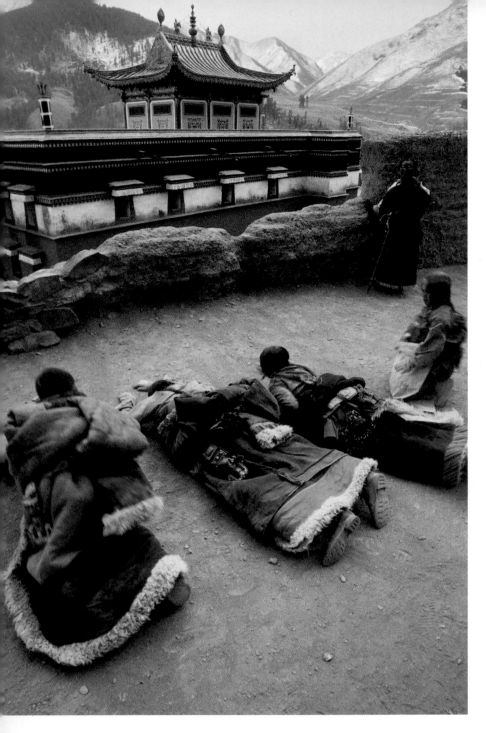

The Labrang Monastery holds a special place in the hearts of the Tibetan people, and it is one of the holiest sites for the Gelukpa or Yellow Hat sect.

wheels and mumbling prayers, they wound their way around the temple complex on bloodied hands and knees. The scent of smoldering juniper branches rose from inside secret chambers as they passed the temples, each circuit bringing good karma and blessings for the New Year. And the New Year was why they had come. From all over Tibet they were flooding in to Xiahe and the Labrang Lamasery, for the lunar calendar was drawing to an end and the Monlam Cham, or Great Prayer Festival, was about to begin.

The new year begins with them in February. . . . And they greet one another gaily and cheerfully saying, very much as we do; "May this year be a lucky one for you and bring you success."

Xiahe is part of a region traditionally called Amdo, which includes parts of Qinghai and Gansu provinces and the fringes of the windswept Tibetan Plateau. Tsongkhapa, the founder of the dominant Gelukpa or Yellow Hat sect and the greatest reformer of Tibetan Buddhism, was born in Amdo—as was the current Dalai Lama.

Tibetan fashion has long involved wearing coats of tiger and snow leopard pelts, but the Dalai Lama has recently asked his followers to stop using, selling, or buying these increasingly rare wild animals.

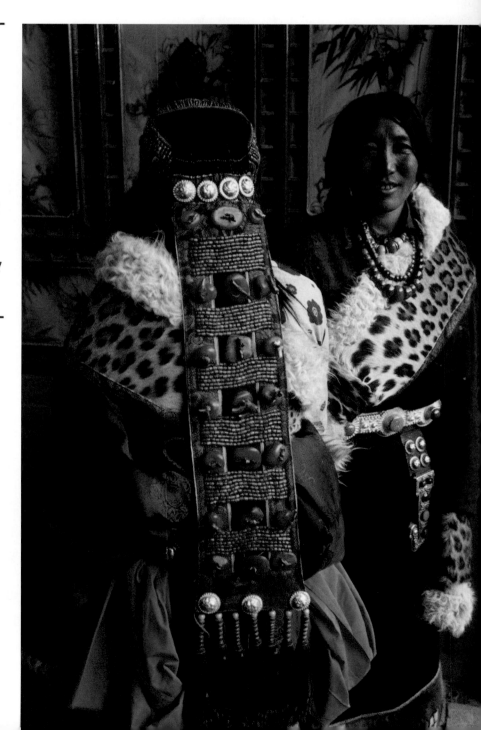

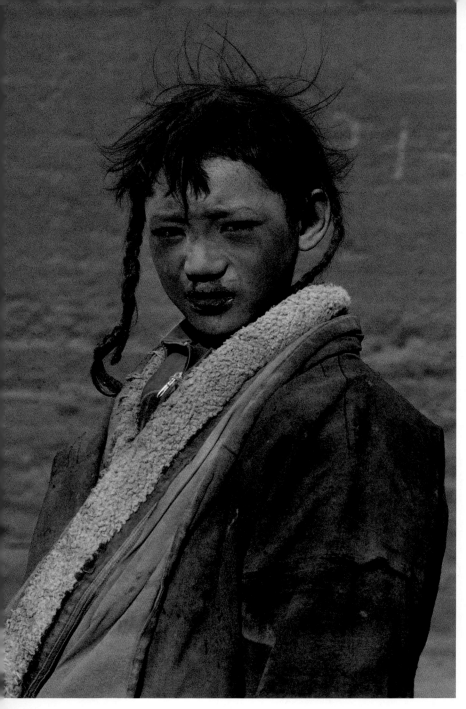

It was Tsongkhapa who initiated the Monlam festival as an annual reminder of the unbreakable link between the Tibetan people and their Buddhist faith.

The struggle to preserve their religion and culture and to recover from the damage of the Cultural Revolution and years of harsh suppression has given Monlam added symbolic meaning. These pilgrims, nomads, and monks were saying, "We are here, as we always have been and always will be."

We found our way to a rugged little shack inside the monastery grounds that was being rented out by a stooped-over monk named Lobsang. We paid for a week in advance and he showed us the outhouses and where to get our coal and dung for the little stove in our room.

A middle-aged white man knocked on our door to ask if one of us was a journalist named Stuart Smith. He had a letter for him.

"Nope." Fran chuckled over my shoulder. "But, I'd be glad to read his letter."

The tall, gawky man at the door had a slight French accent, maybe Canadian, I thought.

"No, I live in Paris but I'm a Greek who was born in Ethiopia," he said. "My name is Ted. Are you guys hungry? I know the best restaurant in town."

Tibetans send their sons to the lamasery to be educated in Buddhist scriptures, Tibetan language, handwriting, literature, and art as well as philosophy, logic, and astronomy.

We walked the muddy lanes until we found a main drag of shops facing each other as Tibetan pilgrims milled about. Over momo dumplings and chrysanthemum tea, Ted told us he was five years into a ten-year book project about Tibetan mysticism. We picked his brains about the upcoming festival and its meanings and origins and walked home through the dark alleyways to the

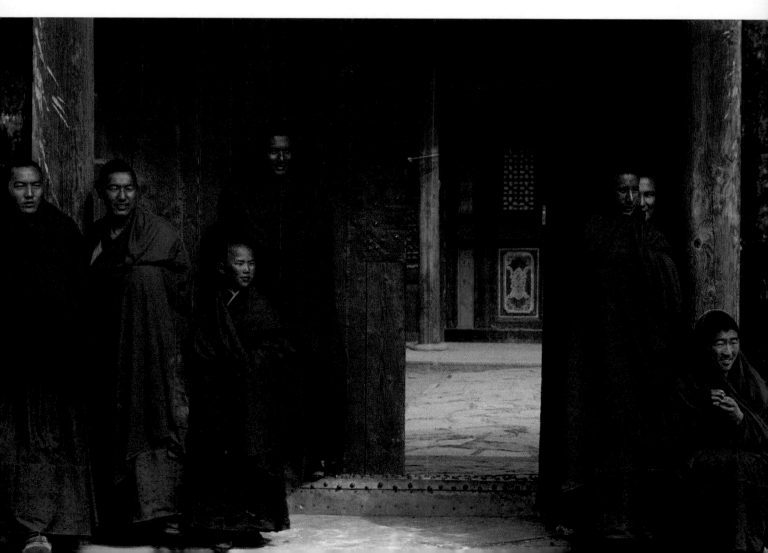

blast of fireworks, which continued all night, some sounding like half-sticks of dynamite exploding just outside the compound walls.

The morning brought snow and with it quiet, so we slept until noon before heading out to watch a hundred or so monks, kids really, playing football in a courtyard facing a temple. They weren't playing soccer per se, but kicking the ball up as high as they could then chasing after it without tripping over their robes. Interspersed among the ball chasers were firecracker-wielding boys with shaved heads who menaced us with their little bombardments as we photographed the whole scene.

According to legend, in the first month of the year, Buddha conquered or converted six holy men of false religions. From New Year's Day until the end of Monlam, people continue to eat, drink, and make merry. The festival culminates with a dance called the Chamba. The Cham dance is meant to scare off evil and bring good fortune for the year to all attendees.

They perform the most potent enchantments and the greatest marvels to hear and behold by the diabolic arts, which is better not to relate in our book, or men might marvel over such.

Ted told us there was a Tibetan tribe called the Soul Stealers of Khum. "They'll poison your tea or *chang* (beer) with a toxin that won't kill you until eight months later when you're home in New York. By that time, they've already offered your soul up to their particular idol."

"Doesn't that go against everything it means to be a Buddhist?" I asked.

"Absolutely," he said. "But older, darker, shamanistic rituals have never left Tibet, making Tantric Buddhism unique among all Buddhist sects. I'll tell you this," he said, pausing for effect as he leaned in and whispered. "There are dark rituals being performed here, now as we speak, somewhere in the bowels of this lamasery, with human skulls and burnt offerings. Black magic calling for the death of the Chinese premier and the fall of the Beijing government." He went on, "When I finish this project I will take my photos of these rituals to Dharamsala to show to his Holiness the Dalai Lama and say, 'What's up with this?'"

I stared at him. We were speechless. The basic tenet of Buddhism is that all life is sacred. To have even bad thoughts is detrimental to your karma. "You don't think the Dalai Lama knows of these rituals?" I asked.

"Of course he does," Ted answered, letting out a girlish giggle, obviously pleased with himself before going on about the Chinese occupation and destruction of Tibetan culture.

"They are very clever," he said of the PSB. "They used to go around destroying temples and shooting and beating monks, but they got such bad press after that,

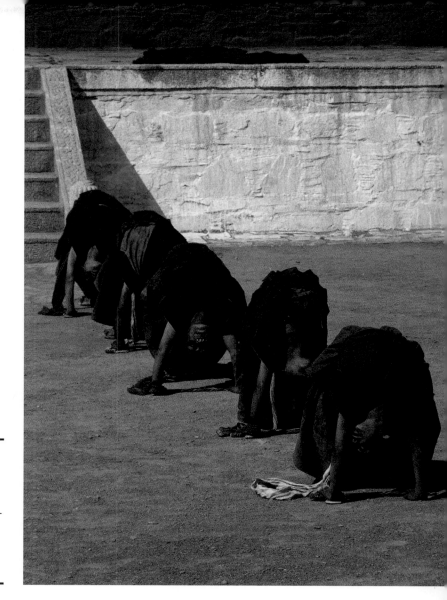

*Under the watchful
gaze of their teachers,
young monks practice ritu-
alized moves steeped in
mythology.*

they've switched tactics and are now silently smothering Tibet with tourist hotels, Chinese workers, karaoke bars, and fast-food chains. They did it at Kumbum—the Taer Si Monastery—in Qinghai Province, and they'll do it here in Xiahe too. . . . Unless the Tibetans fight back and go back to their old ways, they will be assimilated to death."

Until their conversion to Buddhism with its gentle message of compassion and nonviolence, the Tibetans were feared by their neighbors. Their conquered territory included all of Gansu, much of Sichuan and Yunnan provinces, and at one point they even occupied Xi'an, the ancient capital of China.

馬哥孛羅

Our little coal- and dung-fed pot-bellied stove did little to keep us warm in the frigid winter weather. "I'm going for a shower," I told Fran one morning as I pushed the woolen blanket from the door and headed out. We had found a place in the muddy town to take hot showers for twenty cents and had been going as often as possible, just to get relief, however fleeting, from the deep cold and weariness we felt in our bones. When I had finished and was walking back I saw Fran coming toward me.

"What are you doing? Where is my stuff?" I snapped.

We had an unwritten rule, when one of us was out the other watched his gear, wallets, passports, cameras. We never slept at the same time on trains or buses so we could keep an eye out for each other, and we never left a room alone with the other guy's stuff in it. Never.

"Why have you left my gear alone?" I was pissed, and he didn't have a good answer. I went back, got my stuff, and moved into another room. The next morning I knocked on his door. "I'm going to the post office, do you need anything?

"What would I need from a post office in the middle of Tibet?" he snapped back.

"Maybe a stamp, you blockhead."

I heard heavy footsteps behind me as I neared the post office and turned, ready to find Van Gogh with his ear in his hand, but Fran was smiling. We entered the small adobe room heated by a single bukhari stove; it had more Han than Tibetan employees, who were busy pounding rubber seals on everything.

"Look man, maybe I have altitude sickness," he offered guiltily, putting a hand on my shoulder. "I wasn't thinking when I left the room yesterday, I just forgot."

"Listen," I said, still angry but softening. "We haven't been ripped off yet, let's try to keep it that way."

"Okay . . . but just remember . . . if I have to kill you, I'm not shipping you home," he threatened jokingly. "I'll bury you where you fall and keep going."

Fight over.

The town started to get crowded with pilgrims, many arriving from long distances, hundreds of miles on their hands and knees performing what we had come to learn was called parikrama. It seemed that only women and girls punished themselves this way. A scruffy man in rags passed and stuck his tongue out at us. Then another. In fact whenever we made eye contact with people, they'd stick their tongues out at us. We started doing it back and got a lot of smiles in return. It was some sort of greeting.

We passed a small shop with a stand of cassette tapes out front and an assortment of false teeth in various shades behind a glass counter. In the center of the small, square room was an old-fashioned barber chair bolted into blood-stained cement. Tibetan pop music was blaring from distorted speakers. In the chair sat a large Tibetan woman, her silk and fox hat hanging on the wall. Her hair was braided tightly in dozens of tiny rows like you see teenage white girls getting when they're on vacation in the Caribbean. Her head was thrown back, her mouth agape, and a Han Chinese in a dirty white frock was working a hand drill on one of her molars. I didn't see any syringes and assume she wasn't anesthetized; I watched in amazement as he finished drilling then loaded up the cavity with silver. When he realized we were there, the dentist left his patient and started trying to sell us some tapes. We lowered the volume on his boom box and listened as he changed tapes until we showed interest. The patient sat waiting, her mouth stuffed with cotton. She gave her thumbs up to the traditional music we liked and we bought two tapes, leaving him as he filed down his pack job to the lady's liking.

The Panchen Lama's image was everywhere. All the shops sold little postcards of the Chinese-sanctioned number-two spiritual leader of Tibet. "They should make baseball cards of the different lamas," Fran said. "You can have their stats on the back. Like, he was born in 1348 as Tingba and came back in 1789 as Singhma."

"Yeah," I said, "as the sixth Panchen Lama he had sixty-two homers and as the ninth he was a shortstop."

"No, seriously, how come there are no cards with the Dalai Lama on them?"

"Because it is illegal, the Chinese forbid it, making it as rare as a Honus Wagner. You'd need to trade a slew of Panchens for one Dalai."

We found a shop that did have black-market cards of His Holiness. After being taken to a darkened cellar, a nondescript shoe box was pulled from a stack of identicals, no doubt containing shoes. The lid was opened and there he was, in black and white, as a young rookie shaking hands with Mao Zedong. We bought some of him in color, as the world knows him now, older, smiling, his eyes shining from behind those wire-framed glasses, to give out carefully as presents to the Tibetans we befriended.

Our moods lightened with the palpable air of merriment that had brought the town alive. More shops opened. The main thoroughfare grew muddier with horses and their aftermath. Hundreds of pilgrims were walking in, prostrating, jostling, selling, buying, and trading. We swept past a cheery group of men, high on chang, singing off-key, and holding each other steady. Two beautiful twin girls with impossibly high cheekbones and soul-stealing eyes, dressed in rich silken robes and dripping in amber and coral necklaces, shied away from some horses and ducked into a doorway. I made eye contact with one from across the lane and she smiled.

"I am done," I said to Fran. "I don't need eight months to be offered up, she could have my soul right now."

By a small stupa we found a monk standing atop a scaffold and pouring blessed yak butter tea from a dull tin kettle over the crowd of pilgrims. They clutched empty jars and enthusiastically clambered over each other to try and catch a few precious drops.

We ducked into a silk shop following another girl with a magnificent coral headpiece and pretended to browse. The light flooding in through the shop window added drama to the rows of pleated silks, their intense colors emerging from the dark shadows. She was wearing a high-collared blue silk tunic with gold embroidery and stunning coral earrings and necklace.

*They have huge monasteries and abbeys inhabited by 2,000 monks
who are better dressed than other men. They wear their heads and
chins clean-shaven and live an austere life.*

There were shops selling antique Chinese opera costumes; Tibetan jewelry, big
massive silver rings that cover whole fingers with salmon-colored coral beads; leather-
beaded fire pouches that housed flint and tinder; enameled snuff boxes and carved cin-
nabar vases; and silk embroideries and bolts of cloth.

In a matter of days the town swelled, throbbing with commerce and people. After
all the months of gray skies and desolate, uninhabited, monochromatic wilderness, we

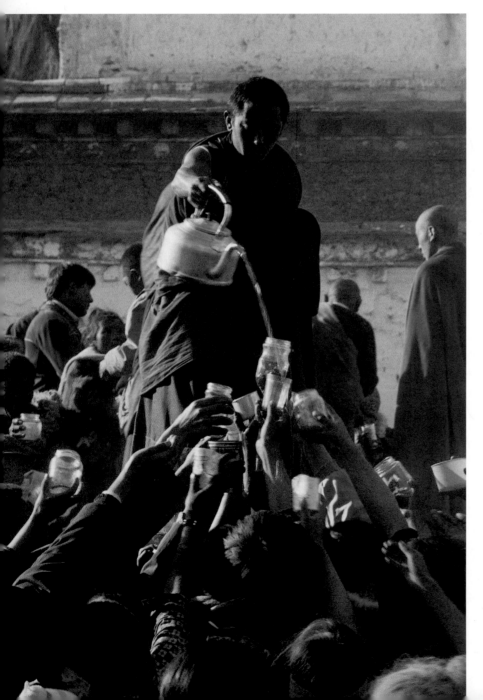

*Tea made from
the water of the
Living Buddha's
well is dispersed
to an eager crowd.
According to tradi-
tion a guest's cup
of salted yak butter
tea should never be
empty.*

felt like Dorothy waking up in a world of Technicolor. It was a dream, for the Tibetans believe the world reflects their collective consciousness. "All things are Buddha things," a monk had told us. "What your mind is capable of imagining, it will create. Everything, the mountains, air, water . . . all matter, has been dreamed up by you, us . . . the collective consciousness."

We felt by entering their world we had entered their dream. Unlike Dunhuang, this place was alive, and we let it become our own quixotic Tibet. Transported back again to a lost world hidden in the mountains, we had entered a forbidden theocratic kingdom, a Shangri-la from the thirteenth century.

We never spoke of it, it was silently understood, but we put on blinders to anything modern that we would encounter. The rare car loudly passing or telephone wires were invisible to us. The occasional foreigner we'd see was deleted from the scene. We inhabited as exotic a place as either of us had ever been, yet we had to make it even more exotic and our own.

A New England accent stopped us dead in our tracks and dragged us temporarily into the present. "Which one of you guys is Attila the Hun and which one is Genghis Khan?" We turned abruptly as if to ask, "Who dares mock us?" to see a twenty-something American kid with shiny, newly shampooed hair hanging to his shoulders from under an olive-green Mao hat. He stood a few feet below in the muddy lane and was looking up at us through round John Lennon glasses. "Who are you guys?"

"Where are you from?" I asked, smiling.

"I'm from Maine. Are you guys Americans?" He stepped up onto the boarded sidewalk and out of the mud and introduced himself as Shawn Mullin. "I'm teaching English in Beijing for a year and decided to take a break and see a bit of China."

"Well, welcome to the Yuan dynasty, lil' buddy!" Fran said as he slapped him on the back.

Adopted on the spot, Shawn found himself checked out of his comfy room with running hot water and a feather mattress and checked in to the plain cell next to ours at the monastery. We stayed up at night, reading from our journals and talking about things that you only learn about yourself when you're traveling. It was good for Fran and me to have a third party around that we both liked, and even better to speak English with someone else. Besides, we knew each other's stories inside out after years of traveling together.

We convinced Shawn to stay for the festival, and over the next few weeks he became our little brother. The three of us explored the lamasery together, peering inside the smoky temples and watching the young monks practice the intricate dances they needed to perform for the Cham. There were courtyards filled with hundreds of student monks preparing for exams by debating in pairs, making windmill gestures with their arms and slapping their hands when they had made their point. The debates are an important part of the festival and the only way to raise a monk's title closer to a lama.

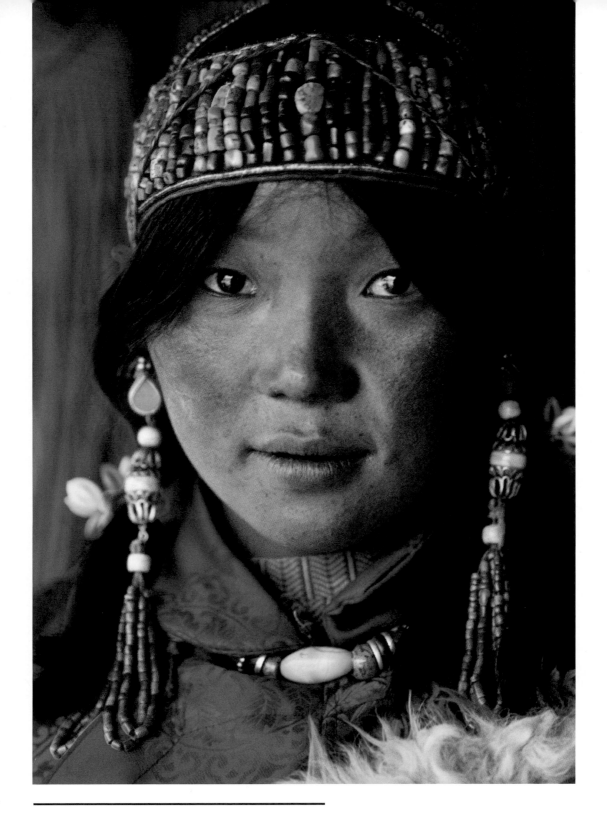

For centuries coral has been prized in the Himalayan regions of Tibet, Nepal, Bhutan, and India. It is sold by weight and is considered by Tibetans to be worth more than gold.

They speak their own language and call themselves Tibet. . . . In
this province coral brings a high price for it is hung round the necks
of women and idols with great joy.

I was people watching, waiting outside the bathhouse for Fran one morning, when a handsome Gan tribeswoman in a giant fox hat stuck her tongue out at me as she passed. She pointed to my camera and with an alluring smile gestured for me to walk with her and two companions to what I assumed was their house. Her beauty was enhanced by the headpieces of amber, coral, and silver medallions all three had intricately woven into their long braids of hair. I tried to explain with sign language that my friend was inside but they kept walking, waving me to follow.

I stuck my head into the showers to hurry Fran and ran back to watch which way they'd headed. By the time he came out they were still visible a quarter mile down the road. We caught up and as we followed a path that ran beside a river to their home, we had a wonderful conversation that neither side understood. They led us to a tidy little cabin in the woods with the aroma of newly cut pine exuding from the paneling and furniture. Their abode and jewelry all signaled their prosperity. The one man in the room spoke little and soon disappeared before anyone could notice.

They fed us a feast of air-dried yak meat on the bone, fried momos, assorted cakes and breads, and endless cups of yak butter tea. It was the first time we had been in a non-Muslim home in a long time; between the music and incense and open flirtation, I was caught off guard. The woman who had beckoned me kept pointing to my nose then to hers and then the bed. I turned to Fran for help but he had disappeared with one of the other women. The others in the room seemed to vanish as well, though I have a memory of their voices, of them being close.

I assure you that a man does not think it an outrage if a traveler
makes free with his wife or daughter or sister or any women in his
house. . . . By this act their Gods and idols are pleased.

馬哥孛羅

The festival officially began when a two-hundred-foot tangka of the Buddha was marched from its sanctuary by dozens of strong-armed monks, who then lugged the giant painting up a steep hill for unfurling. As they made their way through the thousands of gathered pilgrims, men on horseback flanked them. Nobly dressed, they reminded us of knights, wielding lances and beating back the crowds who surged forward in waves to touch and kiss the sacred icon. The largest Tibetans we had seen so far were acting as

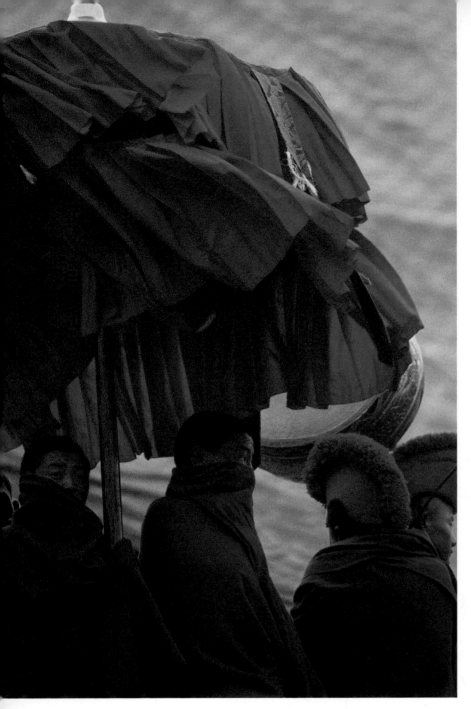

The parasol is one of eight auspicious symbols of Buddhism. Its function is to cast a shadow, symbolizing protection from the heat, suffering, and desire of spiritually harmful forces.

bouncers, pushing people away, their own backs to the awkward tug-of-warlike movements of the tangka-carrying monks. The devoted pilgrims who were in a frantic state to be near it, to touch their foreheads to it, leapt for the tangka, only to be repelled and then trampled underfoot by the crowd behind them.

We scrambled alongside as it snaked its way up like a giant yellow centipede with hundreds of human legs. The dust kicked up by the masses was backlit by the midmorning sun, which had now crested the mountain we were climbing. The monks were struggling under its weight, heaving the unwieldy painting up the embankment. When they reached the top, the enormous tangka was unrolled until the din of the people was hushed. The head lama sat opposite the sacred image under a saffron parasol as prayers were offered and dances performed. After he rose abruptly and left, the monks rolled up the tangka and the crowd dissipated back into the town.

They make lavish feasts for their idols with the most magnificent hymns and illuminations that were ever seen.

On the day of the Cham we arrived in the main courtyard early, positioning ourselves up front. Only one bouncer monk gave us a hard time until he saw our passes and

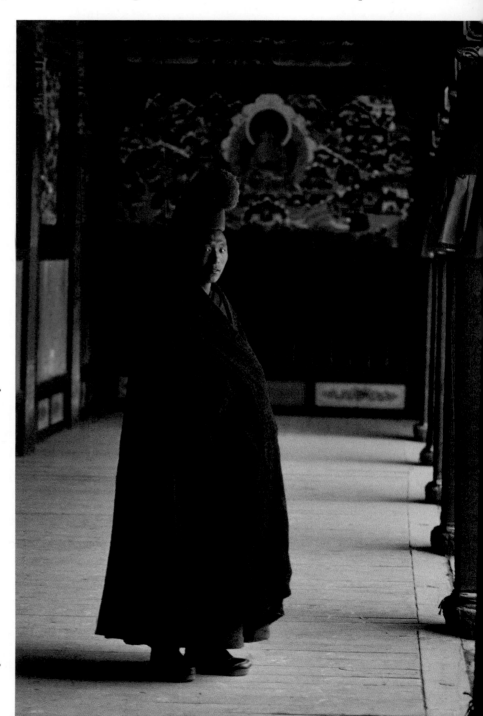

Monks living cloistered from society, heads shaven, the smell of incense and the repetitious chanting of prayers, surely would have struck Polo as oddly similar to those living the monastic life in Europe.

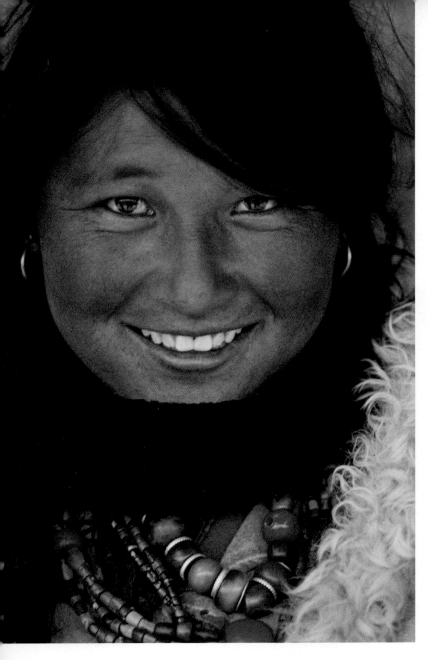

The rosy cheeks of Tibetans may be caused by having more nitric oxide in their blood than people who dwell at sea level. This allows blood vessels to dilate, bringing more oxygen to their extremities in the oxygen-thin air of high altitudes.

we were able to move around the circle chalked into the dirt for the dancers. Thousands of pilgrims jammed the square, quiet and well behaved as the bouncers walked among them with large sticks ready to whack the heads of any rowdies. We sat on the frozen ground for hours until midday, when a procession of monks in bright orange robes came through the center doorway. The head lama took his seat on a balcony overlooking the courtyard. Seated to his right was a young living Buddha. The musicians came and took their places. Giant horns were propped up with cutout dragons and drums painted with evil faces were banged in unison.

A flock of monks, wearing giant yellow crescent hats, entered with a clash of cymbals, followed by throat singers moaning their deep hypnotic chants. A curtain opened and the boy monks we had seen practicing came running out in skeleton costumes to perform ancient steps in a ritualistic dance.

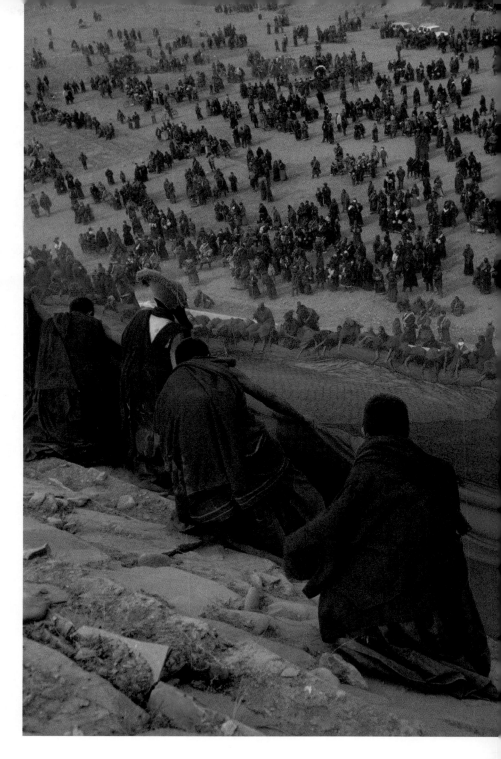

Monks unfurl a giant painting of the Buddha, called a tangka, for the pilgrims flooding into Labrang by the thousands gathered below.

Next an assortment of ferociously masked dancers in green, red, blue, and yellow—zoomorphic creatures with bulging bloodshot eyes, large grotesque noses, and fang-covered lips—danced along the chalked-out lines that enclosed their universe. Benevolent spirits in demonic disguise, they had to be scarier than the evil they chased away.

A priest in silk gowns embroidered with dragons and geometric designs entered the center of the ring and spilled blood from a cup made from the top of a human cranium. Four skull-masked monks representing the four directions pushed dirt over the dark-stained earth and retreated to their corners. The priest opened an orange box

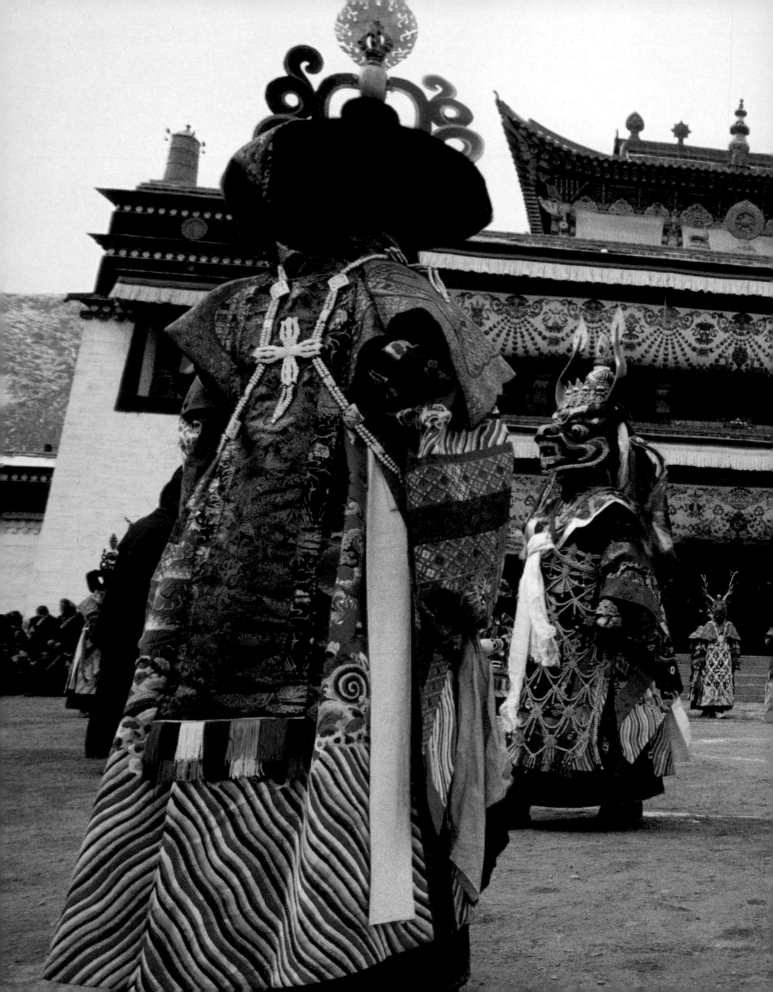

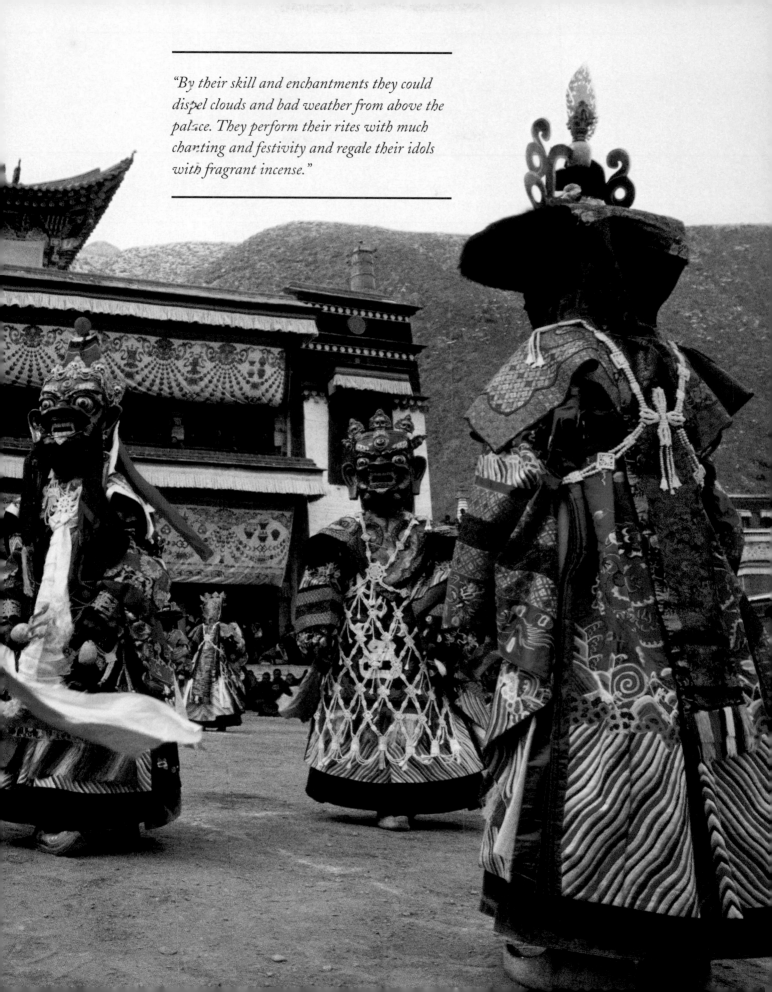

"*By their skill and enchantments they could dispel clouds and bad weather from above the palace. They perform their rites with much chanting and festivity and regale their idols with fragrant incense.*"

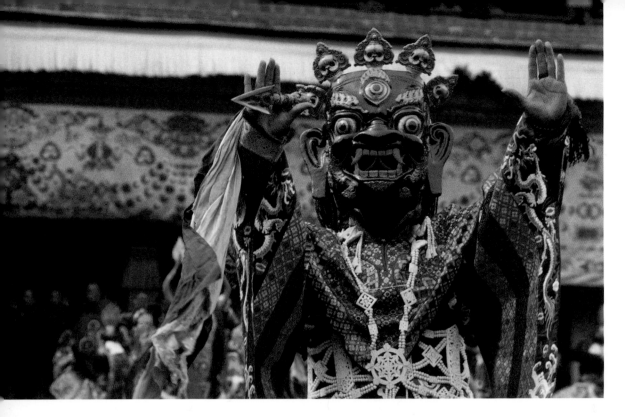

and removed a bloody knife. The masked spirits began again to encircle the priest, moving in rhythm to the music and striking fearful poses when the drums, horns, and cymbals reached a crescendo. The priest made secret gestures with dorje (scepter) and knife, symbols of power and divinity.

The Cham went on like this for hours, the crowd mumbling their prayers and kneading their prayer beads behind us. We sat mesmerized, in awe of the spectacle in front of us, ringside seats to a forbidden rite. Cham is not a form of entertainment. It is a spiritual practice that the dancer undertakes as a meditation in order to liberate other beings from suffering. It is considered very sacred and is thought to bring good luck to those who view it. Pilgrims attend the day-long dance ceremonies, believing in the power of the dance to remove obstacles and bestow blessings upon them. Not unlike the stained-glassed windows of Europe's Gothic cathedrals, the brightly colored masks and costumes assist ordinary people to envision that which they hold sacred, intensifying their religious experience.

It was during these times that I made a conscious effort to burn the scene into my mind: the snow-dusted hills covered with pilgrims behind the lamasery, the otherworldly sounds of the throat singers and horns, the smell of the oily smoke from the burning juniper branches. The photos I took are a record, and just that. These memories are the souvenirs we'll keep forever.

In Xanadu

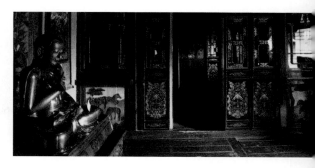

There Was No Stately Pleasure Dome

W HEN THE GREAT KHAN HEARD the Polo brothers were approaching, he sent out a royal escort to bring them to his palace at Shangtu, otherwise known as Xanadu. It had been over three years since the Polos had left Venice, and they had traveled thousands of miles with the sun always setting at their backs. About to meet the most powerful man on earth, Marco later recalled in detail to Rusticello what must have been one of the greatest moments of his life:

> *They knelt before him and made obeisance with the utmost humil-*
> *ity. The Great Khan bade them rise and received them honorably.*
> *. . . He asked many questions about their condition and how they*
> *had fared. . . . The brothers assured him that they had fared well.*
> *. . . Then they presented the letters which the Pope had sent, with*
> *which he was greatly pleased, and handed over the holy oil, which*
> *he received with joy and prized very highly. When the Great Khan*
> *saw Marco, who was a young stripling, he asked who he was.*
> *"Sire," said Messer Niccolo, "he is my son and your liege man."*

Now twenty-one years old and fluent in four languages, Marco enthralled Kublai with stories of the Great Khan's domain through which he had just traveled. So impressed was Kublai with the young European's eye for detail, he became a special emissary to the Khan, sent far and wide throughout the empire so that he could come back and recount the tales of the strange places and marvels he had seen.

> *What need to make a long story of it? You may take it for a fact that*
> *Messer Marco stayed with the Great Khan fully seventeen years;*
> *and in all this time never ceased to travel on special missions. . . .*

And the Great Khan . . . held him in high esteem and showed him
such favor . . . that the other lords were moved to envy.

馬哥孛羅

In Xanadu, we found there was no stately pleasure dome, no lush gardens filled with game, no sumptuous concubines. There was only a windswept plain and the remnants of an outer brick wall that once encompassed the Great Khan's summer palace. Destroyed by the Ming so there would be no memory of the Yuan—we stood there defying them, daring to remember.

Perhaps it was just the stinging wind, but our eyes were tearing as we paid tribute to the historic meeting that had taken place here seven hundred years before. Upon these ruins and in their memory, we poured the holy oil we had been carrying all year from the Church of the Holy Sepulchre in Jerusalem and swore, come summertime, we'd head up to Mongolia to find the living Xanadu.

The Great Wall would appear now and again out the train window as we approached Beijing. It fell below us like a roller-coaster track over the undulating hills only to disappear when the train took an unexpected turn. Our eyes flitted across the screen until the wall showed up again. Months ago near Jiayuguan Fort, we had seen it where it came to an end, at its westernmost extent. A modern

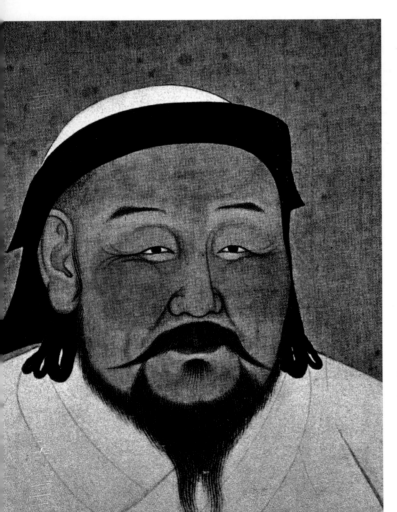

Portrait of Kublai Khan painted in 1295. "Let me tell you of the appearance of the Great Lord of Lords . . . Kublai Khan. He is a man of good stature . . . his limbs fleshed out. . . . His complexion fair and ruddy like a rose, the eyes black and handsome, the nose shapely and set squarely in place."

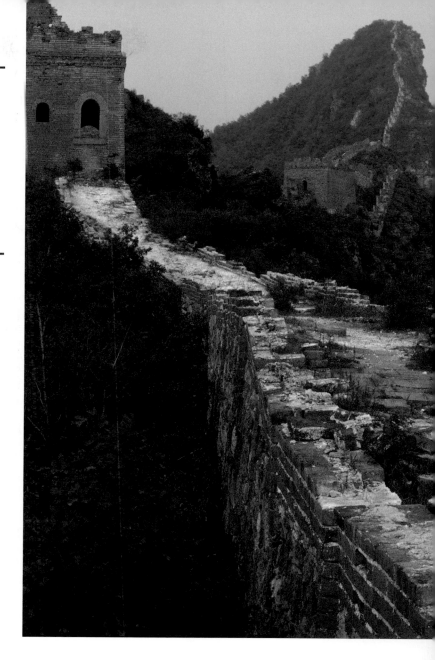

The best-known parts of the Great Wall were built after the fall of the Yuan dynasty, when the Ming emperors determined that China would never again be overrun by the Mongols.

reconstruction had made it appear like an enlarged Legoland set. Later we had come across older forgotten, unrestored sections—places where the wall had been broken to allow farmers to get their tractors through. But now with its familiar and much photographed image stretched across the train window like a giant postcard, its gray bricks absorbing the violets and blues that had come with the evening's arrival, it appeared like an imperial dragon, guiding us into the capital.

One of the biggest criticisms by Polo detractors is his failure to mention the Great Wall of China. Old and all but forgotten, most of the Wall had fallen down by the time Polo entered Cathay. In fact it wasn't until three hundred years later that any Western visitor noticed it, for the Great Wall as we know it today was built during the Ming dynasty in the sixteenth century.

The real marvels of Polo's book are the true things that he correctly conveys for the first time in Western literature, such as the rich island nation of Japan or the Chinese use of paper money. Observations for which, ironically, he wasn't believed.

With the Great Khan's empire stretching from the Yellow Sea all the way to eastern Europe, Marco had met Kublai at the height of his power. The Mongols had just recently subjugated most of China, and though he was the Khan of Khans and the ruler of the largest empire in human history, Kublai knew that China was the most precious jewel in his crown. Therefore, receiving these three emissaries from as far as Europe would help impress the Chinese and lend legitimacy to the throne of this barbarian invader.

To be accepted he must take on all the trappings and sophistication expected of a Chinese son of heaven, and so he made Khan-balik (Beijing) his capital and built, where now stands the Forbidden City, *The greatest palace that ever was. . . . The roof is all ablaze with scarlet and green and blue and yellow . . . so brilliantly varnished that it glitters like crystal.*

When we called home for the first time in months we got the great news that *Smithsonian* magazine wanted us to do an article about Afghanistan for them. It was fortuitous timing, for even on a shoestring budget, we were running out of cash and needed a quick infusion.

Our instincts called for us to go out and meet people, not to mention explore the Temple of Heaven, the Forbidden City, and Kublai's astrological observatory. But we reluctantly locked ourselves in our hotel room and worked in a frenzy. The only time we ventured out of the threadbare, bedbug-infested room was to hit the restaurant across the street to savor its delectable dishes. It wasn't until after we'd chosen the photos and sent off the piece that we set out to see the city.

We exulted in being there and gave Shawn a call at the school where he was teaching. "Where have you guys been? I've been expecting you for weeks!" he shouted over the crackling line.

"Meet us for Sunday brunch at the Hyatt, we're celebrating," I screamed back. "Eleven o'clock . . . don't be late."

It was good to see Shawny as we gobbled down the buffet of sausages and omelets, pancakes and real coffee, fruits and yogurts and salmon. I couldn't believe they had lox . . . and . . . and people were staring at us. Fran was still wearing (along with the dust) his big wolf hat and karakul coat from the Taklamakan. I hadn't cut my hair in over a year and my Russian army overcoat, infused with the stench of camel, wasn't exactly the rage in Beijing. The hotel was full of well-heeled businesspeople and we were ravenous barbarians heaping plate upon plate at our table. After leaving a huge tip, we found the posh lobby and the well-stocked men's room where we filled our pockets with that most priceless of commodities: soft, Western-style toilet paper.

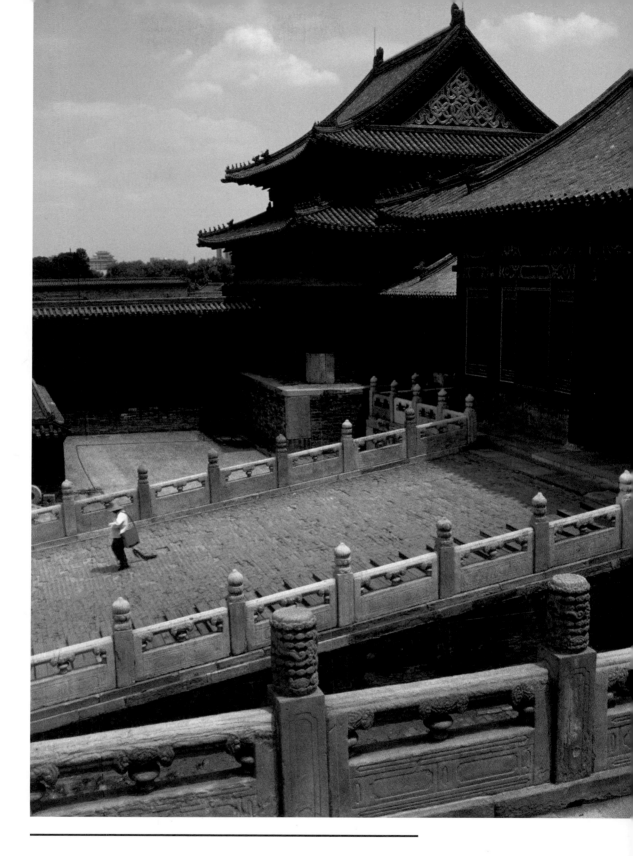

"At each face of the palace is a great marble staircase, ascending from ground level to the top of a marble wall which affords entry to the palace."

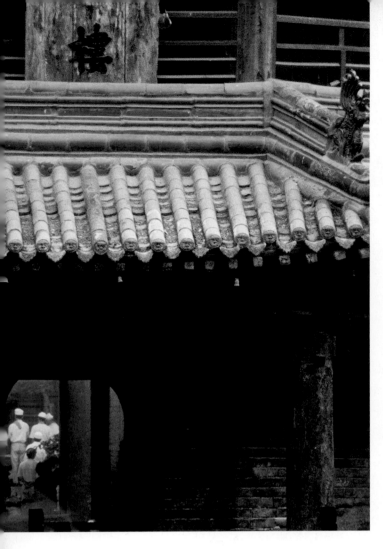

Chinese Muslims pray at the Great Mosque of Xi'an. In the medieval Chinese style, it has pagoda roofs but no domes or minarets, reflecting a long Sino-Islamic history.

We made our way over to the Confucius Temple and Imperial College on the outskirts of town. For centuries this was the place all bureaucrats needed to study in order to pass their imperial examinations to become state officials. Founded in 1287 by Kublai himself, the system wasn't dismantled until the convulsions that shook China early in the twentieth century.

Marco touches on the Confucian system of civil service and family piety when he noted of the Chinese, *They treat their father and mother with profound respect. If a child does anything to displease his parents, there is a department of state whose sole function is to punish those found guilty.*

He was also greatly impressed by the Great Khan's open-minded policy regarding all religions, saying he kept Muslims, Buddhists, and Taoists at court but adding he secretly favored Christianity. This, it must be remembered, came from a medieval European at the time of the Crusades.

His readers, because of Kublai's secret religious leanings, could justify Marco's admiration of the Khan's tolerance. More radical for them would have been Polo's high regard for a strong, authoritarian, royal figure like the Great Khan. For as a Venetian, Marco should have had pure republican blood coursing through his veins.

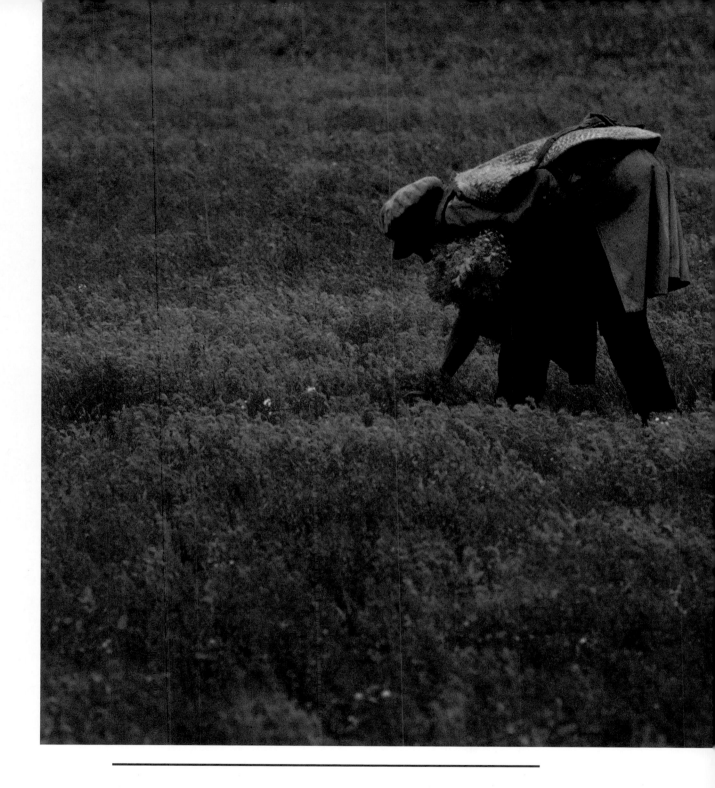

"Now let me tell you of the bounties the Great Khan bestows upon his subjects. For all his thoughts are directed toward helping his people, so that they may live and labor and increase their wealth. When he sees that the harvests are plentiful . . . he builds up a stock of every sort . . . wheat, barley, millet, rice and others in great abundance and stores them in huge granaries, where it is carefully preserved."

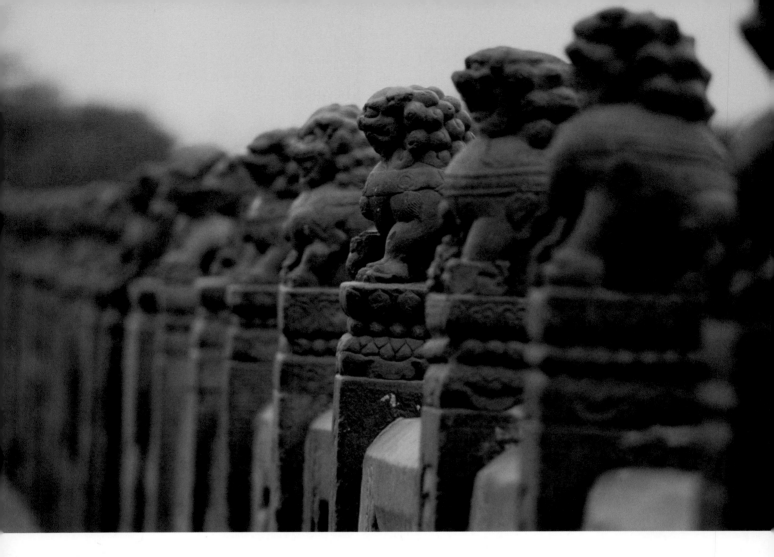

> *"There is not a bridge in the world to compare with it. . . . It has 24 arches and piers and is built entirely of gray marble . . . on either side are columns topped by marble lions of great beauty and workmanship."*

Setting out on one of his missions for the Khan, Polo crossed a structure on the outskirts of Beijing that has come to bear his name today. What he described for his peers and then for all posterity was often taken as just another of his exaggerations. "There he goes again, Il Milione, Marco Millions."

For eight hundred years the Chinese have called the bridge, which crosses the now-diverted Yongding River, Lugouqiao. It was a favorite for lovers, who would come to gaze at the morning moon as it rose over the river during the mid-autumn festival. But to the first Europeans who encountered it years after him, what stood before their eyes was exactly what they had read in *The Travels*, and so it will forever also be known as the Marco Polo Bridge.

LESSER INDIA

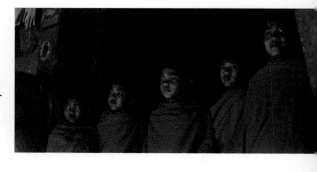

The Road to Southeast Asia

THE TRAIN WE BOARDED FOR XI'AN and the south was not unlike the Central Asian trains, only cleaner, if you can believe that. We got hard seats for the twenty-hour ride and were assaulted by a cadre of scowling women throughout the whole journey. "You have the wrong tickets, pay more." "This is not your seat, pay more." "You're foreigners, pay more."

In the dining car they lined up all the hostesses for a military-style inspection and instruction. These women have to hear the same speech every day, but they stood at attention in their blue uniforms and hats. The Chinese are very fond of uniforms.

Each girl clutched her own little noodle soup in a porcelain-ware pot as the head hostess marched up and down the aisle in a black leather jacket with a red armband and black hat, a Gestapo agent of porters. I couldn't tell what their jobs were; I only saw them when it was time to collect more cash from us. Finally we arranged a sleeper berth but found three drunken Hans playing a game of finger numbers, not unlike rock-paper-scissors. We had come across it often in China, grown men playing drinking games, shouting at the top of their lungs. "Yi, er, san, si, wu" (1, 2, 3, 4, 5), all the while flinging extended digits in each other's faces. You hear them in restaurants, buses, and hotels—everywhere.

"Don't they know that drinking is not a game but serious business?" Fran shouted, mad he couldn't sleep.

馬哥孛羅

At the end of eight days' journey the traveler reaches the great and splendid city of Si-ngan-fu, the capital of the kingdom Si-ngan-fu, which was once a noble realm renowned for its riches and power.

As we often did, we sought out the university, found a good visible spot outside, and waited for classes to let out. In no time we had a crowd of curious students surrounding us.

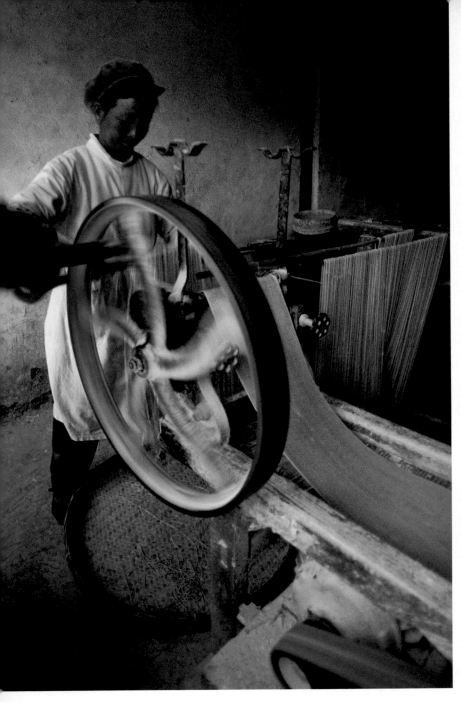

"We are studying your great leader George Lincoln," one said.

"What music do you like?" another asked.

After the crowd thinned we invited the most interested to a dumpling house. Art students, they all had chosen for themselves old-fashioned English names: Edith, Clarence, and Reginald.

"My name is White," said the most cheerful.

"That's interesting. Is that the English translation of your Chinese name?" I asked.

"No," he said, "I just like the word."

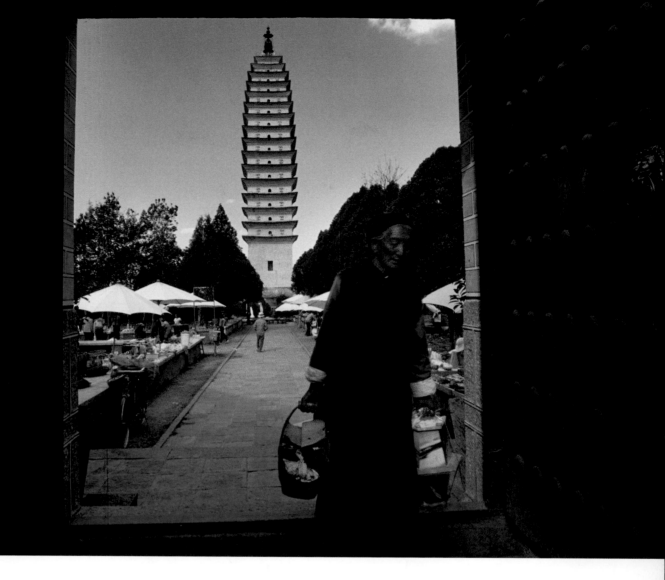

The Qianxun Pagoda at Chongsheng Temple in Dali, Yunnan Province, was already four hundred years old when Marco Polo first gazed upon it.

"Or the color?" Fran asked.

"But white is not a color," White replied.

"Aha . . . exactly!" Fran said. "If black is the absence of color, then white is all colors combined. . . . As an artist, you should love all colors."

The Chinese students enjoyed this, thinking it was very clever, and started taking notes. They were very interested in our travels and even more so because we'd been away from family so long, but in the end, as the hours passed and they ordered the best food from the menu, we learned more about them than they about us.

"Would you like to meet our friend and professor?" White asked as we walked off our meals along the moat surrounding the old walled city. Built in the thirteenth century on the foundations of the original Tang Forbidden City, the walls, ramparts, gates, and watchtowers of Xi'an form one of the oldest and most complete city defense systems still existing in China.

In the city there stands a tower inside which is a big wooden drum, which a man beats from within with a mallet, so as to be heard a great distance. This is beaten as a danger signal in case of a conflagration or a civil disturbance.

"They eat all sorts of flesh, including that of dogs and other brute beasts and animals of every kind, which we would not touch for anything in the world."

He led us to an old hutong just next to the temple complex housing the Big Goose Neck Pagoda, where we found the old man in his courtyard painting the architectural masterpiece that was visible just over his wall. Master Yin was totally blind in one eye and had cataracts forming on the other. He chain-smoked a cheap Chinese brand of cigarettes,

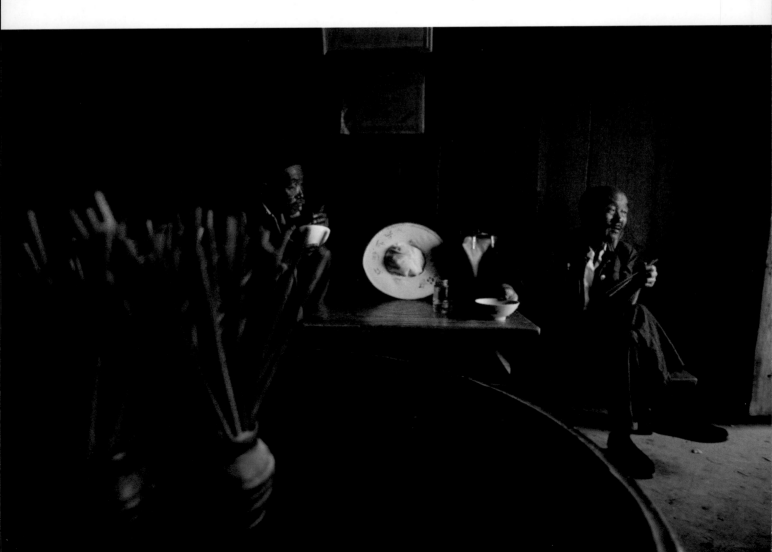

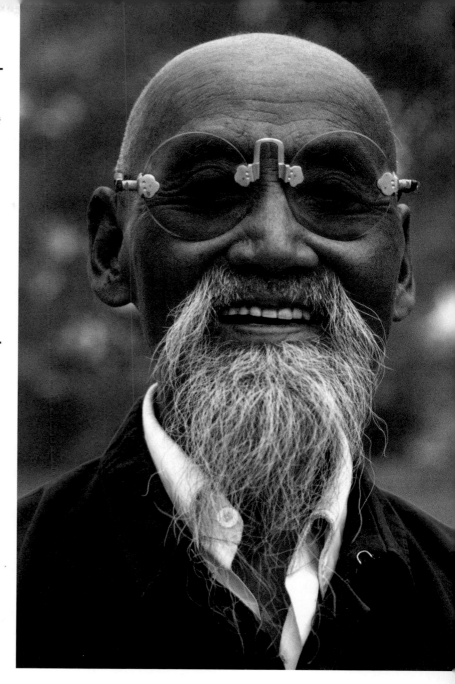

Though tantalizing to imagine, it's a myth that eyeglasses first appeared in Europe when Marco brought them back from China. Spectacles are first mentioned in European literature in 1268 and 1289, just a few years before Marco's return.

had bad teeth, and was obviously very talented. His paintings hung everywhere, classic Chinese ink-brush works on long scrolls with red chop stamps and oils on canvas in a more realistic Western tradition. The subject matter was always the same: the simple, elegant, brick pagoda standing in the temple park just over his wall.

"Hao, hao, hao" (Good, good, good), he said, gesturing for us to sit. After a pleasant and cordial conversation, I got up the nerve to ask him, "Why do you paint the same thing, over and over?"

White translated and the professor laughed. "I've been painting the pagoda for years and it's never the same. Every minute of every day the light changes and I see something different . . . but more importantly . . . it has helped me to realize that I am changing more than my subject. When I am gone it will remain."

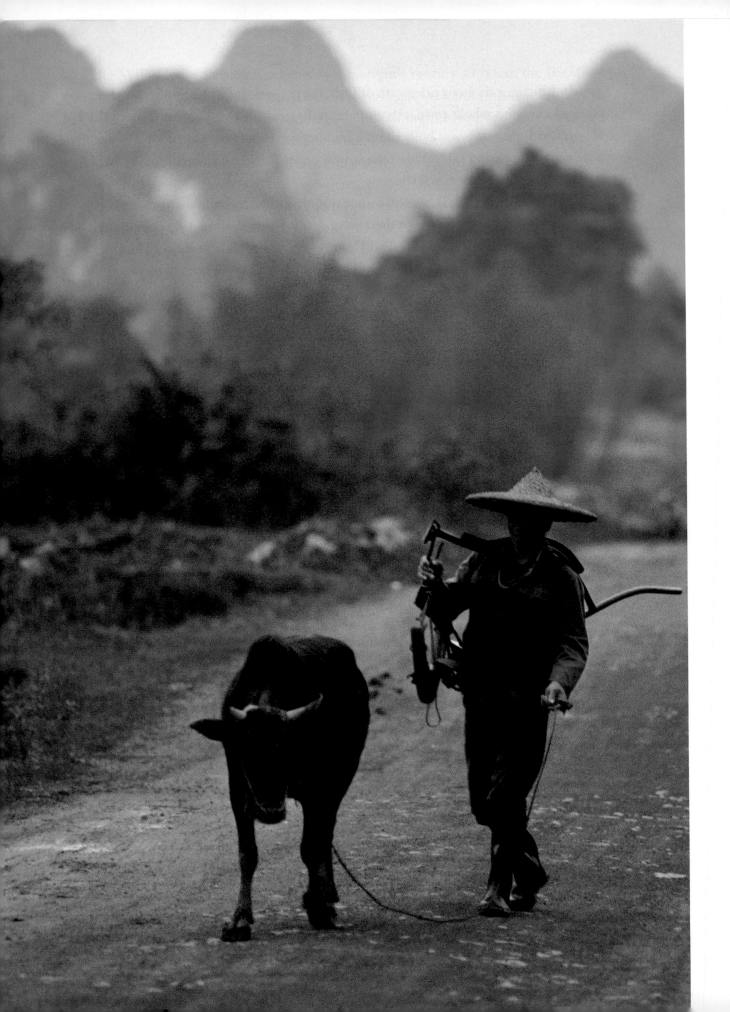

"To the means of life they have no shortage . . . mostly rice, panic, or millet . . . and these three cereals yield an increase a hundredfold on each sowing."

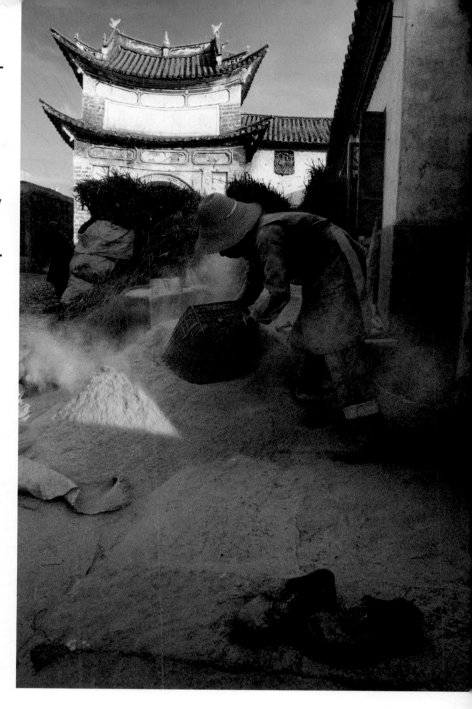

(opposite page) A farmer walks home with his ox near Guilin, Guangxi Province, among the very karst peaks that for centuries have inspired China's poets and painters.

The women wear a special tunic made of felt. The top, near the shoulders, is dark indigo blue, symbolizing night. The bottom half is white, symbolizing day. There are seven circular emblems in the night section, representing the seven planets seen with the naked eye. A tassel hangs from each, reaching the bottom of the tunic and day. There used to be two starbursts on the shoulders representing the sun and moon but they went out of fashion decades ago. Some women padded their backs with extra felt to cushion the heavy burdens they often carry, for though the Naxi are a matriarchal society, the women do all of the work.

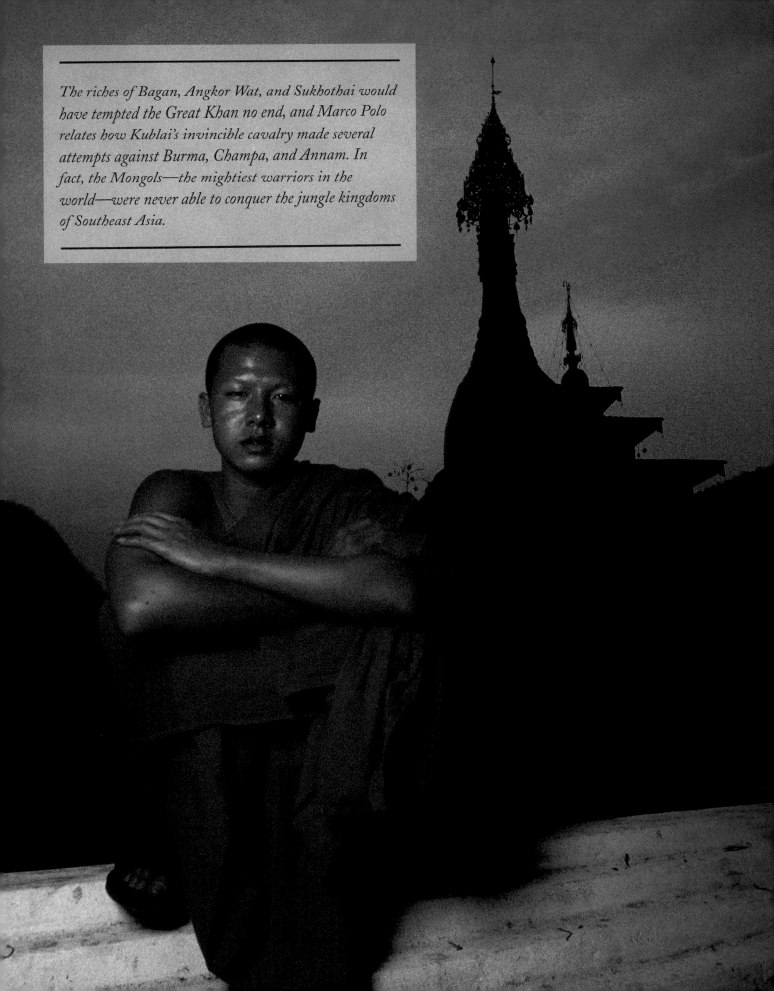

The riches of Bagan, Angkor Wat, and Sukhothai would have tempted the Great Khan no end, and Marco Polo relates how Kublai's invincible cavalry made several attempts against Burma, Champa, and Annam. In fact, the Mongols—the mightiest warriors in the world—were never able to conquer the jungle kingdoms of Southeast Asia.

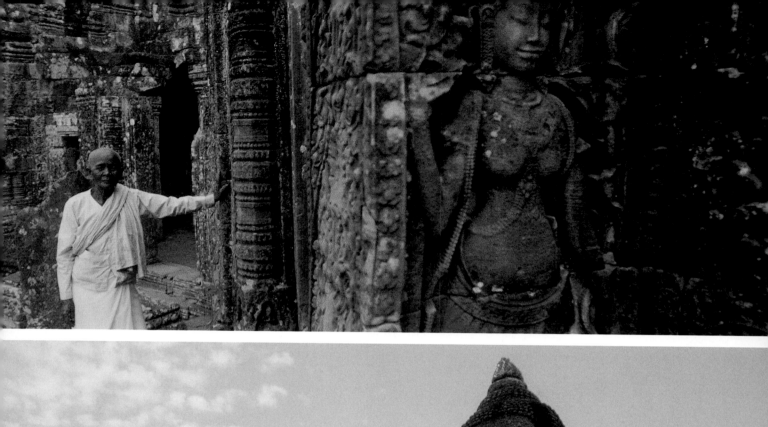

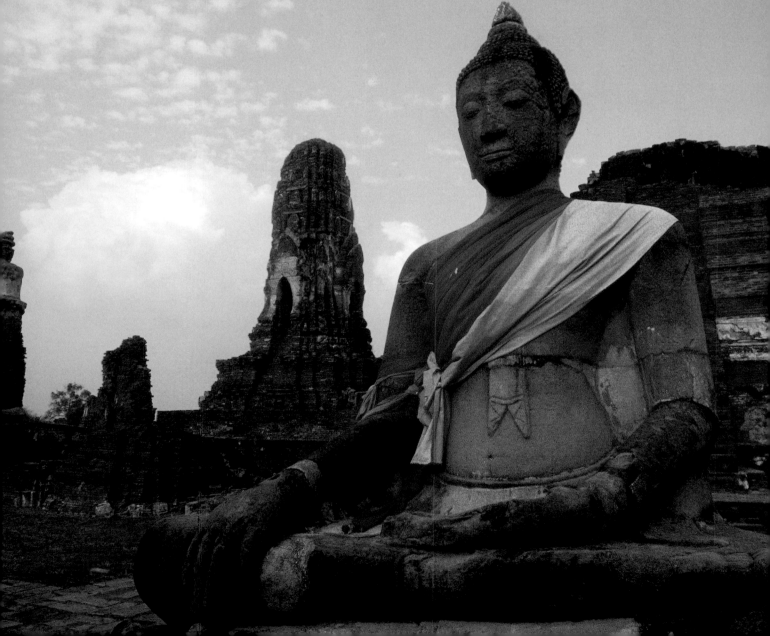

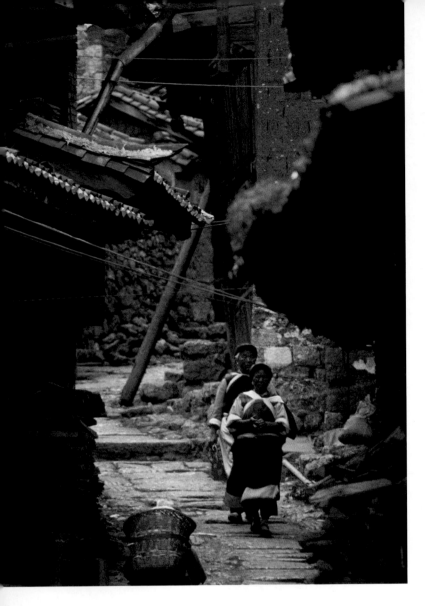

The bride's mother arranges marriages, and the husband, who can visit his wife's house during the day, must sleep in his own at night. The children are reared by her and take her name. She owns all property and can decide to dissolve the union at any time. He has no say. Needless to say, the men of the town had a lot of spare time, playing Chinese checkers, smoking long bamboo pipes, and dabbling in the arts and other leisurely pursuits. We got the distinct feeling a matriarchal society was a man's idea and not a bad one at that.

> *When one of their wives has been delivered of a child, the infant is washed and swaddled, and then the woman gets up and goes about her household affairs, whilst the husband takes to bed with the child for 40 days. . . . They do this because they say, the woman has had a hard bout of it, and 'tis but fair the man should have his share of suffering.*

MONGOLIA

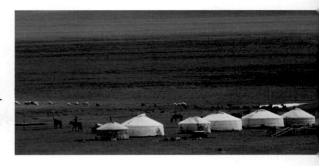

"He Made Up His Mind to Conquer the World"

*Karakorum is a city of some three miles in compass. . . . It is the first
city that the Tartars possessed. . . . And now I will tell you all about
how they first acquired dominion and spread over the world.*

WE RODE OUT TO THE STEPPES and toward Karakorum on top of a truck bomb. It
was Soviet-styled, army green, and resembled a '67 Chevy van my brother once owned.
The back was tightly packed with sixteen sheep and a prepubescent girl covered in the
same yellow dung that plastered the inside of the vehicle. In the front passenger seat sat
an old monk in clean robes.

Fran and I sat up top in the luggage rack, cushioned by bags of goatskins. The
methane rising from the persistently flatulating sheep mixed with the fumes from two
fifty-gallon drums of gasoline we were leaning up against. The driver, the father of the
girl, would constantly stop and fiddle with the engine, to our great concern. One spark
and we'd be done for.

When we were moving again, it was magical. The fumes were chased away by clean
air and sweet grass as we bumped along for miles, gazing at eagles drifting above us like
seagulls chasing a trawler out to sea.

If there is one thing we'll remember about Mongolia it will be the sky. Never before
have we seen such a vast and changing thing. When we came to a stunning valley of
swollen velvet-green hills studded with horses, we banged on the roof. "Stop!"

The driver and old monk looked perplexed as we thanked them and left the road,
walking toward a cluster of yurt or ger tents, a mile or so off in the distance.

*They have circular houses covered with felt, which they carry about
with them on wheeled wagons where-ever they go. . . . And every
time they unfold their house and set it up, the door is always facing
south.*

As we approached, a man appeared and held back the barking mastiffs protecting his flock. We called out the traditional greeting, "Nokhoi Khori!" literally "Hold the dog!" and entered his ger.

It is not permitted for anyone to touch the threshold of the door for it is looked upon as a bad omen, so all who enter must step over it.

In a colorfully painted chair sat an old woman with a shaved head. She grinned at us as the man handed us his snuff bottle. We each took a pinch, snorted it, and sneezed loudly to the delight of the rest of the clan who had now crowded into the tent.

Erdene Zuu Monastery, Karakorum, Mongolia. Before Kublai embraced Tibetan Buddhism, the Mongols were shamanistic, worshipping heaven or the "clear blue sky."

Our host offered us koumiss in a small bowl, bowing graciously while extending his right hand forward and cupping his elbow with his left. We accepted the bowl in the same fashion and he took us in just like that.

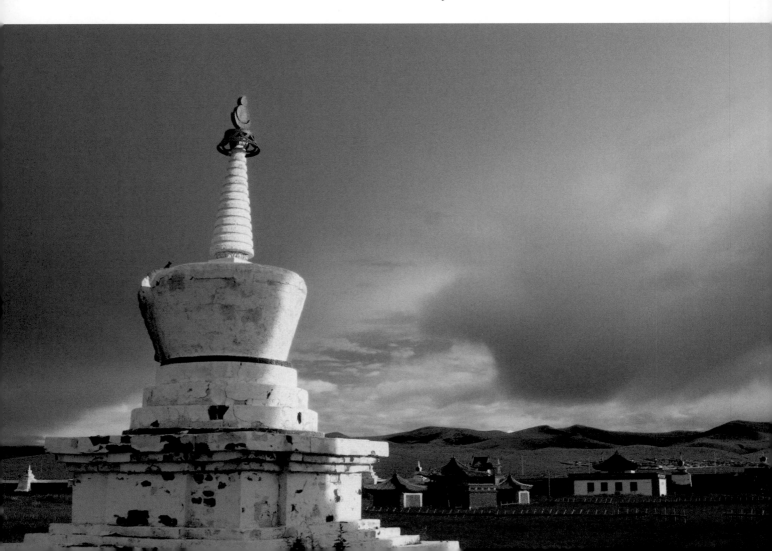

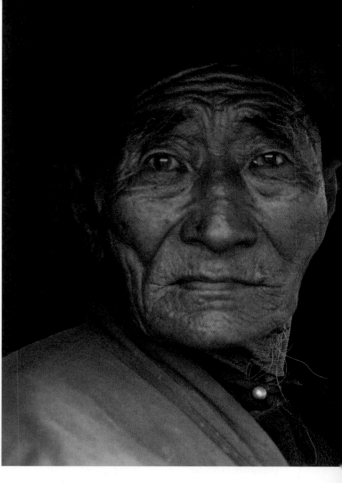

Our traveling companion, somewhere out on the steppes. After the fall of the Yuan, the Mongols went back to their old shamanistic ways before re-adopting Tibetan Buddhism in the sixteenth century.

You should know that they drink mare's milk: but they subject it to a process that makes it like wine and very good to drink, and call it koumiss.

Sitting with the men on their side of the ger as they played drinking games and sang songs celebrating nomadic life and poking fun at townsfolk, we eyed the women on the other side scurrying about making yogurts and buttermilks and ducking in and out of the small door. The prettiest of them served us noodles and tsai, which was basically chai mixed with a rank-tasting hard cheese.

We followed her outside, past the sloping sides of the ger covered with bricks of various cheeses left drying in the sun. A young man in a clean blue del (a long coatlike garment little changed since the days of the empire) and cocked fedora flirted with her as she brought a foal to a mare to suckle. Once the milk flowed she handed off the colt to him and milked the mare herself. Horse milk seemed to be reserved for koumiss and arak but they were busy making sweet curds, cheeses, and hand-churned butter from their cows, goats, and camels for the harsh winter months ahead.

The wives are true and loyal to their husbands and very good at their household tasks. . . . They have dried milk, which is solid like

paste.... First they bring the milk to a boil, then skim off the cream
that floats on the surface to be made into butter.... Then they
stand the milk in the sun and leave it to dry.

We awoke in the morning tired. There had been constant activity throughout the night as if the Mongols had never slept. The ger was empty save a lone girl, not the prettiest, who was ladling milk as it boiled in a huge black cauldron. We found our host, Ogedai, saddling a few ponies as we approached him out by the hitching post. He handed us the reins and we followed him out toward what he called "Seren Dorge," the summer valley of his cousins.

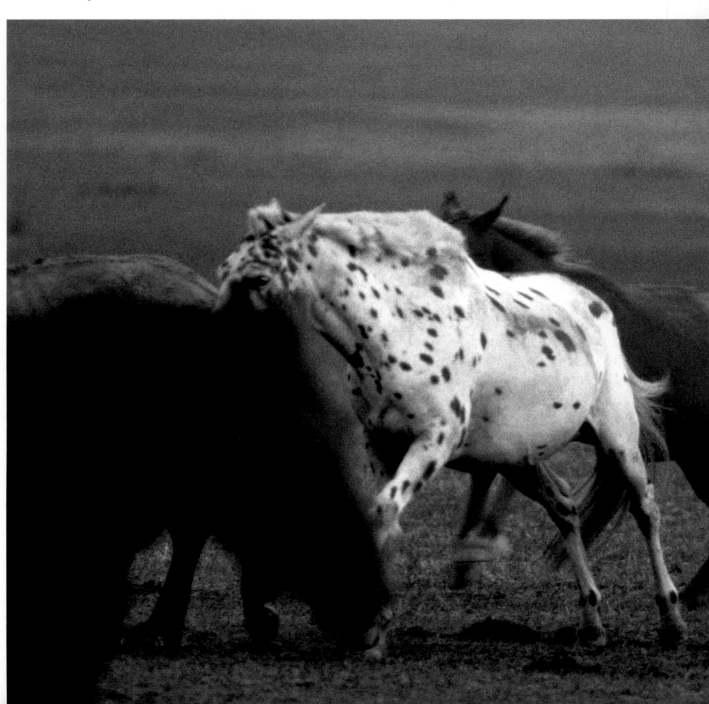

Over the next few weeks we lived with Ogedai's clan and got a real taste of no-madic life. When not helping them prepare for the harsh winter we watched as they practiced their ancient martial arts for their upcoming Nadam festival and coached their sons, some as young as five or six, on how to win the grueling twenty-five-mile

"The Tartars are of all men, the best able to endure exertion and hardship. . . . They will go for a whole month without provisions and can ride a good ten days' journey without making a fire, living only on the blood of their horses."

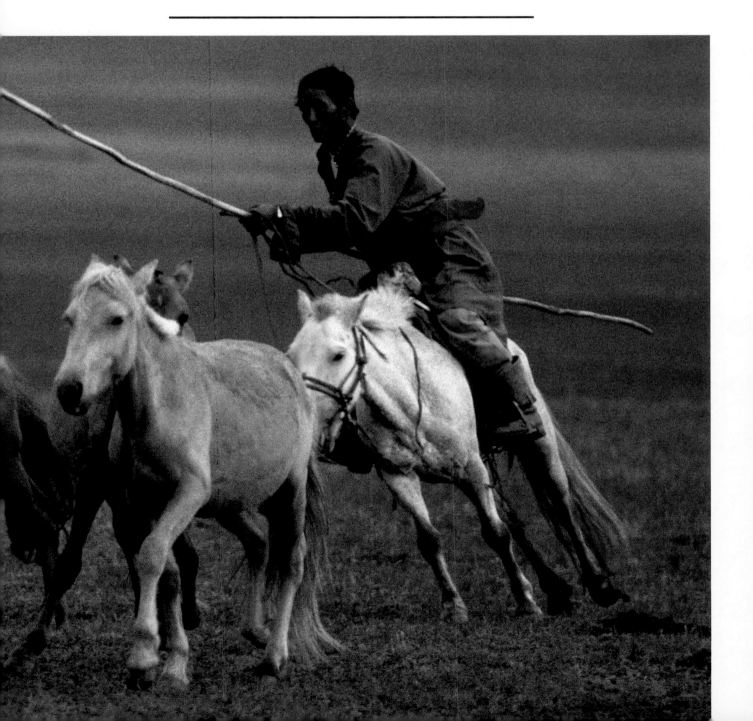

pony race that would be the festival's highlight. The Mongols are virtually born in the saddle and the equestrian skills of even the littlest member of the family dwarfed ours.

"They are the horse people," Fran said one evening as we watched the men breaking in ponies, the sky growing black with rain.

In summer they live in cool regions where there is good grazing and pasturage for their beasts, among mountains and valleys.

"Among the Tartars . . . if any king, prince or other . . . wishes to take a wife . . . they pay no regard to the nobility of her birth but only to her charm and beauty."

Though he was now ruling as a Chinese emperor, it's said the Great Khan had steppe grass sown in his courtyard in Beijing to remind him of his Mongol origin. So, it is easy to imagine the Khan captivating Marco with tales of his childhood and culture, so moving the young Italian that years later Polo would dedicate more chapters of his book to the history and lifestyle of the Mongols than he would to the Chinese.

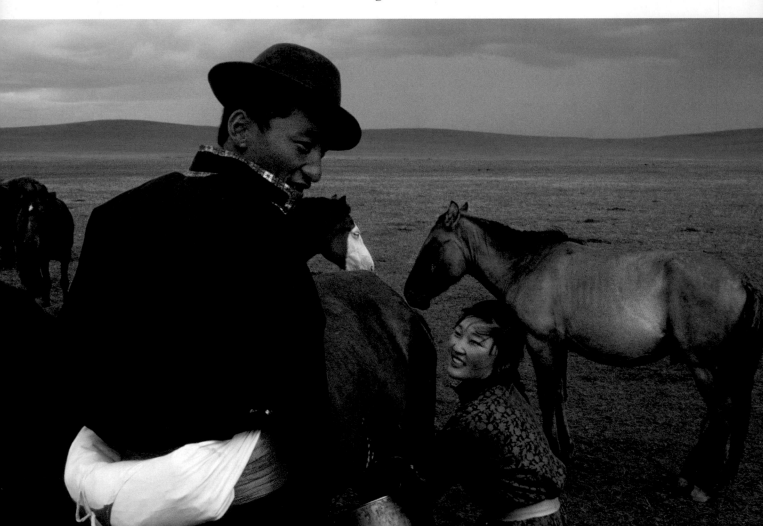

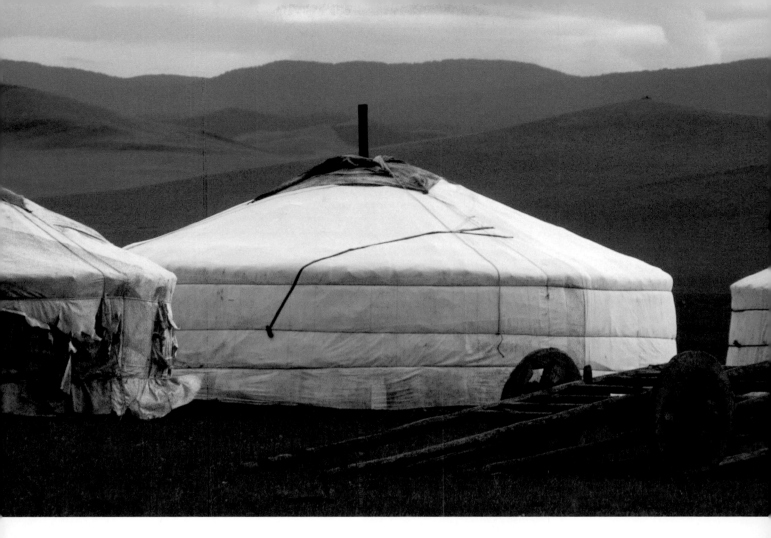

Yurts are perfectly tailored to the nomadic life of the steppes. The portability, shelter, and comfort they provide have allowed these structures to stand the test of time.

In 1206, all the various Tartar tribes gathered at their ancient holy place on the plains of Karakorum and chose a king to rule over them. His name was Genghis Khan, grandfather of Kublai—a man who, Polo tells us, *When he had amassed such a multitude of followers that they covered the face of the earth, he made up his mind to conquer the world.*

The once mighty empire, which retreated back to its nomadic origins in the steppes, had only recently gained independence from the Soviets and didn't need to look far to find a hero. Ogedai even seemed to believe he would return like a messiah.

"Soon Genghis will come back to lead the tribes," he told us one night after the effects of endless bowls of arak had kicked in.

"Will he conquer the world again?" we asked, feigning fear by shaking in our boots.

"No, no, the spiritual Genghis will come and unite all men in peace."

"Genghis Khan will unite the world in peace?" we scoffed. "Now that's what I call being born again," I said to Fran.

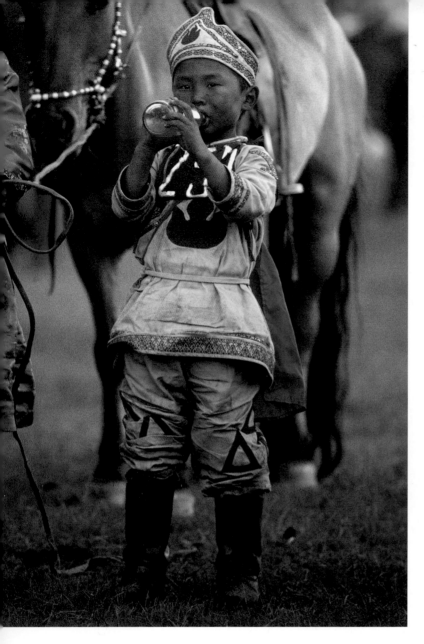

Horse-racing in Mongolia dates back to the Bronze Age, and at the Nadam festival children as young as five race at breakneck speeds over a twenty-mile course.

"I guess he's had close to a millennium to think about what he's done and correct his ways!" he cried, slapping Ogedai's back.

"That's right," I said. "A giant *time out* for that naughty boy!" We started laughing until it became obvious that we were insulting our friend.

"Have you heard of his lost tomb?" we asked Ogedai, changing the subject by referring to one of the holy grails of archaeology. He just smiled. "They will never find it," he said. "It is hidden in the western hills."

> *You should be told that all the grand Khans . . . are carried to a mountain that is called Altay to be interred. . . . Let me tell you a strange thing, too . . . the convoy that goes with the body doth put to the sword all whom they fall in with on the road, saying: "Go and wait upon your lord in the other world!"*

It seemed a cult was beginning to form around Genghis, whose image and memory had been outlawed by the Russians, who feared a rise of nationalism or perhaps, more painfully, because they'd never forgotten the ravages of the Golden Horde.

The night before we were to leave, a sheep was slaughtered in our honor. Taking the animal between his legs, Ogedai made a five-inch incision into its chest, then reached in and ripped out the aorta, throwing it on the ground. Hardly struggling, the sheep was dead in seconds. Ogedai carefully set aside the organs, and his wife carried the stomach far from the ger to be buried. Next, the blood was scooped out of the chest cavity where it had pooled.

"These are the tactics by which they prevail in battle. . . . They have trained their horses so well that they wheel this way or that as quickly as a dog . . . at top speed they twist 'round with their bows and let fly their arrows."

"Oh man, we get to have Mongolian barbeque," I said to Fran as Ogedai skinned and butchered the flesh. Our mouths watered at the thought; we'd eaten nothing but noodles and unpasteurized milk products for weeks and were looking forward to some lamb chops. Ogedai's wife flushed out undigested grass from the intestines, then filled them

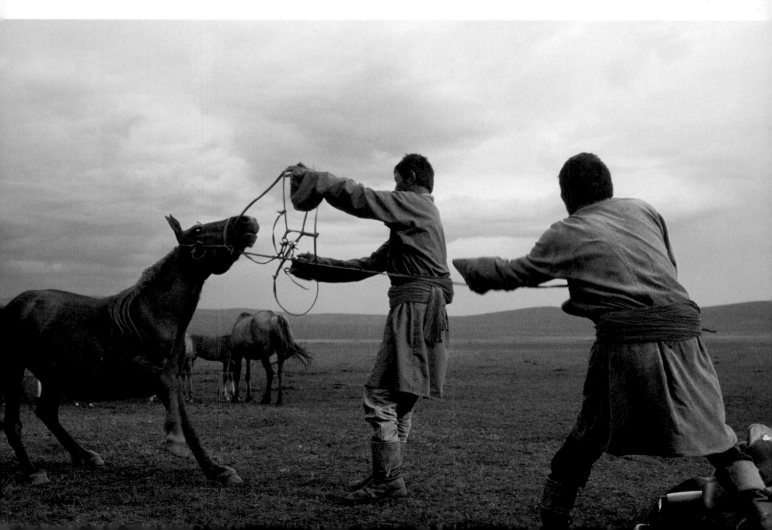

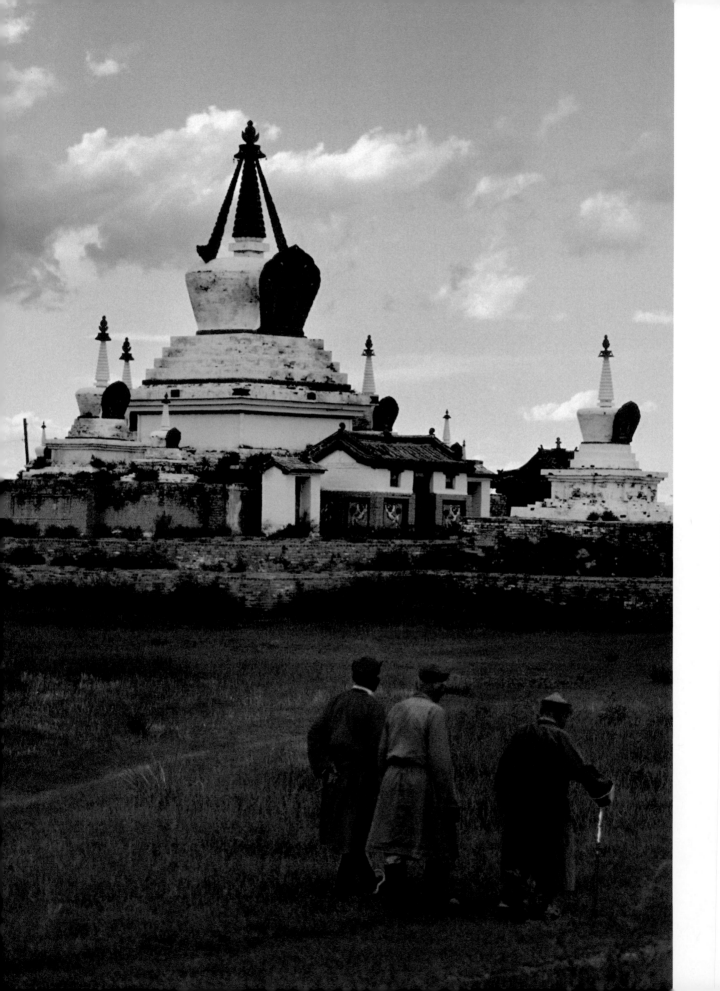

with the blood to make sausages. Nothing seemed to be wasted. They boiled all the organs and blood sausage with a handful of salt and served us first. We pretended to enjoy the heart and liver the most, not wanting to insult their generosity.

"As nomads," Fran said, trying to alleviate my disappointment, "they've served us the most precious food they have." High in protein, the prized organs needed to be eaten right away. The meat, once jerked, could be eaten any time.

I tried smiling as Ogedai handed me an eyeball and insisted that he have it instead. We went back and forth like this, the customary three times, before I gave up and to his glee swallowed it in one full swoop. "Umm," I offered without gagging, as we wistfully watched his son hang the fresh meat inside to dry in the summer heat.

Their sheep and rams are entrusted to the care of shepherds . . . according to the law of the Tartars they do not cut the throats of animals, but slit their bellies.

The passages in Polo's book that moved us the most are those that describe the people he comes across. In a real sense he was the world's first anthropologist or ethnographer. So, when we looked through our lenses into the eyes of the descendants of the very people he so accurately described, it felt like time travel.

The Mongol short stirrup changed the face of medieval warfare by allowing a rider at full gallop to lift himself off his saddle and accurately shoot an arrow.

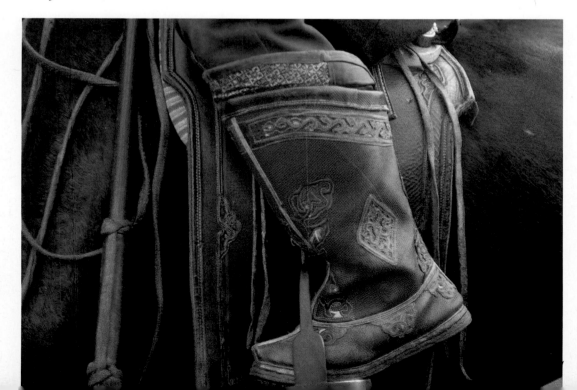

That night we scaled an embankment to watch the final play of light on the peaceful valley. Looking out alone at the group of tents, smoke billowing from their tops, dogs barking at nothing, cattle and sheep grazing, prehistoric-looking horses roaming past others tied up to hitching posts, Fran threw his arm around my shoulders.

"I don't want to leave. I could see myself getting a Mongol princess and settling down. . . . Xanadu is here, now, it's alive. These people are really living!" He went on, "Maybe it's us, the overcivilized in modern societies, who are merely surviving. To be a nomad and roam this gorgeous countryside with no need for money or a vacation. You kill one of your sheep to feed your family for a week; your wife and kids milk the animals to make your food and drink. . . . I just don't know if I'll be able to fit back into my old life after being here."

"I know what you mean," I said. "We go into a supermarket, buy a steak wrapped in plastic and Styrofoam, totally disconnected from the simplest truths in life. I wonder what else we are missing. Prop the kids in front of the TV so you could gossip on the phone or put grandma in an old-age home because she's better off. The Mongols sit around and tell stories and sing songs. They walk in and out of each other's tents and treat each other's children as if they were their own. . . . So, I don't blame you for wanting to stay," I said, "but if you do, I'll have to kill you, pack you up in salted pork like St. Mark, and ship you back to Venice with me."

Marco's account of the Great Khan's extensive harems being stocked with the females of his vanquished enemies' tribes was confirmed by a 2003 DNA study that found one in twelve Asian men is descended from Genghis Khan.

Il Milione on the Grand Canal

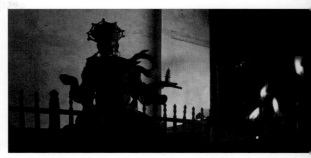

"I Am Afraid to Tell You ... for Fear I Should Be Branded a Liar"

The Khan has built a huge canal of great width and depth ... and made the water flow along it so that it looks like a river. ... It affords passage for very large ships. ... By this means it is possible to go from from Manzi to Khan-balik.

ALTHOUGH THERE IS NO MENTION OF HIS NAME in official Chinese records, Marco recounted that after years of loyal service to the Khan, he was appointed to an important post—the governorship of Yangzhou, a busy city on China's inland waterway, the Grand Canal.

In contact now with a culture that had existed for thousands of years, Polo noted that among the Chinese *are wise philosophers and physicians with a great knowledge of nature. ... They are men of peace, being so pampered by their kings, who are of the same temperament. ... For I give you my word that if they were a war-like nation, they would conquer all the rest of the world.*

But he can also feel the tension: *They cannot bear the sight of the Great Khan's soldiers, knowing that through them they have been deprived of their own natural kings.*

Even though he was an official of an occupying force and would hardly be welcomed, he seemed to get a close glimpse of Chinese life. *The men and women are fair skinned and good-looking. Most of them wear silk all of the time, since it is produced in great abundance here.*

The sheer numbers in China stunned Marco, earning him his nickname. But he was right; China was the economic superpower of the Middle Ages. Present when a Mongol census of the city of Hangzhou was given, Polo claimed there were over 1.6 million homes; this at a time when Venice, the richest and most populous city in Europe, was inhabited by only 100,000 people.

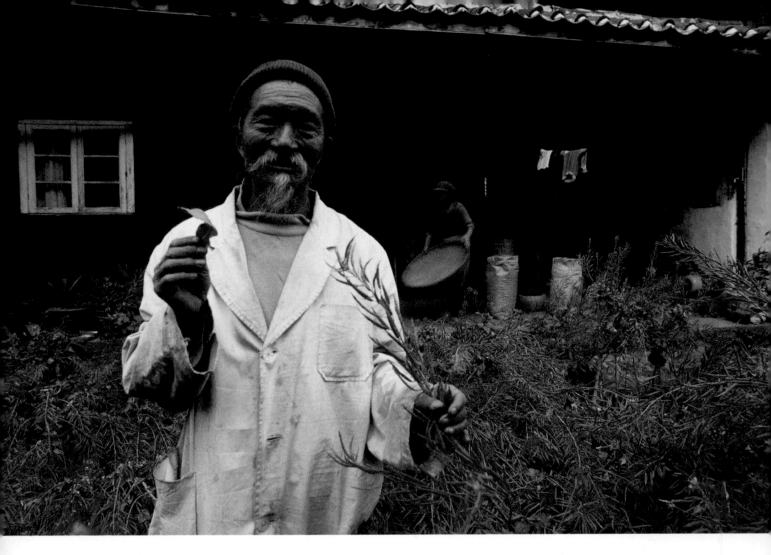

The world-famous Dr. Ho in his garden at the "Clinic of Chinese Herbs" in the Jade Dragon Mountains.

And on the Yangtze he prophetically saw his future when he stated, *I am afraid to tell you how many ships there are on this river, for fear I should be branded a liar . . . for I assure you that the amount of merchandise transported through Cathay by this multitude of craft is staggering.*

From our slow boat to Hangzhou on the Grand Canal we watched timeless scenes occurring on both banks of this famous waterway as houseboats, commercial barges, and cargo vessels shuttled back and forth.

The puttering of an engine and the cries of a small child carried across the smooth river from the bow of a barge, the boy's father propelling the craft by long pole. People crouched low under a stretched tarp at midboat, their faces low in their rice bowls, chopsticks flying to scoop in their evening meal. We headed for sunset to the oldest bridge in Suzhou, a Tang dynasty masterpiece of engineering. Long and multi-arched, it stretched across the canal with a heightened section that allowed small vessels of its time to pass underneath. Grass grew now from between the bricks on its pathway.

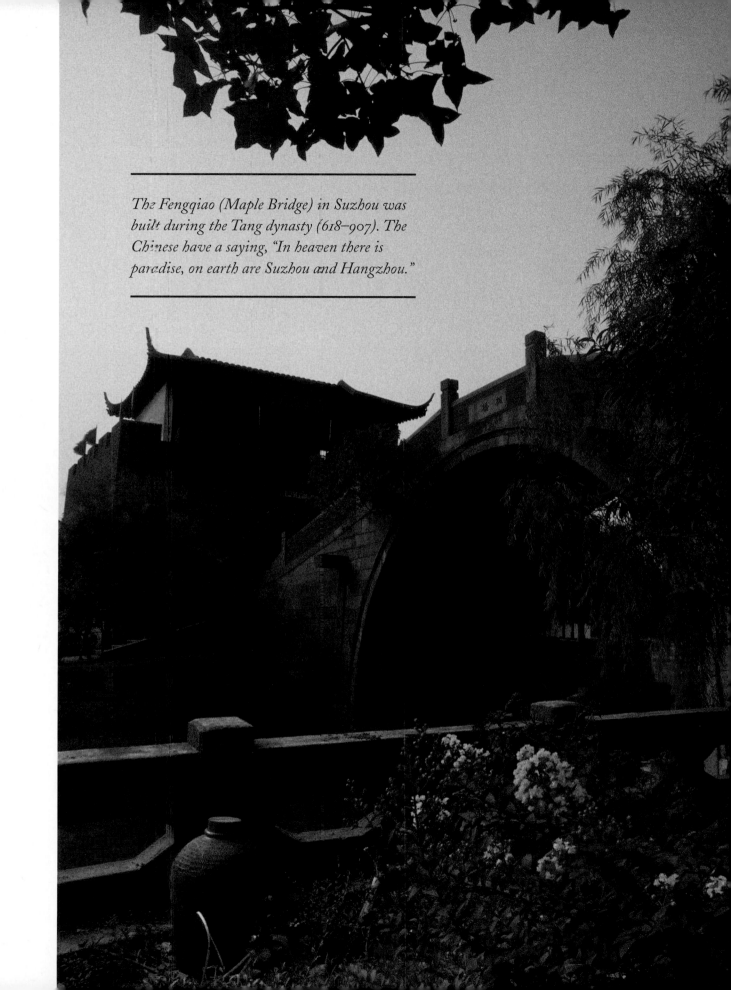

The Fengqiao (Maple Bridge) in Suzhou was built during the Tang dynasty (618–907). The Chinese have a saying, "In heaven there is paradise, on earth are Suzhou and Hangzhou."

馬哥孛羅

At 1,100 miles long with 24 locks and 60 bridges, the Grand Canal of China is not only the most ancient man-made waterway in the world, it is also the largest—bigger than the Suez and Panama canals combined.

Polo surely must have thought of home and Venice when he saw the bridges that grace the cities of heaven and earth, Hangzhou and Suzhou: *In Suzhou they have stone bridges that are fully 3 miles long and others that are so lofty and well designed that big ships without their masts can pass under and yet carts and horses can pass over them.*

Even though he offered the Western world these rich details of Chinese life for the

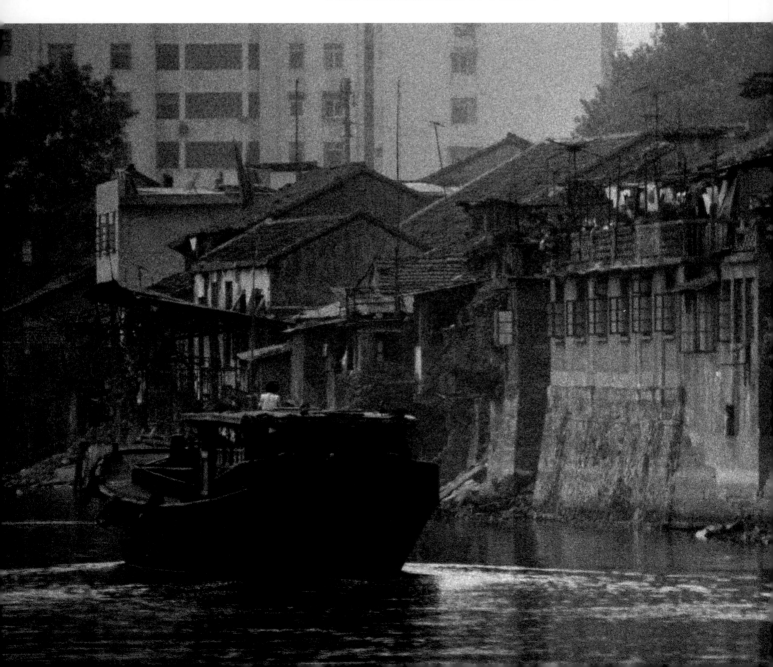

first time in history, the basis of his critics' disbelief still rests on a few omissions in his book. He didn't mention tea, foot binding, or calligraphy, and he didn't learn the Chinese tongue. However, only Chinese in the southern regions drank tea, and its use would hardly have impressed Marco, as there would have been no market for it back home. More remarkable to him was the nationwide consumption of rice wine: *They make a drink of wine and excellent spices, it is beautifully clear and intoxicates faster than other wine because it is very heating.*

As for foot binding, perhaps Polo was alluding to this painful practice when he wrote, *The maidens walk so daintily that they never advance one foot more than a few inches beyond the other.*

Also, at that time foot binding was restricted to a small group of elite women who were confined to their homes. Again Marco answered his critics himself, *The young*

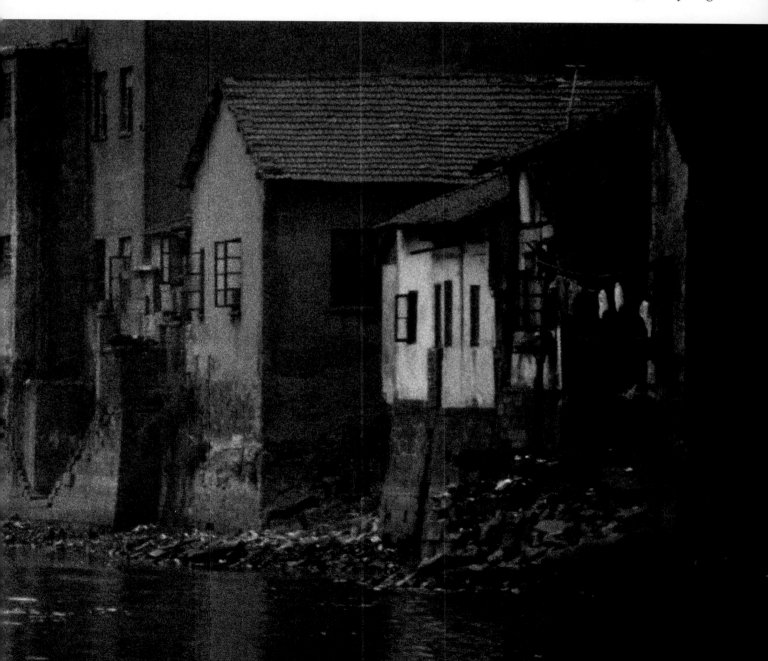

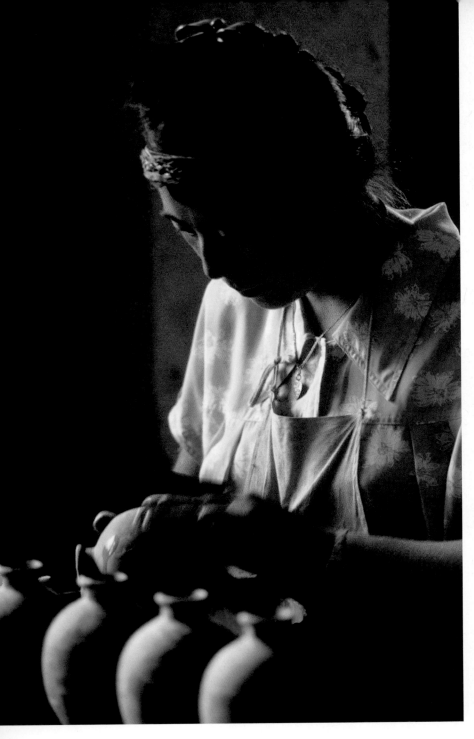

"In this province . . . they make vessels of porcelain, large and small, of incomparable beauty . . . and from here they are exported all over the world."

ladies of Cathay excel in modesty. . . . In their own chambers they remain . . . seldom presenting themselves to the sight of their fathers and brothers.

Despite his omissions on the art of Chinese calligraphy and not learning the Chinese language, again Polo was quite observant when he told us that throughout China there are different dialects to the language but only one form of writing. He had mastered four Asiatic languages already: Mongol without question, in addition to Persian, Turkish, and probably Arabic. He could speak and write and be perfectly understood by the people most important to him, the Mongols. Indeed, the emperor of

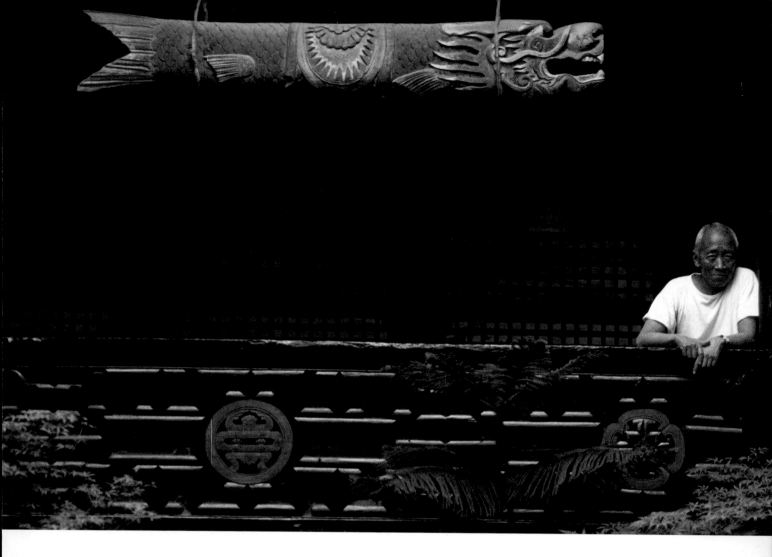

The Chinese mu yu *or slit drum is hollowed out from a solid log, usually in the shape of a fish, and it used ritually in Buddhist and Taoist temples.*

China himself, Kublai Khan, never bothered to learn Chinese.

After being away so long, the Polos began to yearn for home and begged the Khan for leave to return to Venice. They were rich in gold and jewels and had other motives as well, for the intrigues at court over who would succeed the aging Khan of Khans had begun. Being as close to Kublai as Marco claimed only put them at risk from his rivals when he died. They had to go. But Kublai wouldn't hear of it: *He liked so much to have us near him that nothing on earth would persuade him to let us go.*

Whether it was for personal or political reasons, Kublai kept the Polos until it served his purposes. As it happened, his nephew needed a wife. Hand-picked from a certain clan in the steppes, the royal Mongol princess needed to be escorted and delivered safely to Persia. Here was Marco's chance, as he was given his last and most personal mission for Kublai.

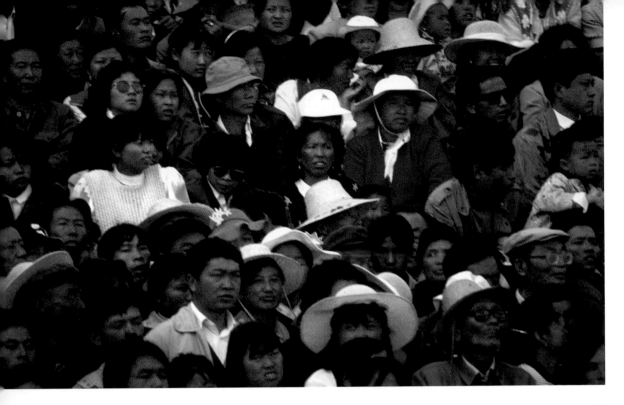

"Here at every hour . . . are crowds going to and fro on their business, that anyone seeing such a multitude would believe it impossible to feed so many mouths."

Our only chance was to drum up enough hype about our journey in the media and hope someone would help out. Using our by now well-honed street smarts, we'd talked our way into a free stay at a five-star hotel called—of course—the Marco Polo. As a payoff for the management, we suggested they arrange for some publicity and found ourselves plastered all over the local newspapers. But still, it looked like we were going nowhere. That was, until we went to see P&O Lines. By chance the representative from P&O had heard our interview on a talk radio show. "We turned Michael Palin down a few years ago when he was doing 'Around the World in Eighty Days,'" he told us. "We'd like to make up for that, so we're going to give you guys a hand." They arranged to ship us to Indonesia, and we signed on as crewmen aboard the *Kowloon Bay*, one of the largest classes of container ship. She was as long as three football fields and held up to three thousand containers. We were happy but apprehensive, knowing this would be just another hollow victory if we couldn't get visas for Iran.

Having voyaged before in the strange seas to India, Marco says they were *fitted out with a fleet of fourteen ships with four masts each and as many as twelve sails.* Given the largest and most seaworthy cargo vessels of their day, the Polos set sail from southern China with hundreds in their royal armada. Little did they know what lay ahead.

They put to sea and sailed fully three months till we came to an island lying towards the south named Java.

SUMATRA

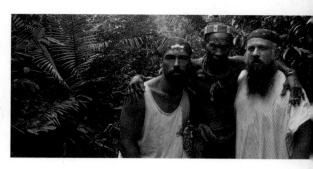

The Tree of Life

THE PARTY FOUND THEMSELVES STRANDED IN SUMATRA, forced to wait for the trade winds to blow in the westerly direction. In the meantime, they built a fort in the jungle to protect themselves.

> *The people are out and out savages and live like beasts . . . if they get hold of a stranger, they seize him and if he cannot be ransomed, they kill him and devour him on the spot . . . for I assure you that they eat human flesh.*

馬哥孛羅

In Singapore we left behind our nautical posts aboard the *Kowloon Bay* and from Indonesia's Riau archipelago we caught an old boat and traveled four hours to the Sumatran coast. Stilt houses cut from rough jungle timber flanked the coastline for miles, reminding us of Brazil and the Amazon. After transferring to another old tub we entered a river that flowed into the heart of the rainforest. Night approached as we huddled on top of the small wooden vessel, claiming our spot among a stack of bananas being transported to Pekanbaro, in the center of the island. The river, muddy and fast, drifted us further in. Palms and other tropical plants bent and clung to the muddy banks. Mangrove roots, wholly exposed during low tide, clung fast to the mud with spidery, dead-looking limbs that supported lush green vegetation above. We lay back and let the sounds of birds and monkeys hidden on the misty banks waft over us.

"Hey, take a swig of this." I took my eyes from the stars floating above my head to see Francis handing me a bottle.

"Alright, good timing," I grunted, sitting up. "You know, I kind of feel like we're in a scene from *Apocalypse Now*. Even the low-key chug of the engine reminds me of it . . . did you know that was inspired by Conrad's *Heart of Darkness*?"

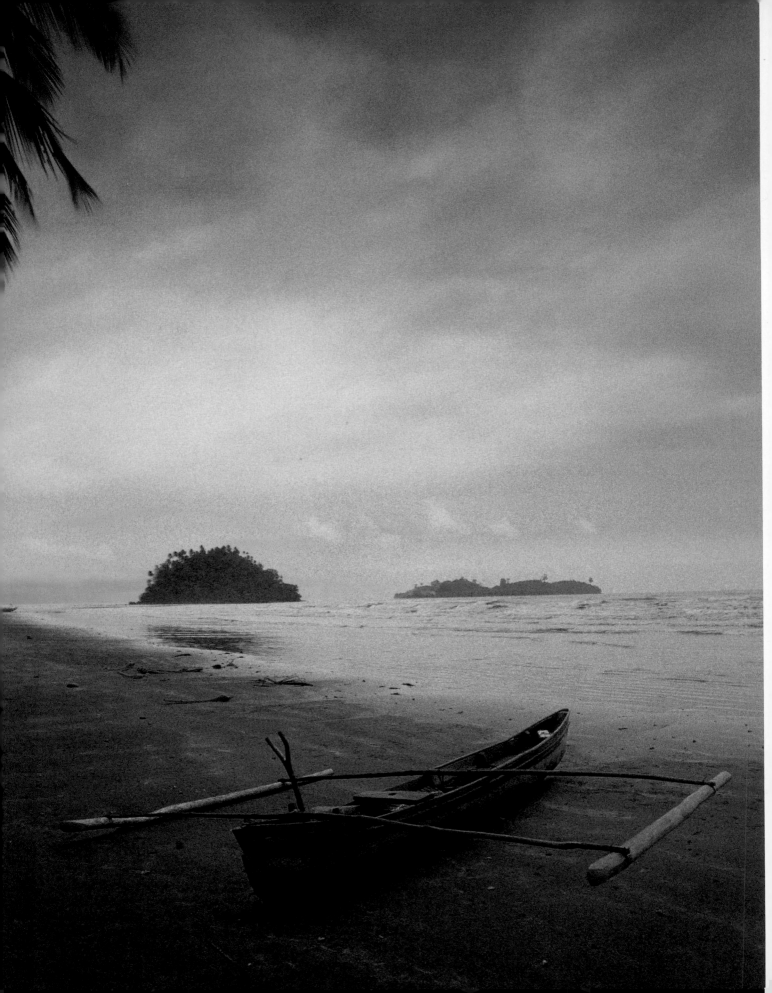

(opposite page) Marco Polo was perhaps the first to explain to Europeans what a monsoon was: "It takes a full year to complete the voyage.... For only two winds blow in these seas, one that wafts them out and one that brings them back."

A cloud of gnats hanging over the boat forced our mouths shut and temporarily killed the conversation. I passed the bottle back in silence, stood to take a leak off the side of the boat, and nearly got whacked in the face by a huge bat feeding on the gnats mid-flight.

"Did you ever see *Lord Jim* with Peter O'Toole?" I shouted over my shoulder, my voice thick now from the alcohol. "It's amazing . . . they filmed it at Angkor Wat."

We docked in the predawn haze and caught a bus for a nausea-inducing ride through winding, mountainous roads to the other side of the island and the coastal town of Penang.

Like most of Indonesia, the island of Sumatra has for the most part converted to Islam, the religion brought by Arab traders, but there are still a few small islands where the way of life has changed little in thousands of years, let alone since the Polos were here. One such is Siberut, lying ninety miles off the coast and part of the Mentawai island chain.

The old barge didn't seem that seaworthy, but a local assured us it's the one he always took when he returned to the island to visit his family. With some trepidation we crossed the gangplank leading to the hold. Everything below the water line was bursting with supplies, and they were still loading. There was a center aisle running the length of the hull with racks of hardwood bunks stacked three high. Dark, dank, and smelly, it looked like the hold of a slave ship, dangerously overcrowded with people, some three or four to a bunk.

The island lies in a sea so turbulent and so deep that ships cannot anchor there or sail away from it, because it sweeps them into a gulf from which they can never escape.

We pushed off into the incoming surf, riding large, rolling swells. I was hoping these would ease up once we got out to deep water, but they kept coming relentlessly, and I was seasick within a half hour. Crawling into a top bunk, I remained in agony for the next fifteen hours. There was an old-fashioned brass porthole two feet from my face and I assured myself that if need be I could unhinge its corroded latch and squeeze through, but every time I lifted my head from the hard wooden berth it felt like a magnet was sucking it back down again.

To say the ride was rough is an understatement. The swells weren't hitting us with even patterns; some unorthodox waves rocked us from the sides as well. I shut myself down and went into a self-induced coma that left me with only a patchy memory of that

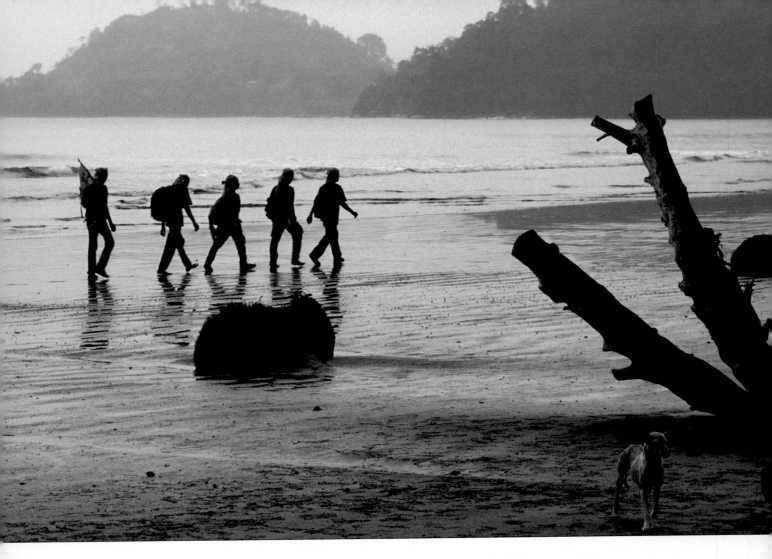

"The people . . . used to be idolaters, but owing to contact with Saracen merchants . . . have all been converted to the law of Mahomat." Today over two hundred million or 88 percent of Indonesians identify themselves as Muslims, which makes it the most populous Muslim-majority nation in the world.

terrible night, of the water splashing around the hold, the incessant creaking of the boat, the giant cockroaches scurrying over me, the moaning of the other passengers and livestock, the smell of diesel and sick.

I don't even remember disembarking; before I knew it we were jumping out of a dugout canoe on a sunlit beach, our barge now sitting in a quiet bay. I stumbled as I waded through the clear turquoise water and toppled under a tall, hovering palm. The sand under me was heaving and rocking and I puked for the last time. Fran had fared only slightly better.

"Dude, that was the roughest sea I've ever been in—and I was in the Marines," he let out breathily. "I was so sure we were going down, I rode the whole friggin' way top deck, on the bow. It was so bad I had to lash myself down with the bowlines . . . but at least I would've had a fighting chance. I wanted to come get you but I couldn't move. . . . I'm sorry, but I thought you were a dead man."

I lay back with my arm covering my eyes and pounding head and listened. "I'm telling you," he went on, "we were pitched almost vertical sometimes, some of those swells must have been fifty foot. . . . I was swamped—waves crashing over me!"

When I was able to focus on him I saw that he was soaking wet, his long beard gnarled in encrusted knots, his black T-shirt patched with white where salt had crystallized. I had a vivid vision of that little toy boat going under in those giant swells, with him lashed to the bow, cursing madly and spitting back at the sea, like Ahab and his terrible leviathan. I let out a chuckle, we locked eyes and burst out laughing until we could take it no more, it hurt too much.

A tribesman walks the dense jungle paths of Siberut, part of Sumatra's Mentawai archipelago.

When we were able to get up, we found a shack selling warm orange sodas and chugged a couple down. Ochok, a rail-thin man with an upbeat personality, befriended us and we instantly took to him, hiring him as interpreter and guide. He led us to a man in a dug-out canoe

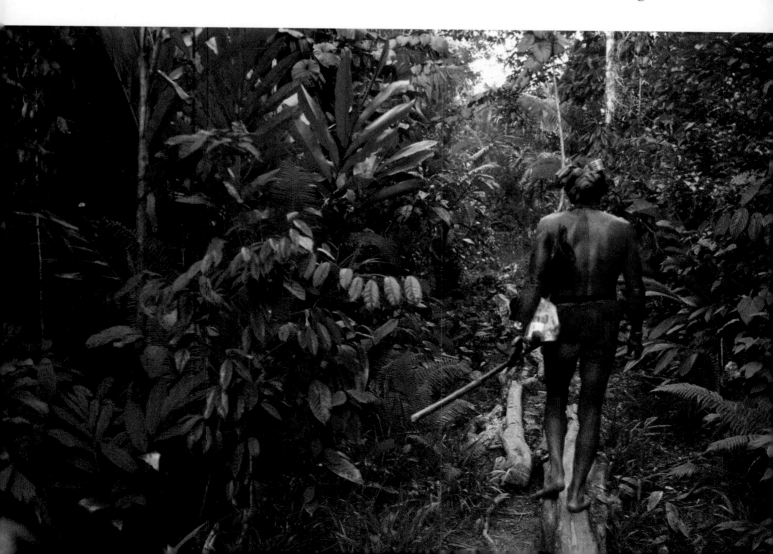

with an outboard, and we headed into the dense tropical rainforest to the isolated hunter-gatherer communities that are scattered along the island's river valleys. In one of the last truly wild frontiers on earth, the ride was spectacular.

The narrow, muddy river snaked its way in, barricaded on both sides by the teeming, thick jungle. We sat quietly for hours until the river got shallow, nearly tipping the long, hewed-out canoe on a sandbank. We got out and waded waist-deep in the mucky river, pushing the boat along with our gear inside, occasionally getting dunked when stepping into a sinkhole. Without the drone of the motor the jungle came alive, its symphony playing off the water we were now pushing through.

Then, from the corner of my eye, what I took to be just another mud-encrusted log on the riverbank sprang to life and in a mad dash splashed into the water in front of me.

> *They are loathsome creatures to behold. . . . Their mouth is big enough to swallow a man in one gulp. Their teeth are huge. All in all, the monsters are of such ferocity that there is neither man nor beast but goes in fear of them.*

"Croc!" I screamed. "Croc!" Nearly capsizing the canoe as I flung myself in. I instinctively looked for Fran, only to find him already in the boat.

"That's a Komodo dragon—you see the size of him?" he said, pointing as the giant lizard swam swiftly upriver.

"Yeah, right. That's no consolation," I shot back, a slight crack in my voice. Ochok and the boatman were still laughing at us as we hesitantly made our way back in the water.

Fran went on, "I know it wasn't a Komodo because they're only found on that island, but that's not far from here and that monitor must have been over six feet long. Did you see how fat he was?" I didn't answer; I was too busy scanning the sun-speckled banks that lay ahead.

馬哥孛羅

A true lost world, Siberut was cut off from the main island more than half a million years ago, giving it one of the highest concentrations of endemic flora and fauna populations on the planet. Over 60 percent of what lives here is found nowhere else in the world, including (incredibly for its small size) four species of primates.

If Polo broke ground in anthropology then he was also an early naturalist. He was clearly taken with Indonesia's wonders, describing plants never seen and collecting seeds and nuts long before his more famous followers in the early nineteenth century.

The superstitious medieval readers of Marco Polo's book would have expected to be told certain fantasies about the East, such as dog-headed men and other mythological

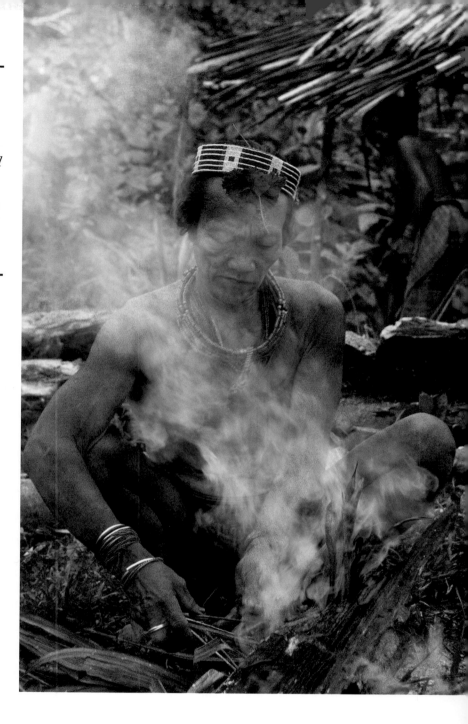

The Mentawai are
Austronesians, the
original inhabitants
of Southeast Asia, and
have long resisted as-
similation; they live a
lifestyle little changed
since prehistory.

creatures. Though he, or for that matter Rusticello, sprinkled a few fables in, like desert
ghosts and giant birds that could lift elephants, Marco was eager to tell the truth and
dispel the legends most popular to Europeans at the time. Here, for instance, he told
them that the unicorn, a mystical image in the Middle Ages, was not at all the creature
trapped by hunters in the chains of virgins, but in actuality just a rhinoceros.

In today's information age, it's hard to image that not too long ago little was known
of our cousins, the great apes. The mountain gorillas of central Africa were not discovered by scientists until 1902, making Marco's tale of orangutans (meaning "men of
the forests") all the more remarkable. Stories of man-beasts living on the fringes of the

known world are not unheard of today; think of the Yeti and Bigfoot. But in Polo's time such legends were common; savage, dangerous beings lived out there that could devour the unwary. Yet, to the people who share the forests with them, apes were former humans who, for various mythological reasons, had been transformed.

> *I may tell you moreover that when people bring home pygmies which they allege to come from the Indies, 'tis all a lie and a cheat. For those little men, as they call them, are manufactured on this island, and I will tell you how.*

Again, instead of perpetuating myths of unusual strength and sexual depravity that made their way into the twentieth century with King Kong, Marco said, *You see there is on this island a monkey which . . . has the face just like a man's. They take these and pluck out all the hair except the beard . . . and then dry and stuff them and daub them with saffron and other drugs until they appear to be human. This is all a trickery as you have heard. For nowhere in the Indies nor in wilder regions still was there ever men seen so small as these pretended pygmies.*

Astonishingly, ancient legends of an Indonesian island inhabited by little men were confirmed in 2003 with the discovery of the smallest human species ever identified, a three-foot-tall adult skeleton found in a cave on Flores Island. Dubbed *Homo floresiensis*, these little people may have lived as recently as 18,000 years ago, possibly coexisting with *Homo sapiens* (modern humans) who remembered them in their oral traditions.

Finally, we turned a bend to a remarkable sight. A group of natives had gathered on the hilly shore to greet the once-a-week shipment of goods that had accompanied us. Tattoos covered their bodies and colorfully beaded headdresses and necklaces adorned them.

Lightheaded, I stepped out of the boat into knee-deep mud. A tiny, naked man with a spear, mahogany skinned and muscular, helped me up the mucky embankment and gave me a warm hug when I finally righted myself. All he wore was a loincloth made from some kind of soft, fibrous plant material. We followed him and a few others into the forest on fallen trees that were lined end-to-end and acted as a causeway over the thick, muddy jungle floor. We couldn't keep up with the little Mentawai; they scurried along barefoot at a breakneck pace as we stumbled on the slippery logs with our oversized boots and feet, getting stuck in the quicksandlike mud. After a few hours we came to an uma, literally, a "house that contains ancestral heirlooms." Hewn from rough timber and thatch roofed, it sat on stilts and provided shade for the ten or so pigs living under it. A man afflicted with rheumatism sat at the entrance and we climbed the simple steps hacked from a log to sit next to him. His wife and some teenage children arrived and lit up hand-rolled cigarettes made from what looked like banana leaves.

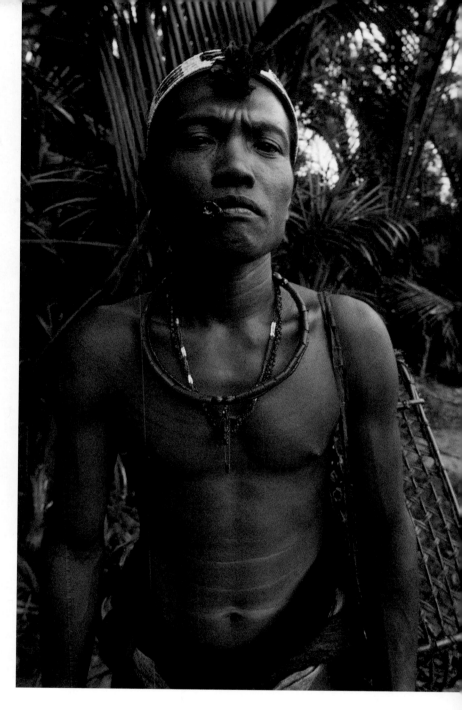

Although war parties and headhunting were abolished not too long ago, inter-uma rivalry is closely woven into Mentawai society, and there are intricate laws and fines to be paid (mostly in the form of pigs) for any transgressions.

"They are the chain-smoking people," I said. "Even the little kids are lighting up."

"Yeah, but look how happy they are," Fran said, and he was right, they were aglow, and our visit had become an impromptu happy hour.

"I stand corrected. They are the happy chain-smoking people."

The woman was perhaps forty, but looked much older. In what must have been a painful rite of passage, all her teeth had been filed to sharp points, giving her smiling face a fiercely incongruous look. Her breasts hung to her belly, nursed dry years ago by many children. Her tattoos ran from her neck down her chest across her breasts and into her sarong, bands were inked on her biceps and calves, and her hands were covered in an intricate design.

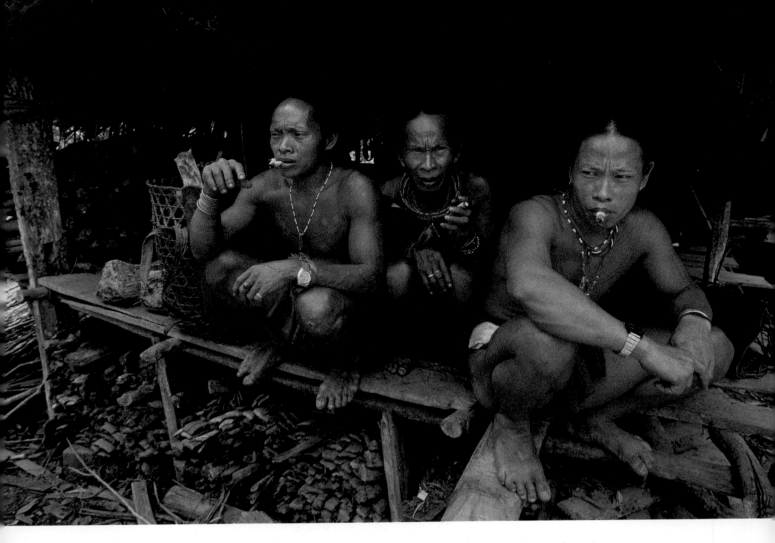

The Mentawai believe that every day they must seduce their own souls not to leave their bodies. They do this by wearing adornments of either flowers or jewelry.

The Mentawai are Austronesians, the original inhabitants of Southeast Asia. With hardly any body hair, they marveled at ours and were free and at ease cuddling up to Fran and stroking his long beard.

"You are tired, we stay here?" Ochok half-stated, half-asked. Although we were still reeling from the sea voyage, we decided to trek on under the shade of the canopy, crossing many shallow, leech-infested streams.

"Why aren't you tattooed?" we asked Ochok during a break.

"The young peoples is rejecting the old ways. They laugh and point at us when we go over to the main islands. . . . And it's hard to find work," he explained. "We get them when we are married but I will not be tattooed until my father lies sick and dying. Then he can see I will carry on the traditions of my ancestors."

After a few hours we came upon another uma with only women inside; a toothless granny was grinding sago while the younger ones sat nursing armfuls of children. We could have pressed on but decided to spend the night in this house. The inside of an uma consists of two or three adjoining rooms running the length of the building; at the thresholds of each room either monkey or boar skulls dangle from crossbeams. Everywhere hung countless bird fetishes made with real feathers. Monkeys and reptiles were carved on the posts and a large turtle emerged from the center of the floorboards in high relief, its teardrop shell scooped out from the thick hardwood plank to serve as a permanent bowl.

The skulls of monkeys that have been eaten hang in an important part of the uma. It is hoped the souls of dead animals will like the uma and tell their living relatives to join them, which means more meat for the house.

I coveted their naive style of primal art, highly representational and stylized and infused with mystery and magic. I imagined myself a modern Gauguin, collecting these great works from the noble savages and bringing them back to awe my fellow artists in civilization. An arrogant white man's fantasy of paradise lost and found, I know, and one that should have died a century ago, yet there I was having it.

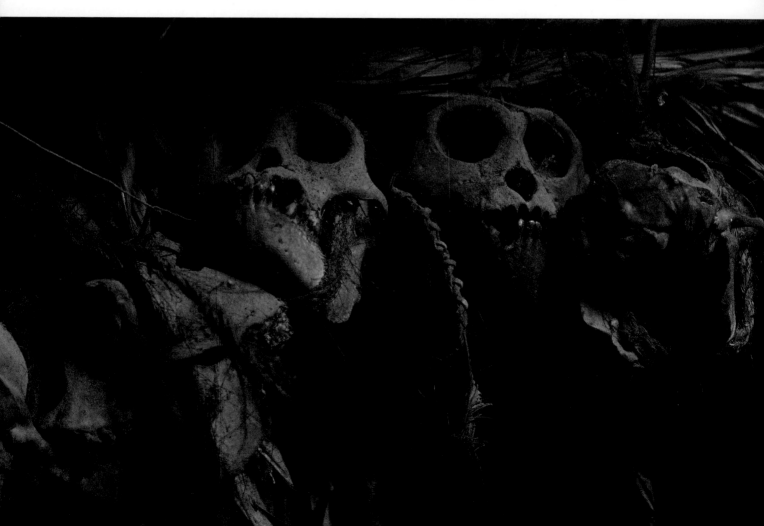

I pointed to a crude image of feet painted on the timber. "That means someone has died from this uma," said Ochok. "Their feet are there, so their spirit can never enter again."

Though no longer cannibals, the Mentawai of Sumatra are still animists, believing all that exists has a soul. The natural world is their religion. The forest has many spirits and it is where their ancestors dwell. To offend any spirit is to bring sickness and evil into the uma that only the shaman can cure because it is he and he alone who can mediate with the realm of spirits.

At dusk a man showed up and hugged us with a high-pitched nasal greeting and a tremendous smile. Ochok introduced him as Laka (Red), of the Sakalio clan. There were hibiscus flowers in his headband and he was wearing the red waistband and coral necklace that signified his status as a shaman, or sikerei. He had been in the jungle all day collecting roots, plants, and flowers to make a medicine for his wife, who had pains in her chest.

"How long has he been foraging?" Fran asked a puzzled Ochok.

"*Foraguh*, what?"

"What time did he leave this morning?" Fran asked again, pointing to the cheap, glittery Casio watch that dangled on Laka's wrist. Ochok nodded comprehension and turning to Laka, let out a stream of their language that took way too long to be a translation. The shaman paused for a time, looked at the sky, and pointed to the east just above the tree line, saying he had left when the sun was over there.

"Oh right," we said, amazed, realizing his watch was just a trinket.

> *You must know that when one of them falls sick they send for magicians who claim by means of their enchantments and diabolical art to know if he will recover or die.*

We followed Laka to the banks of a stream that ran behind his house. He squatted in the water to wash the plants he had collected, placing them gingerly on a giant elephant ear leaf he had cut from the banks. We watched as he grated the plants over a branch with studded spikes that acted as a natural rasp. He poured water over the shredded pulp, squeezing it into a ball until the juices filled a plastic cup, and brought the cup to his wife to drink, rubbing her whole body down with the soaking pulp as he sang a prayer for her sick spirit as well. It was an act of such intimacy and love that we felt like voyeurs and stepped outside the uma to search the skies of the Southern Hemisphere for constellations we've rarely seen.

The shamans of the primal forests retain ancient knowledge that can benefit all mankind. Who knows what cures to diseases grow here that have become as endangered as the ways of these people?

I assure you that in all these islands there is no tree that does not give off a powerful and agreeable fragrance and serve some useful purpose.

Laka and his wife Megeba (Poor) had five children; the eldest male was called Kopisusu (Coffee with Milk). He, his wife, and three-week-old son lived in the uma as well. Kopisusu couldn't tell us how old he was but my guess was early twenties. Like his father he had tattooed symbols for either the sun or stars on his shoulders. Blue-black lines followed both cheekbones and ran down his neck. A single line ran from below his lip and straight down his entire torso and was crossed by other lines running around the entire barrel of his chest. Multiple horizontal strands of beads around his neck formed a

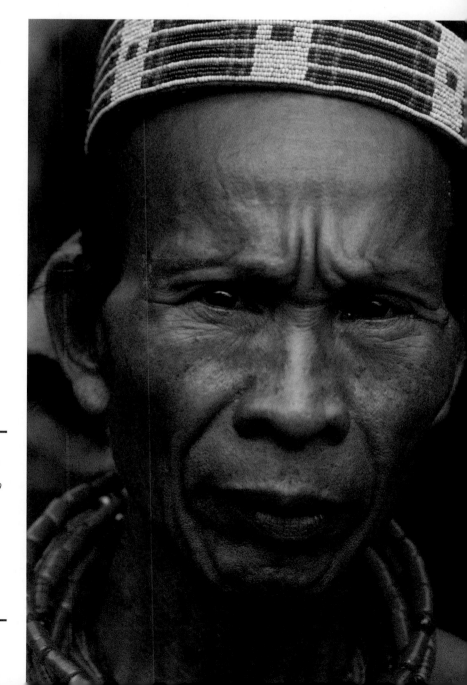

Laka was a sikerei, or shaman, of the Sakalio clan. The Mentawai believe it is only the sikerei who can communicate with the realm of spirits.

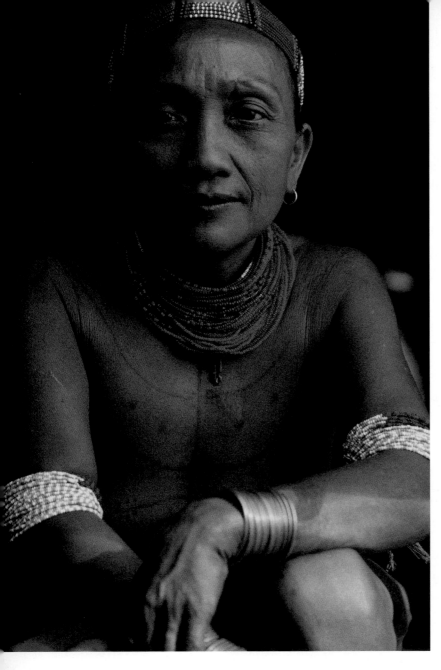

permanent necklace. His arms had striped vines running their lengths and his legs and feet were covered as well.

A lone gaslight illuminated his face from the darkness that had enveloped the uma, adding drama to the scene as he explained their creation myth. "We cover ourselves like this, so that we are no longer naked. Our kabaranan (origins) speaks of our ancestor, a boy who once transformed himself into the first sago tree, the Tree of Life. A sacrifice for our people, that they would never go hungry. So sacred is this tree to us, it is tattooed on the body of every sikerei. The stripes on my legs are its trunk, these long lines running down my arms are the branches, on my hands and feet its bark, and the curved lines on my chest, the sago flower."

Male and female have their flesh covered all over with pictures made with needles in such a way that they are indelible. They make these on their faces, necks, bellies, hands and legs . . . the more elaborate anyone is decorated the more handsome he is considered.

Fran showed off his various tattoos, which caused quite a stir in the uma, the girls of the house rubbing the geoglyphic Nazca spider on his leg and the dragon on his chest.

We tried to sleep on the hard planks like the rest of the family, but between the grunts and squeals of the pigs beneath us and the swarms of mosquitoes hovering over us waiting to attack the one sliver of flesh not smothered in repellent, we found it

"Without our tattoos we would be naked. They are our clothes."
(Kopisusu)

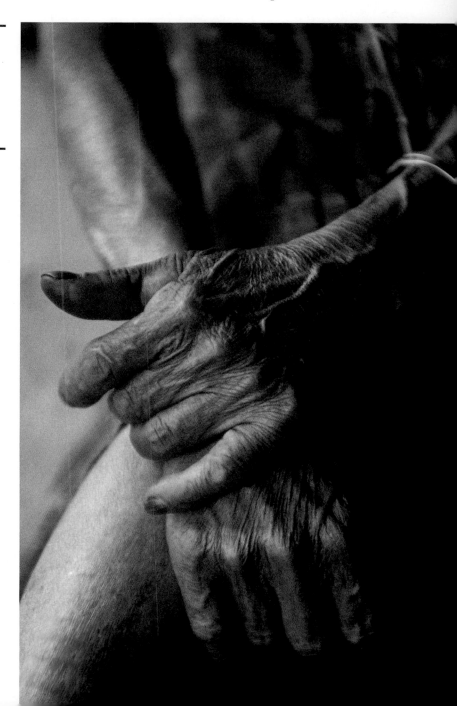

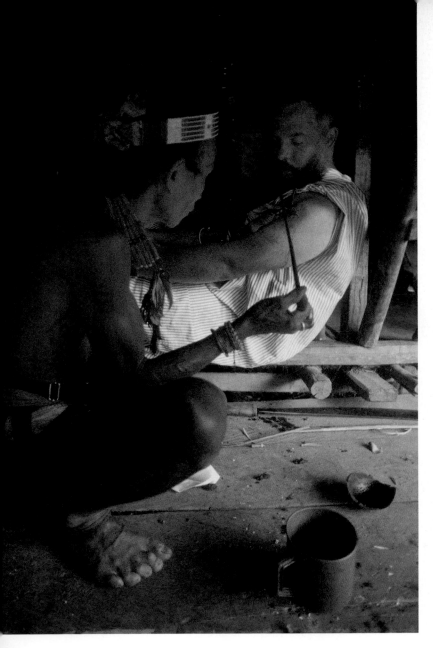

With a tap stick and ink he made using carbon from the fire, Laka gives Fran an authentic tribal tattoo.

impossible. In the morning we followed Laka and Megeba through the forest to recover a log of sago that was either being preserved or fermented as it lay on the bottom of a watery swamp.

> *There are trees here of great height and girth that two men could just embrace. This wood can be split in a straight line from top to bottom. . . . It is heavy and when thrown in water sinks like iron. . . . After stripping off the bark, you find inside this pith consisting of flour . . . this is put through refining, seasoned and made into cakes and paste dishes, which are exceedingly good for we often ate of them.*

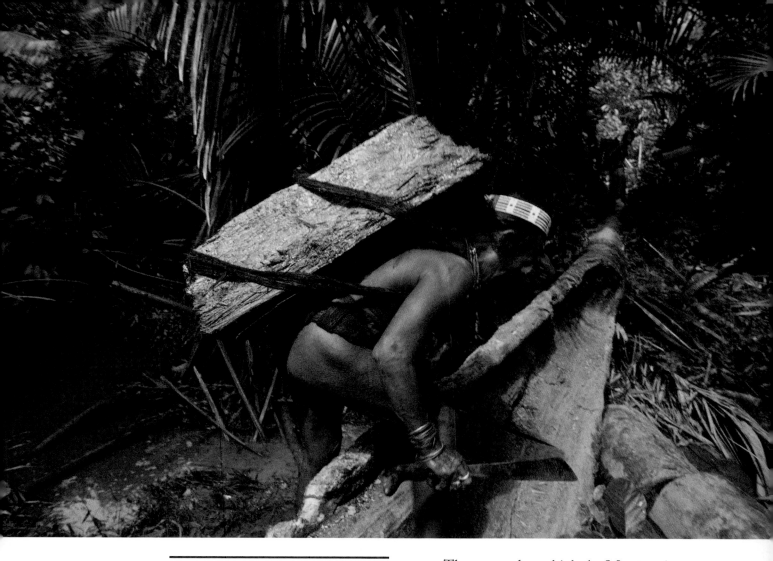

While his wife waits on a causeway made by fallen trees, a Mentawai tribesman retrieves a heavy section of sago he had stored in the swamp behind him.

The sago palm, which the Mentawai venerate and harvest with great care and ritual, is still processed as Polo observed. A single tree produces 1,600 pounds of carbohydrate-rich flour, enough to feed an uma for six months. The paste dishes have the consistency of wallpaper glue and are sometimes mixed with live grubs. The pith has a sour stench like rotting vegetation and tastes better when mixed with bananas or when baked. We ourselves can attest to this for we often ate of them.

After bathing in a pristine waterfall, the sounds of the forest lulled us along. It felt sacrilegious to talk too much on the jungle paths; when we did it was in a hushed tone, making sure not to miss Laka stealthily pointing out a colorful frog, the rustling of a dead leaf as something slithered by, or the hauntingly beautiful song of the gibbons, high up in the canopy. When we heard the commotion in the faint distance, Laka stopped dead in his tracks, and then took off in its direction. We chased after nervously, not knowing what it was. As we grew near we realized it was a pack of dogs, their incessant

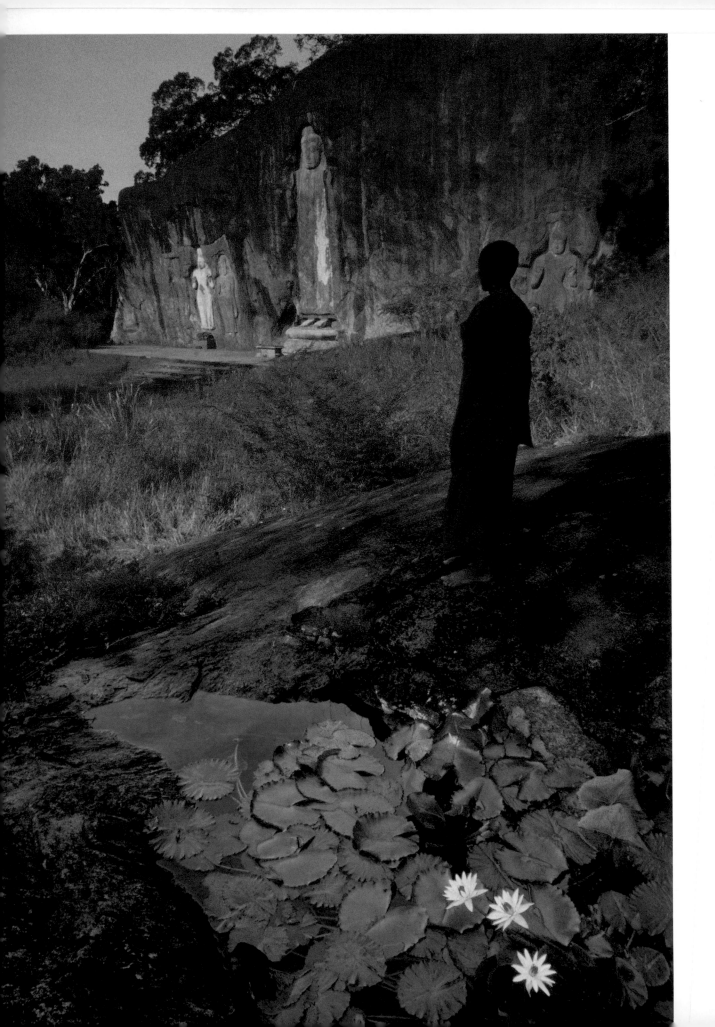

(opposite page) *After the Taliban blew up the standing Buddhas in Bamian, the one sculpted out of the living rock at Buduruwagala became the world's tallest at fifty-one feet.*

day. In the afternoons we bought small tunas from the returning fishermen, spiced them with atomic chili curries, and roasted them up on the beach.

It was easy to be captured by Ceylon's serenity. Polo was right, it is an island paradise, but on that very day just a stone's throw away to the north, thirty-seven soldiers were killed in the long-running civil war between the Sinhalese and Tamil Tigers.

"A Buddhist-Hindu war just doesn't sound right to me," I said to Fran one night as we watched sea turtles bodysurf breaking waves.

"I know what you mean," he said. "All war is wrong and religious wars even more so, but somehow Islam versus Christianity is easier to understand than this one."

"It's the Buddhist thing for me," I said. "Everyone knows there are Hindu fanatics, remember that temple riot in Gujarat?"

The inhabitants of Ceylon are not fighting men. . . . If they have need of the services of soldiers, they hire them from abroad, especially Saracens.

Aukana Buddha, carved in the fifth century. In the second and third centuries, when missionaries brought not just the religion but the culture of Buddhist India to Sri Lanka, they couldn't have imagined the culture wouldn't survive in India itself. Today, Sri Lanka is the oldest Buddhist country in the world.

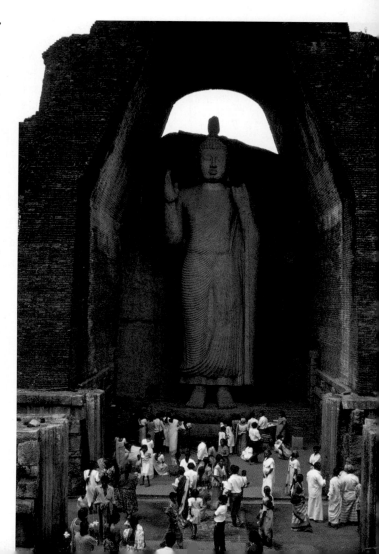

In Ceylon, Marco gave the West the most in-depth study yet regarding the life of the Buddha, correctly retelling his life story. How he was raised a prince and shielded by his father from the sorrows of mortal life. How, when he was older and discovered the truth that all things suffer, decay, and eventually die, he would embark on a personal quest for spiritual knowledge that would eventually lead him to enlightenment and nirvana. And, in a radically open-minded statement for a medieval European, Polo even dared to say, *For assuredly had he been a Christian, he would have been a great saint with our lord Jesus Christ.*

Polo even correctly told us that here was kept a tooth relic of the Buddha held sacred by people whom he called idolaters, who came here on pilgrimage from very distant lands.

馬哥孛羅

And it is a fact that in this island is a very large mountain . . . it is said that at the top of this mountain is the monument of Adam, our first parent.

As usual, I was nauseous from the switchback roads that sliced through the hill country and had had enough. When we could see Adam's Peak jutting above the terraced tea fields from the overcrowded minibus, we asked the driver to stop.

"Let's walk the rest of the way, it only looks about ten miles," I said to Fran. But after only a few, we grew weary and followed a group of women in bright saris off the muddy road and into the tea fields. They had hand-woven baskets on their backs and were plucking only the lightest green, newly grown leaves from the tops of the tea bushes. Adam's Peak loomed in the background as we made our way down the terraces toward the crash of a waterfall to take a dip.

We approached the guesthouse at the base of the peak by late afternoon. The innkeeper was happy to see us; it was off-season for pilgrims and we were his only guests. "Welcome, welcome," he offered through teeth stained ox-blood red from betel chewing. He led us to a Spartan, mosquito-infested room to dump our packs.

The Saracens say at the top of the mountain it is the monument of Adam, but the idolaters say it belongs to a prince whose name was Sakyamuni.

Today the pilgrims flocking to the peak are still Muslims, who see in the indentation of a boulder Adam's very first footprint on earth, and Buddhists, who believe it is the Buddha's last footprint before leaving it. For us, the peak held another man's footprint and was just another site on a grander pilgrimage.

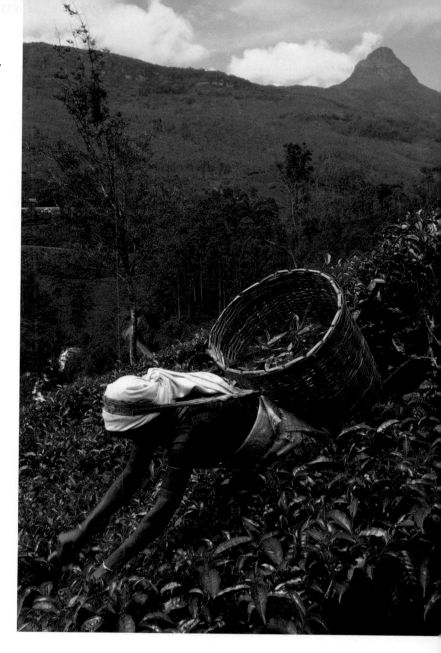

A tea-leaf plucker works terraced fields in the shadow of the 7,359-foot-tall Adam's Peak, which is the world's only pilgrimage site to be held sacred by four religions: Buddhism, Hinduism, Christianity, and Islam.

There was a woodworking shop adjacent to the house and the innkeeper followed me in. "Are you the carver?" I asked, walking among his Buddhas and elephants and lacquer ashtrays.

"Yes, these I sell to the pilgrims, but . . . ," he pulled out a photo album, "this chair took me five months to carve from ebony."

I leafed through the shots of an intricately carved black throne as he explained that before he began his masterpiece he covered the shop floor with holy ashes and cow dung. Then at a precise hour of an auspicious day he made his first strike of the chisel. When he had finished, he lugged the chair to Colombo and presented it to the president in honor of his grandfathers, who had for centuries carved all the thrones of the Sinhalese kings.

He showed me a yellowed newspaper article with the caption: "Carver of 1.7 million-rupee chair doesn't even own one in his house." The article said the president auctioned

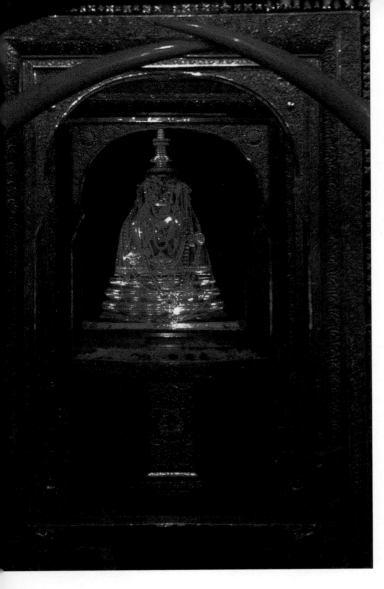

Temple of the Sacred Tooth Relic, Kandy, Sri Lanka. A tooth of the Buddha is encased in seven gold caskets studded with precious stones, which have been given by various rulers over the centuries.

off the chair and gave the money to charity. A rich gem merchant had bought it for the staggering sum of $34,000 and the carver didn't get a dime.

"Why don't you make another and sell it? You could be a rich man," I said.

"No, no . . . never, just the one, special . . . just one," he replied in his halting English. "I do this for my soul, not money . . . I am rich man here," pointing to his chest and wiggling his head side to side with that happy twitch that is peculiar to the subcontinent.

For dinner the innkeeper served us a fiery vegetarian meal while we asked him questions. "I was born this village," he'd answer, or "The biggest change? More pilgrims because of the new roads, and the chains came off the mountain ten years ago."

"The chains!" we said in unison.

> *The cliffs are so sheer that no one can climb it except for one way . . .*
> *for many iron chains have been hung on the side of the mountain*
> *. . . by their means a man could climb to the top.*

"Yes . . . you will see some of the old chains when you climb up tonight. Before they built the stairs, people would make their wills before climbing the chains. Not everyone made it back down."

We left at 2:00 a.m. with a couple of flashlights he loaned us and began the ascent to catch the sunrise. We climbed silently at first, the scent of jasmine drifting over the stairs etched into the side of the mountain.

"We should have counted how many steps there are," I said to Fran during a break.

"Is that what's going through your head?" he asked, bewildered.

"Yeah, why?"

"I don't know . . . I just thought"—he paused—"I just thought that you'd be feeling it too."

"What?" I blurted, still really only thinking about how many stairs there were.

"Just . . . I don't know . . . my mind is racing with questions: How many of the guys got killed with Waseq? Why are we the ones to do this? Were we chosen?" We stood

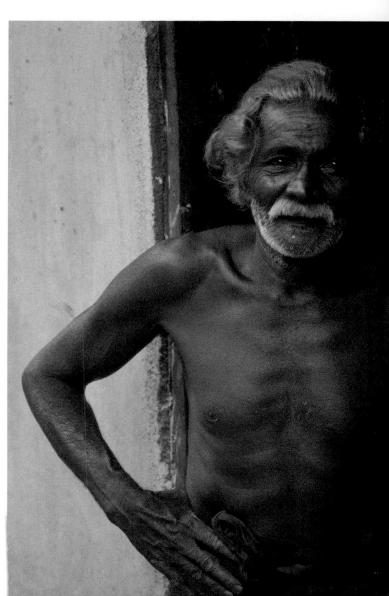

The innkeeper—a man of peace. The Sri Lankan government estimates that over seventy thousand people have been killed since 1983 in its civil war with the Tamil Tigers, who want independence in the north and east of the island.

watching the eastern sky start to grow bright, and at this hour, I had no answers for him. "I was thinking about that guy down there, how he doesn't care about money or fame or recognition. He does his art for the spirituality of it."

"Yeah, that is pretty enlightened of him." I laughed. "He's no Arthur C. Clarke."

"It's more than that!" Fran said. "He's like the gatekeeper, the holder of sacred knowledge. To toil with no expectation of a reward for his efforts but to be in his bliss is so alien a thought to us . . . I guess maybe . . . I guess I'm re-evaluating my motivations for taking this journey."

I shut off my flashlight and sat down, knowing this was going to take awhile. "Did you smoke something and not tell me?" I asked him, not so sure I wanted to get into such a deep conversation.

"C'mon man, I'm being serious. Don't you feel the power of this place? It's like the axis mundi or something, the center of the world. . . . Don't you feel the stillness? There are no sounds, not even a cricket is chirping."

I agreed with him, but the only thing I was feeling were my thighs burning.

At the summit, pink and purple clouds clung to the hills below, cutting through valleys like rivers of cotton candy. Turning our backs to the sun that had crested the hills, hovering above the horizon like a giant spotlight, we could see the triangular dark shadow cast by the seven-thousand-foot peak as it stretched its summit over the lowlands all the way to the sea. We gazed at the forty-mile-long shadow in silence until the sun rose and the shadow raced back to us, pooling gently at the foot of the peak.

"Axis mundi, huh?" I said to Fran. "I get it."

馬哥孛羅

We were anxious as we walked across the capital's crowded square to meet Raja. The ship was leaving in a few hours and we still needed to get to the sea consortium's office to sign the indemnity. A political rally was taking place in the square and the police had barricaded the streets. It took us over an hour to get out of the center of Colombo and down to the docks as Raja weaved through the slow traffic and hordes of people filling the streets.

It was not until later, after we had signed on and boarded the rusty feeder ship, that the captain told us the news. At the rally, a candidate for the presidential election, Gamini Dissanayake, and fifty-eight others were killed by a suicide bomber, a female Tamil Tiger.

> *When the traveler leaves Ceylon and sails westwards for about 60 miles he arrives in the great province of Malabar . . . indeed the best part of India.*

INDIA

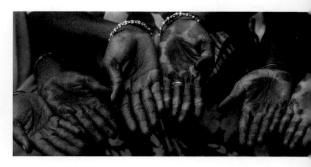

"The Richest and Most Splendid Country in the World"

ALL SHIPPING IN THE STRAITS WAS BANNED to stop arms coming in from Tamil Nadu, so we were forced to circumnavigate the island. Two days later we sat anchored off the Indian coast in rough water waiting for a berth to open up in port. It took over a week.

"Mister Denis, you like I make you a nice fried chicken and vegetables for dinner tonight?" Edgar the cook asked me one morning as he slopped on my breakfast of fish-head stew. We had been eating nothing but fish for days and my mouth watered.

"Yes Edgar, that would be—"

"Only one problem, Mr. Denis," he interrupted me. "We have no chicken or vegetables." Red-faced, I sat down with the laughing crew.

We should have been forewarned. The first thing the captain had said to us was "Er . . . ah . . . hope you guys eat squid." The paint-peeled, rusted hulk stank of the cephalopod. Every corner of deck that received sun had palm-sized squid drying on lines. We passed the days lazily reading books, playing chess, and fishing off the bow for yet more squid with the friendly Filipino crew.

One morning, agents from customs and immigration came aboard to take our passports and grill us on our itinerary. They wanted to know exactly what kind of book and film we were making. Either the captain had told them something or P&O had explained our quest through their office in Colombo when we signed on as crewmen.

"What difference does it make, we have valid visas, just let us off the boat!" I said in frustration to the agents. They left the ship in a huff, but when they returned in a few days, they brought a new problem: bubonic plague had broken out in India and there was to be a quarantine.

"The plague is in India, we are arriving not leaving! Why would we need to be quarantined?" Fran asked a clueless agent before they sped back to shore with the harbor pilot, not to return until a few days later when we had a berth in port.

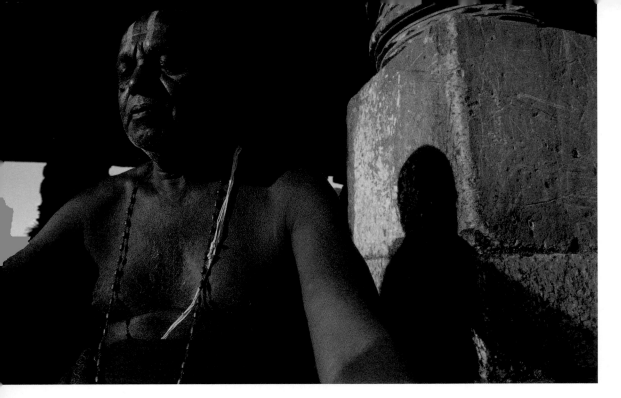

"The Brahmins are known by an emblem which they wear, for they carry a cord of cotton on their shoulder and fastened across the chest . . . and live virtuous lives."

"You have been denied entry into India, because the law stipulates that no sailor may disembark from a cargo vessel as a passenger," the captain informed us. "You'll need to sail back to Sri Lanka with us and fly to India."

Why should they care that we couldn't fly? We had to think of something fast. "Can I call the American consulate?" I asked. "Sri Lanka has been under martial law since the assassination last week and we feel our lives would be in danger if we went back."

"We'd rather jump ship and take our chances getting arrested," Fran added, the captain's grimace a clear indication what he thought of *that* idea.

"Yes, call the Americans, see what they can do."

I found a phone booth on the dock and rang the consulate, begging for help.

The next morning that captain called us to the bridge. "They are permitting you to sign off as crewmen on one condition. You leave India in seventy-two hours."

"That gives us a three-day head start to get lost," I said to Fran as we walked through the gates of the marina. "And . . . I couldn't think of a better place to get lost in."

"Yup," he replied, a huge grin on his face. "They'll have to catch us."

(opposite page) "They believe no sailor can be trusted. . . . For they say, a man who sails by sea must be a man in great despair."

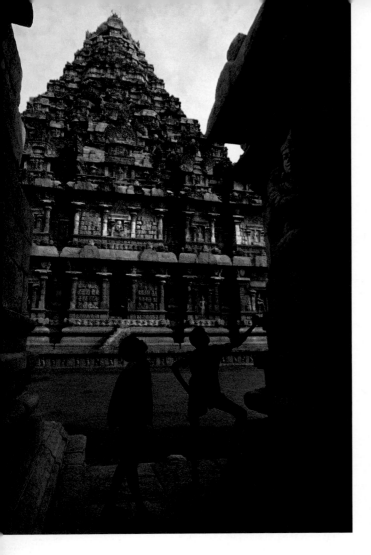

The temple at Gangaikondachol-apuram (the town of the chola who captured the Ganges) was erected to commemorate the victories of Rajendra Chola I in 1022. The city remained the capital of the Cholas until the kingdom declined, not long before Polo arrived.

The monsoon rains that poured upon the face of Madras were relentless. The streets were rivers of waist-deep brown water with live electrical lines dangling in them. I tried not to look at the flotsam and jetsam of sewage I waded through, keeping my eyes fixed on a garishly painted Bollywood movie billboard. It sat twisted and crumpled and ripped off its posts by the ferocious winds.

We rode out the storm in the servants' wing of a former Mogul palace that had been converted to a guesthouse, hardly venturing out of the Jodhpur-blue painted room for days. Everything from our morning chai to our evening suppers was ordered in from the boy touts who were forever knocking on our door. It was a fittingly dark backdrop for what happened next.

"I just called home for the first time in months and my poor mother had to tell me that my father is dead," Fran said one afternoon as he entered dripping wet into our room. He was as white as a sheet. "I can't believe it. I missed the funeral and everything. . . . I'm full of remorse and guilt for not being there to comfort my mom and sisters."

"Ah Franny . . . I don't know what to say. I'm so sorry. . . . What do you want to do?"

"I don't know," he said sadly. "I can't think in here. Let's just go to the basilica and do our jobs and I'll light a candle for my dad."

馬哥孛羅

Let me tell you a marvelous thing about the burial place. The Christians who go there on pilgrimage take some earth of a red color from where the saintly body died.

Polo is the first storyteller to place the tomb of St. Thomas the Apostle, "Doubting Thomas," in southern India, saying he was martyred there by rival Hindu priests.

As we waited for an audience with the Bishop of Mylapore in the basilica that houses the tomb, we found a nun, Sister Isabel, who was kind enough to show us the holy relics: a spear point believed to have pierced Thomas's side and some of his bones.

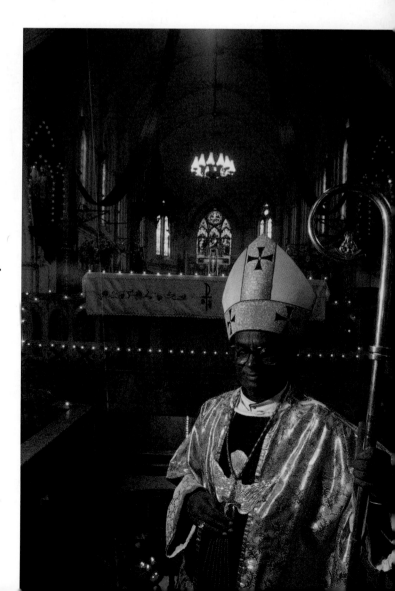

The Bishop of Mylapore at the tomb of St. Thomas the Apostle in Tamil Nadu, India. There are only three churches built over the tomb of an apostle: the Basilica of St. Peter in Rome, the Cathedral of Santiago de Compostela of St. James in Spain, and the Basilica of St. Thomas in India.

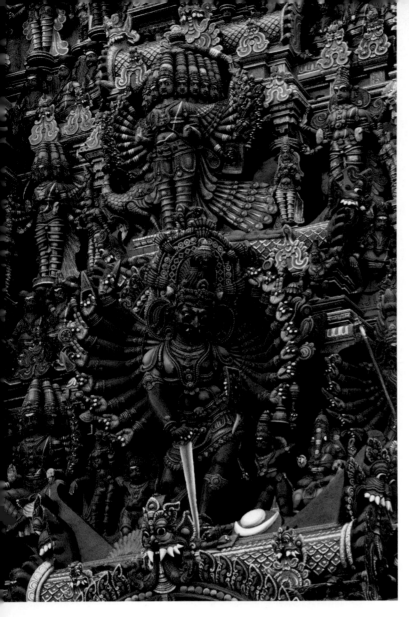

Meenakshi Amman Temple, Madurai, India. There are a large number of deities or murtis in Hinduism. These beings are either aspects of the supreme being, Brahma, or powerful deities known as devas. The murtis appear with many arms and hands, each grasping a symbol that depicts their various powers.

"My grandfather converted from Hinduism and the family disowned us," she said in singsong English. "We've only recently reconciled when my cousin anointed his head at his funeral in the Hindu tradition and we didn't object. I pray for them though, for they are lost." She went on ironically about the Hindu pantheon as we walked past devout Catholics piously kissing the toes of various saint statues lining the walls of the church. "They have a god for everything and will pray to any idol."

> *They have idols with the heads of four faces and some with three heads, one in the right place and one on either shoulder. Some have four hands, some ten and some a thousand.*

The bishop extended his ringed hand to us. We shook it but did not kiss it. "We'd like to take your grace's portrait beside the tomb for our book," I said after explaining

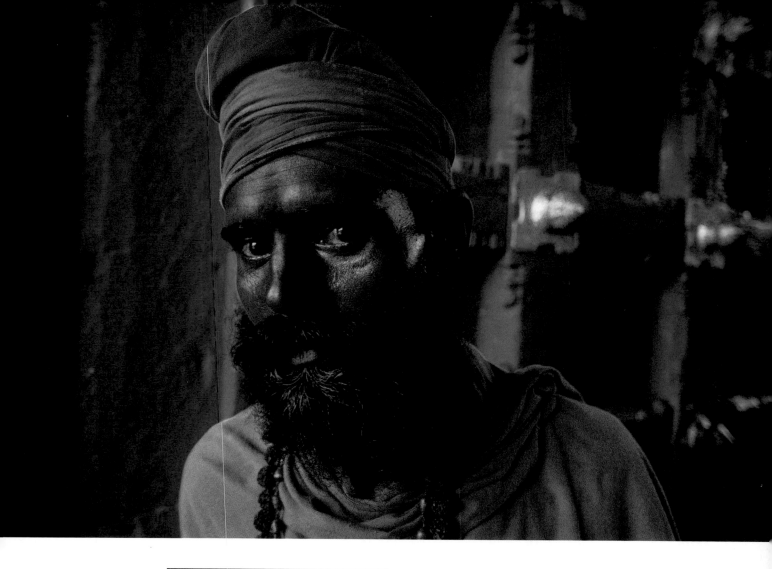

The saffron robes of a sadhu represent his renunciation of the material world. In Hinduism spiritual enlightenment has always been the highest goal in life, so these wandering ascetics are revered.

the project, but he seemed reluctant. "My uncle Paul is a Maryknoll missionary," I quickly added, trying to seal the deal.

"Where is he?" he asked.

"Back in Guatemala now, after being forced out at gunpoint for sticking up for indigenous rights. He's one of the bravest people I know."

He leaned back in his chair, twirling the oversized ring on his finger. "I have much respect for Maryknoll's work, but I am so busy now preparing two hundred children for confirmation next Sunday."

"We understand," I said. "Thank you very much for seeing us." He got up and walked us to his door.

"Your eminence," Fran said. "May I ask a favor on a more personal matter? I just learned upon arriving in India that my father passed away. Could you please remember him in your next mass? It would have meant a great deal to him."

"Yes, yes, all is maya." He laughed.

We followed them for a week or so, sleeping under the stars and being fed by villagers, whom the wandering ascetics paid in kind with blessings and prayers.

They anoint themselves with powder no less than Christians in the use of holy water. If anyone does reverence to them in the street, they anoint them with powder on the forehead in token of blessing.

They showed us how to sit and meditate. "Practice," the kindly guru said, "step by step, five minutes a day, then ten, then fifteen, then a half an hour and so on. Between four and five in the morning is best, but you can do it anytime, just find a quiet place." He put his fingers in his ears to stress his point. "And concentrate on nothing but your breathing." He held his right nostril down and inhaled deeply then switched fingers and held his left to exhale, looking momentarily distinctly unholy in the process, his long white beard tied in a knot at his chin and his forehead smeared with dung ashes.

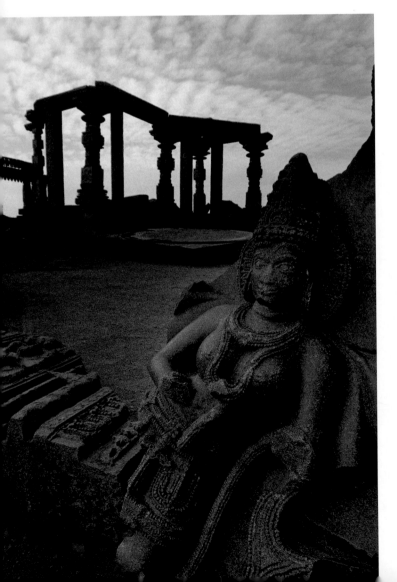

The ruins of Warangal where Rani Rudrama Devi ruled from 1261 until her death in 1296, the year after the Polos returned home. Devi, masculine for "lord" (Deva is the feminine), is in her title intentionally, for she ruled as a king.

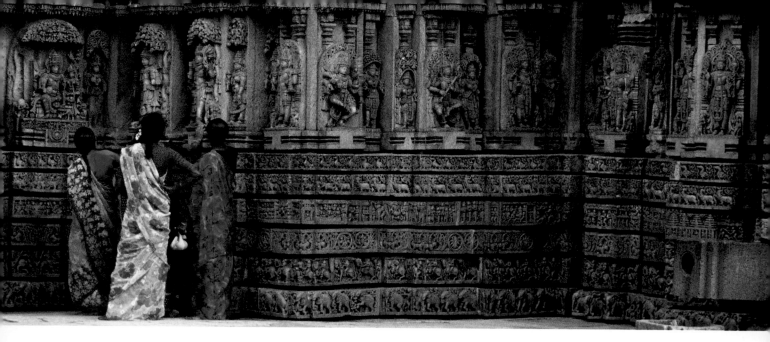

Built in 1268, the Keshava Temple at Somanathapura is adorned with a riot of human figures that gave us a snapshot of daily life in the Hoysala kingdom at precisely the time Polo was there.

One night, after following the sadhus to a funeral ghat beside a river, we watched a cremation. The eldest son of the family, his head shaved in mourning, circled the body of his mother three times before putting his lit torch to her mouth, which was stuffed with sandalwood shavings. We sat quietly as flames slowly consumed the body until all that remained were her unburned feet, and then they too were pushed into the embers.

"I'm feeling more spiritually connected to my dad here than when I was in the church. It's as if the universe knew I needed a lesson in mortality," Fran said to me, his face lit by the orange glow of the funeral pyre. "A lesson on the impermanence of all things. . . . I know my father loved me. He nurtured my passion for travel and history and he would have wanted me to continue . . . so, I'm rededicating the rest of this journey to his memory."

They hold that as soon as a man is dead he enters into another body; if he conducted himself well or ill in life, he will be reborn and pass from good to better or from bad to worse.

馬哥孛羅

"They're Enfields," the guy we bought the motorcycles from said. "If you break down you can get parts anywhere in India, and when you're done, they'll be easy to sell."

We shelled out the few hundred dollars for the bikes and sped off to tour the splendors of thirteenth-century Indian architecture.

By traveling north you find a kingdom ruled by a queen, who is a very wise woman. I can tell you throughout her 40-year reign she governed well with a high standard of justice and equity, as her husband did before.

A female ruler would have been a curiosity to any medieval European, but because he took the time to write about her, Polo gave voice to a woman otherwise lost to history. Modern archaeology has confirmed that the queen, a certain Rudrama Devi, ruled in Warangal when Polo visited.

"There are great numbers of maidens who are dedicated to amusing their male and female idols, to which they sing and dance and afford the merriest sport in the world." This practice—giving young girls to the temples as Devadasis (slaves, or servants, of God)—was outlawed in the 1950s.

We saw so many temple sites in the ensuing weeks that they became blurred into my memory as one experience, an amalgam of old rocks and incense. We would ride into a small village, find lodging for the night, get up at the crack of dawn, and have the place to ourselves. It was sweet light, the bewitching hour, and I was walking among ruins with my friend Francis, talking history, one of my favorite things to do.

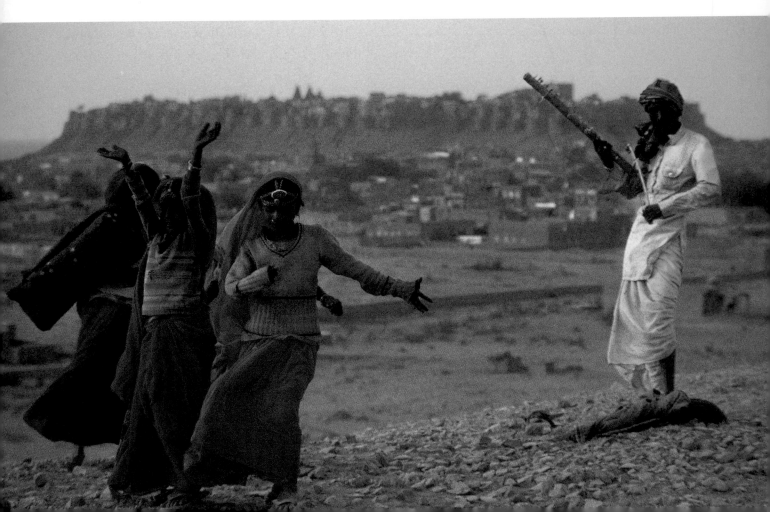

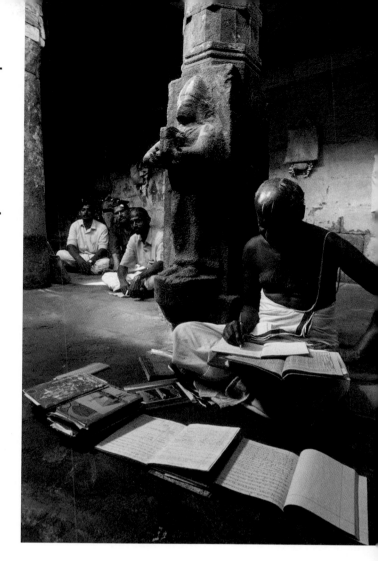

Fathers wait anxiously to have their newborn children's charts read and recorded by a Brahmin astrologer in an eight-hundred-year-old temple in Tiruchirappalli, Tamil Nadu.

"This one was built by a king who ruled from 1260 to 1291, our exact time frame," Fran said at one, reading from a lonely idiot guide he had borrowed from a chance-met backpacker. "I'm blown away by the sculptures, every possible niche is crammed with figures and not just deities," he said as we walked around the star-shaped complex.

I pointed out, high up in a niche, the figure of a woman giving birth; and there were others having sex, washing their hair, and dancing. "These scenes are snapshots of everyday life at precisely the time Marco was here, a very rare thing," I said. "What's up with the twelfth and thirteen centuries? I mean, there is this explosion of architectural and artistic creativity going on all over the world. Here in India you have the Chola and Hoysalas, and then you have the temples in Angkor Wat and Bagan in Southeast Asia and the great cathedrals of Europe, all rising within a few hundred years of each other."

"And don't forget the Seljuks in Turkey, the Samanids of Persia, and the Toltecs in Mexico," Fran chimed in.

At an eight-hundred-year-old temple, we watched as couples waited for a Brahmin priest to write down the horoscopes of their newborn children.

As soon as a child is born . . . .the parents have a record made in
writing of his nativity, that is the day, month, lunar cycle and
hour of his birth . . . this they do because they guide all their actions
by the council of astrologers and diviners who are skilled in the art
of magic and geomancy.

Fran talked me into having my horoscope read, but I did so skeptically. The Brahmin began by saying I would die when I was seventy-five-years old. "I was personally planning on more, but I'll take it for now and renegotiate when my time's up," I joked, but he missed my sarcasm.

"Your wife will be a strong person and very supportive of you. She will make you a better man. You will have two boys, who will grow up to be strong and well educated."

"Sounds good, can't wait to meet them," I said, rolling my eyes for Fran as we switched places.

"Ah . . . you are a Jupiterian man," he said to Fran as he sat in front of the priest, handing him a paper with his birth numbers. "I could tell by your forehead." He delved into his books and after a while looked up. "You will do something great, like Christopher Columbus himself."

That was it, I was a believer, and not least because I wanted to live to see seventy-five, for I was convinced one of the most dangerous things to do in this life was to take to the roads of India, either on a bus, in a car, or scariest of all, on a motorbike.

Village life in India takes place in, on, and right up to the edge of the barely paved roads, and when not weaving through darting children, chickens, and holy cows you must be wary of other motorists who seem hell-bent on running you off and into a ditch. Which is why, when I couldn't keep my eyes off a group of tribal women standing out in a crowded street, I motioned for us to stop.

They wore brightly colored clothing, perhaps the most elaborate we'd ever seen, with tiny mirrors embroidered into the patchwork and large, silver, coiled necklaces and earrings. Mantles covered their heads, draping down their backs and almost touching their feet. Cowrie shells, bits of ivory, and animal bones were sewn into their blouses and woven in their hair, and silver anklets clanked as they walked along barefoot. Needless to say, we stopped traffic when we started photographing them.

Excited to discover they were Lambadi, the ancestors of the tribe that migrated from India to Romania, around the time of Polo, to become known as gypsies; we were surprised to find their fellow Indians looking down upon these colorful people.

"Why do you want a photo of the Lambadi?" a man asked dismissively.

"Where are you from?" shouted another.

Before we knew it there were sixty or seventy incredulous Hindus encircling us. The Lambadi started to dance at Fran's request so he'd get something good on video, form-

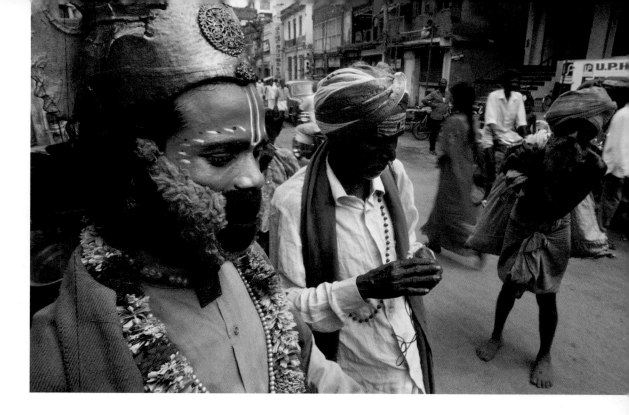

ing a circle and singing, silver-coined fingers clasped low, then raised high, causing armfuls of bangles to jingle. I saw their men already calculating how much to charge us for the impromptu show. There seemed to be just two of them but it was hard to tell, for like most tribal people, only the women wore traditional garb, the men preferring cheap Western-style polyester suits and black leather wingtip shoes.

After explaining we never paid for pictures, we bought them a simple lunch of dhal for twelve cents each. I'm not so sure they understood the difference. I'm not so sure I do.

"Hey, dude," Fran said after we took off again, huge grins on our faces from the encounter. "I'd rather have a Lambadi in front of me, than a frontal lobotomy."

I almost lost it in a ditch.

馬哥字羅

You either love or hate India: A land with 17 percent of the world's population but less than 5 percent of its wealth; a country with nuclear power and weapons, while much of its economy still runs from the backs of ox carts; the world's largest democracy, where stories of human bondage and slavery are not uncommon. All of humanity is stripped bare in India, laid out for raw public consumption.

Beggars, some with heartbreaking diseases like leprosy, constantly barraged us. We couldn't begin to relieve their suffering with a handout, but we couldn't turn away either.

We'd look them in the eye, talk with them, and treat them with dignity. They'd usually smile even if we didn't give, but I must confess, it hurt. The kids always got to us, we'd try to buy them something to eat but not when there were a lot of them . . . it was just impossible.

"You must have compassion with detachment," the guru had told us just weeks before. "You must embrace it all."

馬哥孛羅

India is the richest and most splendid country in the world. . . . You must know that pepper of great quality grows here in abundance and ginger too, besides plenty of other spices which are shipped all over the world for good profit.

Not only was he a trailblazer of the Silk Road, Polo pioneered uncharted territory on another famous avenue of trade, the Spice Route—giving the West its first account as to the origin of these most precious of commodities. Spices, to Marco's readers, meant herbal medicine, incenses, perfumes, as well as seasonings, all worth their weight in gold.

This would be vital information to future explorers, for centuries later, when the Mongol Empire had collapsed and the Muslims were once again the middlemen controlling the Silk Road to the East, Europeans like Christopher Columbus would set sail during the Age of Discovery to try and get to the riches they'd first heard of from Marco Polo.

馬哥孛羅

When you quit Malabar and go 500 miles towards the south-west you come to the kingdom of Coilum. The people are idolaters, but there are some Christians and some Jews.

We walked down the cobblestone streets of Jew Town Road in Cochin until we spotted an old white man coming toward us. "Excuse me, sir. Do you live here?" I asked.

"Yes, I do," he said, trying to look up but half bent over his cane.

"Are you Jewish?" I asked bluntly.

"Yes, I am," he replied. "Are you?"

"Yeah, sure," I said. "I'm from New York . . . so, I guess by osmosis, you could say I am." He chuckled and invited us to walk with him to his home. It was a classic three-hundred-year-old colonial house, more Nicaraguan than Indian, with high doors at the street opening to a cloistered courtyard with a tiled fountain and garden and thick teak planking for floors. The familiarity of it soothed me, a mini-vacation from Asia. We sat under the portico in plantation chairs while he poured us teas from a samovar.

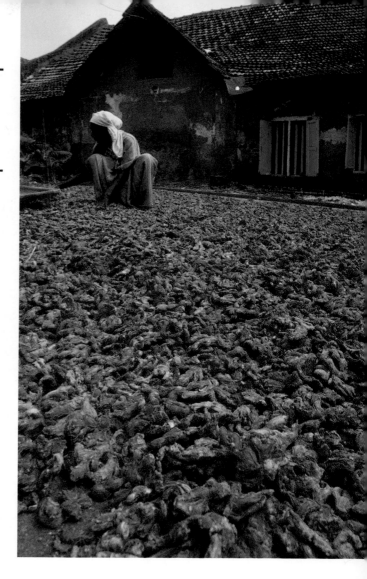

Spices, such as this ginger left to dry in the sun of a courtyard, were worth their weight in gold in Polo's era.

"We are Sephardic," he said, wiping excess tea off his mustache with the back of his hand and handing us business cards simply printed with the words "I. S. Hallegua."

"Sir, I'd like to explain what my friend here and I are up to . . ."

"You don't have explain a thing," he cut in. "You're young! I know exactly what you're up to . . . and you should stop that!"

When we regained our composure, I said, "I can't believe you've lived here your whole life. You could have worked the Borscht Belt with Henny Youngman, maybe even Vegas."

He spoke energetically of the Jews of India and Iberia: "Spices, that was the business; it's why we came, but that's all done with now. Everyone's gone. I'm one of the last, and no . . . I will not pose for a picture and no one in the community will either. Don't ask me again."

He told us the man in charge of the shul, the oldest synagogue in India, was his cousin. "His father and mine were brothers and our mothers sisters, you don't get closer cousins than that," he said. "But we don't talk, I'm a communist and he's a democrat."

He sat down Indian-style on the hardwood floor and popped a video into the VCR. "Watch this, the BBC did it about fifteen years ago." A commentator began with the history of the Cochin Jews. The last thing I heard before the old guy started talking again regarded the newest influx fleeing the Inquisition in Spain, arriving after da Gama in the sixteenth century.

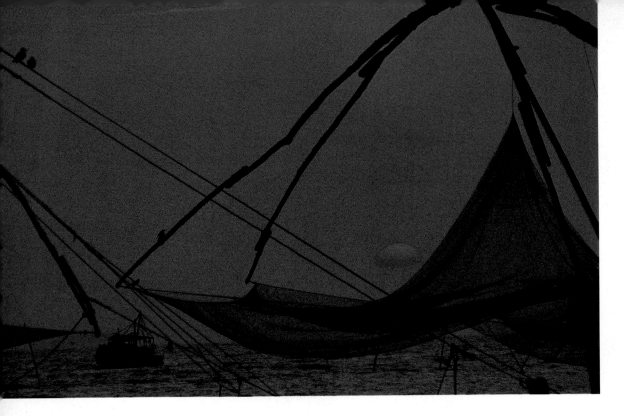

The unique design of the fishing nets still in use today in Cochin, on India's Malabar Coast, was brought from China during the Yuan dynasty and perhaps even on the very same cargo vessels on which Polo sailed.

Silent black-and-white footage came up and he stopped mid-sentence to point at the screen. "That's Isaac Castile, there's Hyman, and that's Uncle Moshe," he said excitedly as he tapped the monitor with a withered finger. An old man walked past the camera with a long white beard and turban, looking more Muslim than Jewish. "That is my grandfather," Hallegua said. "God forbid he ever found out someone was taking films of him," he cried.

"Why?" Fran asked. "If they hadn't, you couldn't sit here today and watch him."

"Don't you think I don't love to see my grandfather walking like he was still alive?" he shouted a bit testily. "But . . . he'd turn in his grave if he knew."

Well, that explains why no one will be photographed here, I thought. It's some sort of taboo.

He shut the tape off, rewinding it, never stopping his chatter. "There used to be eighty-two families of white Jews here and now there are just eighteen people; if you come back in ten years there will be none."

Before he could start a new sentence, I jumped in. "What do you mean by white Jews?"

"We, . . ." He hesitated. "We took slaves here, until I was about eight years old, we had slaves. We called them black Jews

(opposite page) Color in India has spiritual meanings: red, the color of blood, represents life and is considered good luck for brides; yellow and saffron are the colors of the dead and of yogis; pinks denote wisdom and divinity; and indigo and purple are for royalty and splendor.

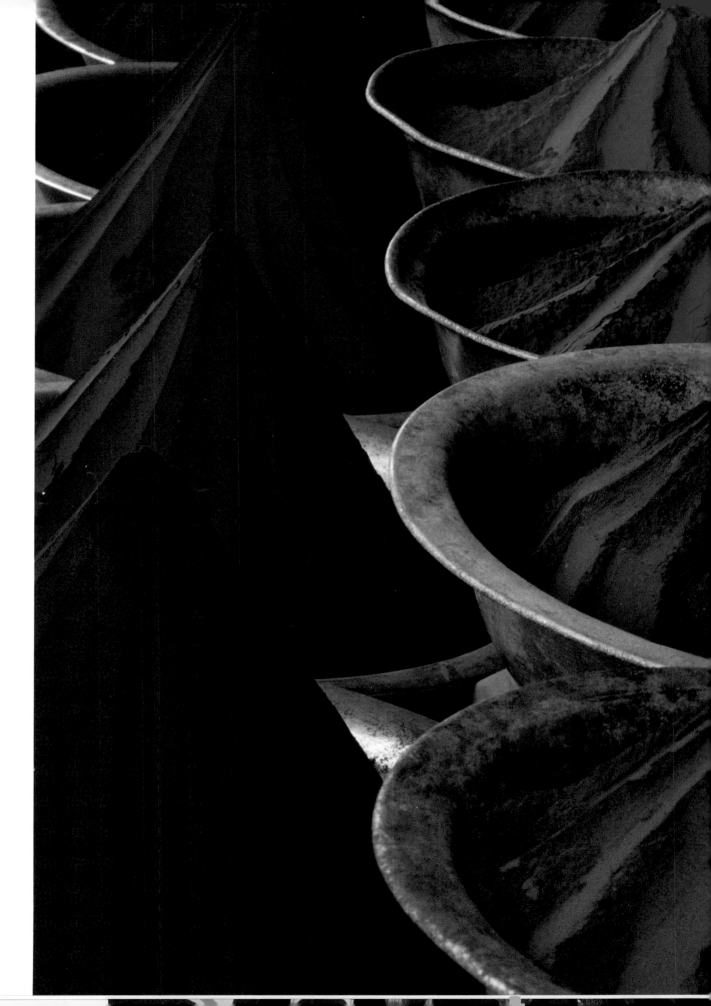

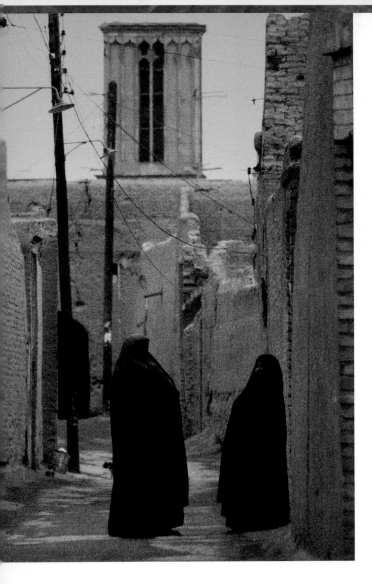

Medieval air conditioning is still used in the central desert city of Yazd, Iran. Vents opened to the four directions force air down the wind catcher, or badgir, cooling the house, and in some cases sending the air over cisterns or pools of water, which cools the air.

has been destroyed during the revolution in Iran . . . uh, um . . . I mean, the cultural revolution in China!"

I couldn't believe what he'd just said. After all we've been through and it came down to this, a slip of the tongue, a nervous mistake. There's nothing like reminding these guys of their revolution when they think you might be in the CIA. There was utter silence at the table.

What came next happened in the blink of an eye but has become epic for me. Fran pushed himself dramatically back from the table, screeching his chair and with eyes bulging at me like Jackie Gleason, blurted, "Whoa, dude . . . help me out over here!"

The climate is excessively hot—so hot that the houses are fitted with ventilators to catch the wind. The ventilators are set to face the quarter from which the wind blows and let it blow into the house. This they do because they cannot endure the overpowering heat.

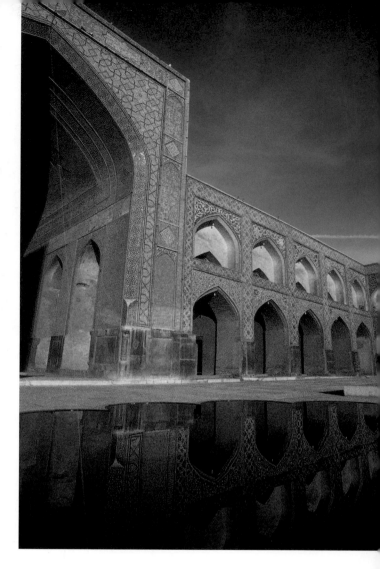

Poetry has a long and respected history in Persia and it's easy to see why, gazing into the lyrical reflecting pools of the Masjid-i Jami in Esfahan.

The whole delegation snapped their heads as if at a tennis match and stared at me. I felt I was in a surreal comedy skit and wanted to fall off my chair laughing but somehow held it together.

"What my friend was trying to say was nothing thrilled us more than the times when Polo's book came alive. But, unfortunately those times were rare in China because they destroyed much of their own history, unlike the Islamic Republic, which by your very presence here with UNESCO and WTO, shows your dedication to Persia's own rich cultural heritage."

"Don't worry about it," I told him later. "Faux pas aside, I think we did well."

"Oh man, as we came to their table I felt like I was walking on giant marshmallows, my adrenaline was flowing . . . I was trippin' or something," he said.

"Listen, just look at it this way," I said, "if we get the visas, those few psychotic seconds will be the funniest of our lives—something to smile about on our death beds—but, if we don't . . . "

馬哥孛羅

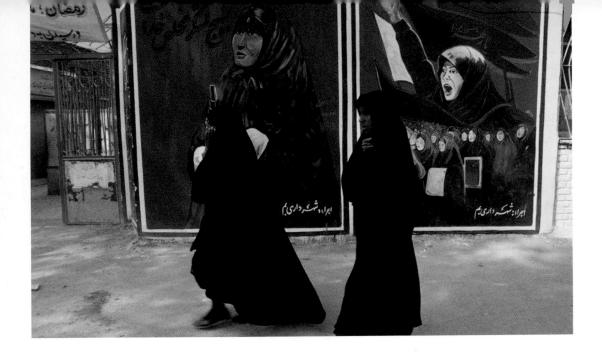

The train through the Baluchistan desert was virtually empty, and we had a whole compartment to ourselves with plenty of time to think. I thought of high school and yellow ribbons tied around trees, of how I wore a button then that said "Fuck Iran" and pronounced it I-Ran instead of E-Ron, of the hostages and the anger I felt at seeing them blindfolded, of the day Reagan was inaugurated and they were released, and . . . of all the things they could do to us now.

At the border we were anxious: would they confiscate our camera equipment, would they even let us in? We jumped down to get stamped, and besides a minor frenzy among the border guards, who it seemed had never seen an American passport and practically tore them out of one another's hands in amazement, they were downright pleasant. Our packs were never searched; they simply asked if we had any hashish or heroin and then welcomed us to Iran. That's E-Ron. I'd had more trouble crossing into Canada.

Since we were so few getting off the train, our driver was on us in a second. Part of our deal for being the first Americans given visas to the Islamic Republic since the revolution was that we'd agreed to pay a driver and interpreter for our stay. Nikbakht, the interpreter, was older, nervous, and twitchy. The driver, an Azerbaijani, was cool, laid back, and looked like Al Pacino in *Serpico*. We were under no illusions they weren't working for a security apparatus of the regime.

"It says on your itinerary that first you'd like to go to Hormuz," Nikbakht said after we were already racing across the bleak desert.

According to *The Travels*, the Polos' long voyage from China had been racked by disaster: *Now let me tell you the simple truth. When they embarked, they numbered fully 600 souls, not counting the seamen. Of this number every one died on the voyage, except only eighteen.* The royal entourage limped into the Persian Gulf and the port of Hormuz, probably in the summer of 1293. Twenty-one years earlier the Polos had stood there and made the decision to continue east on the Silk Road rather than risk their lives on ships Marco had said were unseaworthy.

But before we followed Polo to Hormuz, we wanted to visit Bam, an important stop on the caravan routes between the Persian Gulf and India. Bam, the medieval sandcastle of Cecil B. DeMille's wildest dreams, was the best ruin we had ever seen, and we'd seen a few. We watched in our minds' eyes as Ali Baba and the forty thieves played out on the empty lanes of the citadel rising from the golden desert.

"Persia," we said, as we drank in the sweet light dancing over the walled ruin.

"I can't believe we are here," I said as I gave Fran an exuberant hug.

"A great beginning to the ending of a journey of a lifetime," he said, striking a pose like a silent film star, waiting for his close-up.

In the morning we bought dates from a small kiosk, and two teenage boys approached us, asking where we were from. "You're lying," they said, dumbfounded when we told them, but were even more so when we guessed they were Hazaras.

"They call us the yellow race here," one of them said.

The blue-and-white-glazed ceramics that most people think of having come from the Ming dynasty and copied profusely in Europe—think Delft tiles—were in fact a Persian invention. The Chinese called it Mohammadan blue in homage to its origin.

"You are the descendants of Genghis Khan," we told them. "Be proud." They walked off smiling.

When we jumped back in the car, Nikbakht was freaked out. He'd watched the whole exchange from the curb. "You must never tell people where you are from!" he insisted. "We must tell them you are with the UN."

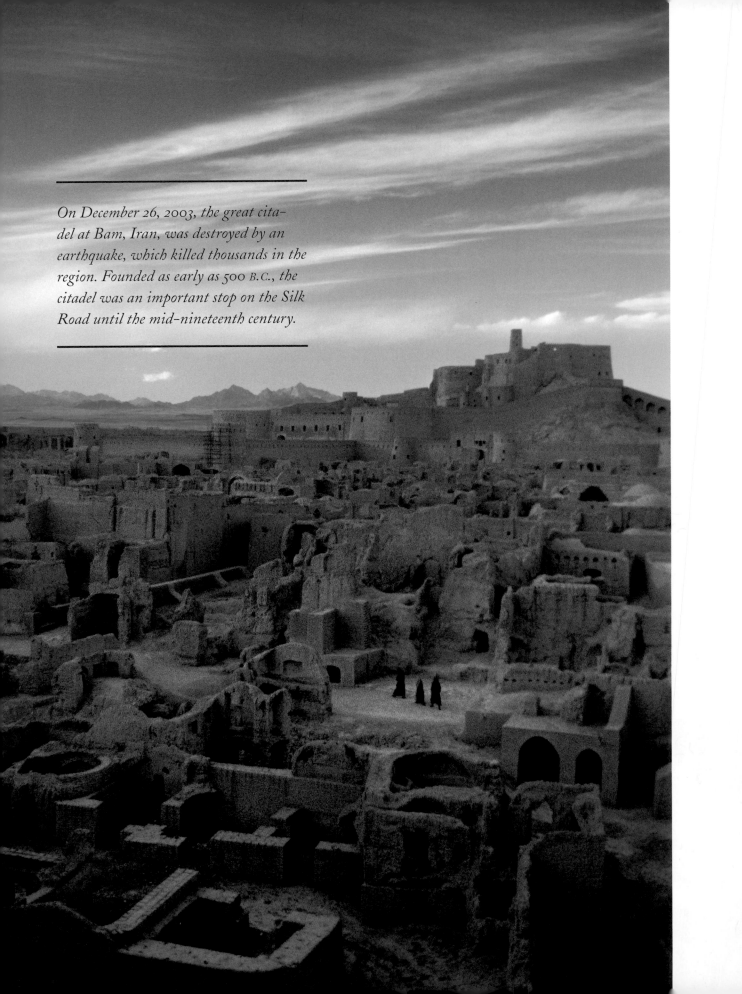

*On December 26, 2003, the great cita-
del at Bam, Iran, was destroyed by an
earthquake, which killed thousands in the
region. Founded as early as 500 B.C., the
citadel was an important stop on the Silk
Road until the mid–nineteenth century.*

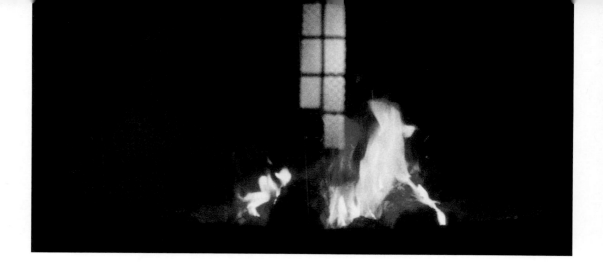

The Zoroastrian fire temple in Yazd, Iran. "If it ever . . . goes out, they go 'round to others who hold the same faith and worship fire also, and are given fire from that church. This they bring back to rekindle their own."

There were police and military checkpoints in and out of every town and some in the middle of nowhere. At every one, Nikbakht showed them a paper stating we worked for UNICEF. It was as if the Iranians were smuggling us across their own country.

"You will be in danger if they know you are Americans," he snickered, pucker-faced and nervous.

We took to ignoring him after that, speaking with Reza the driver in Turkish, which Nikbakht couldn't understand, annoying him to no end.

When we were alone, Fran and I agreed we had to ditch them somehow. We hated traveling like this, wanting to be free to speak with the inhabitants just as any journeyer would.

We came upon a town of fire-worshipers. . . . The inhabitants here told me that in days gone by three kings set out from this country to worship a new-born prophet and took with them these gifts—gold, frankincense and myrrh.

For over twelve hundred years, the fire burning in the Zoroastrian temple in Yazd has been kept alive by a long lineage of priests, log upon log and ember to burning ember.

The ancient Zoroastrian religion is perhaps the first monotheistic faith. Centuries before Christianity, the Zoroastrians believed that their God would send a savior, born of a virgin, to triumph over darkness and evil. Great astrologers, the Magi of Persia, also believed that the sign of his birth would come from the heavens. Their veneration of fire as a sacred channel of God's eternal light and purity is still practiced by a small group of followers in Iran today.

Nikbakht bristled at our telling everyone where we were from, and he was beside himself that we insisted on staying in the $2-a-night local hotels instead of the $30-a-night official ones, not least because we were paying and he was uncomfortable. "We just don't have the money," we'd told him. When we got to Shiraz, Fran feigned sickness and we said we needed to stay for a few days, for him to recoup.

"Look," I said to Nikbakht, "he needs time to get better and we can't afford you. We'll make our way to Tehran in a few days and call your office." And that was that. They left.

"I can't believe how easy that was," I said to Fran. "Ha . . . maybe they were just tour guides and not spooks after all."

"Are you kidding me?" Fran said. "I'll bet they think we're up to something and are luring us into a trap. They probably have another team in place ready to follow us."

"I don't care, let 'em. What are we doing except drooling over all the old ruins we come across and taking pictures of seven-hundred-year-old ceramic tiles?"

馬哥字羅

On the sixteenth anniversary of the Islamic revolution that toppled the shah and brought theocracy to Iran, we entered the Meidan Emam, Esfahan's gem of Islamic architecture and one of the largest public squares in the world. It was packed with half a million demonstrators. Every atom in my body was screaming for me to turn around and flee in the opposite direction, and yet I knew that was impossible.

Drawn like moths to a bright flame, we freely joined the throngs of people and, following the loudest and most fervent chanting deep into the belly of the beast, we found a pulpit arrayed with microphones. Fanatical clerics took turns rousing the crowd in chilling chants of "Death to America" and "Death to Israel."

An army helicopter appeared and hovered close, spilling thousands of small Iranian flags and anti-American propaganda leaflets into the crowd as young children and women scrambled for them like kids over a piñata. The roar was deafening and we were jostled deeper in by the surging masses.

> *They make a great to-do about mourning. They assemble with their kinsfolk and neighbors and give themselves up to loud wailing and keening and lamenting. . . . There are even women among them who specialize in lamentation and are daily on hire to bewail.*

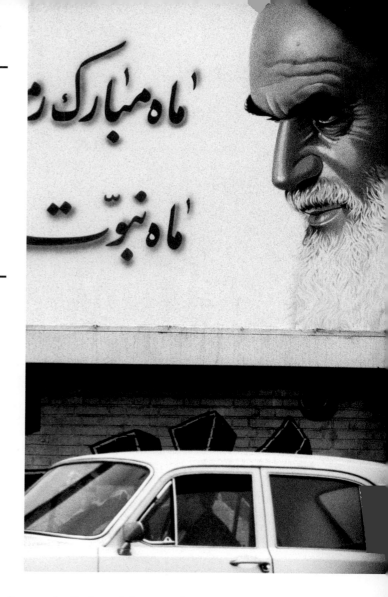

On the day he became supreme leader of the Islamic Republic of Iran, Ayatollah Khomeini proclaimed it the "first day of God's government." Over the next ten years until his death, he reigned over a cultural revolution that turned Iran into a theocracy.

They were burning American flags and effigies of the president and Uncle Sam, but they weren't too preoccupied to notice us, the foreigners with cameras. The police arrived in seconds, demanding we go with them and causing a scene. We tried baffling them with English, saying we were with the UN, but to no avail, they started dragging us off. We made the hasty decision to hand over the cameras and film rather that be arrested, knowing we had extras at the hotel. They took our gear, and we got swallowed back up and lost in the crowd, passing a gathering of women, all dressed in ominous black chadors wailing or ululating with their tongues, a mournful, high-pitched call that sent chills down our spines.

But in truth, besides the policemen, we never felt personally menaced. Once we got away from the main square and its TV cameras, it seemed most people were just happy to have the day off from work. In fact, the Iranian people are among the nicest and most hospitable we have ever come across. They'd come up to ask what country we were from and never believed the answer. More often than not they shook our hands and quietly said they despised the mullahs and wished for a change.

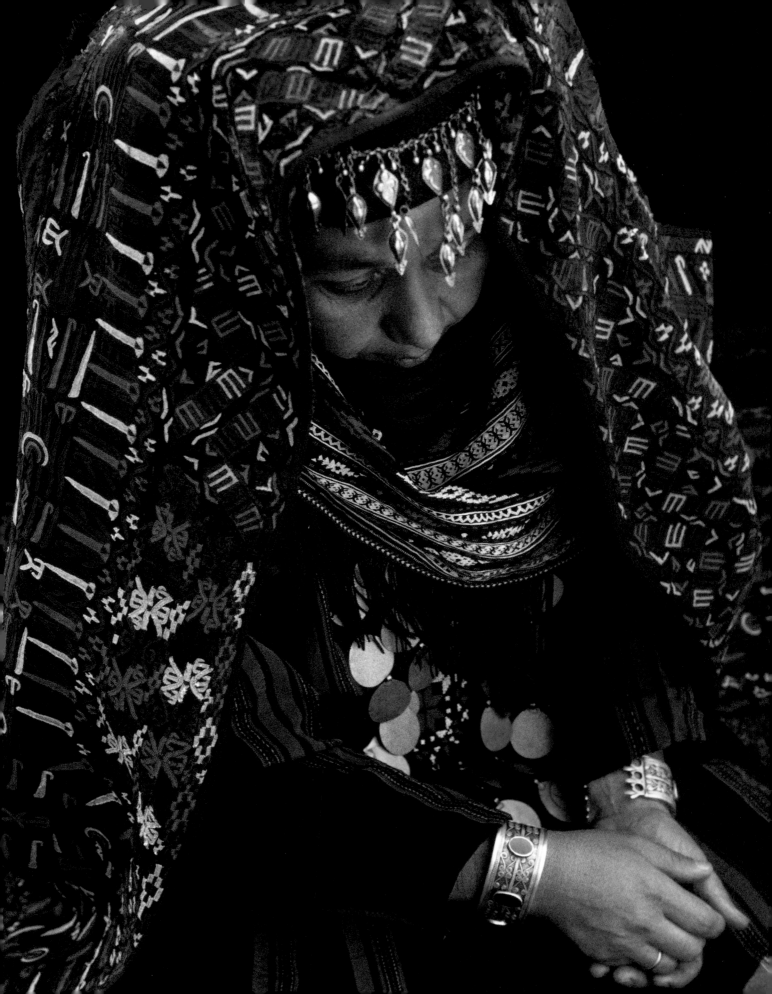

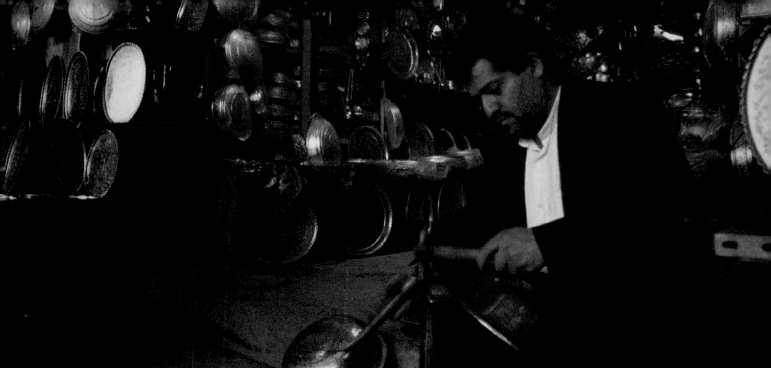

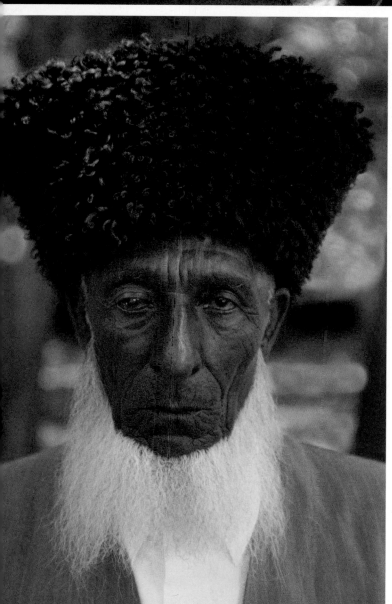

(opposite page) A Nokhorli tribeswoman believes her breath belongs only to her husband and only by accident will her mouth be exposed in public.

(above) An Azerbaijani coppersmith in a bazaar in Tehran.

(at left) A Turkoman of the Nokhorli tribe wears a traditional telpek made from karakul.

When Polo said Persia consisted of eight kingdoms, he was alluding to its ethnic diversity. Turks are Iran's largest minority, which includes among other tribes the Azeris and Turkomans, who all migrated into the region in the eighth and ninth centuries from northern parts of Central Asia. In the eleventh century they converted to Islam and, led by the Seljuks, entered the Caucasus and Asia Minor, where they eventually defeated the Byzantines and established the Ottoman Empire.

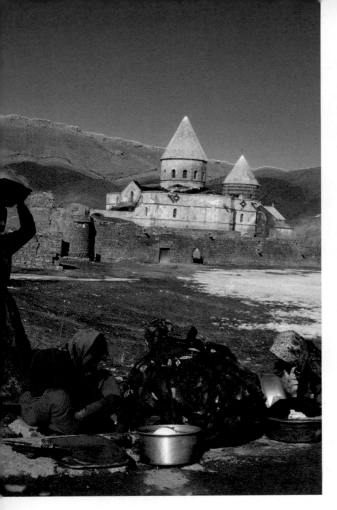

The Armenians may be gone, but Kurdish girls still wash dishes in a small stream in front of the Kara Kalissa (black church) in the Azerbaijani region of Iran. Reconstructed after an earthquake in the 1300s, the church is revered by Armenians worldwide.

"We used to pray in our homes and socialize in public," one student said. "Now we pray in public and socialize in our homes." Young people, who made up 70 percent of the population, were chafing under the restrictive religious laws imposed by Ayatollah Khomeini, whose brooding image was everywhere.

I will tell you a story just as I, Messer Marco have heard it told by many people. . . . There was a sheik called Alodin who had made in a valley between two mountains a garden like the paradise Mahomet promised the Saracens . . . planted with fine fruits and flowing with rivers of milk and honey. . . . Here he would drug young men and surround them with beautiful damsels who sang and danced and ministered to all their desires. When they awoke from their dream, they longed for death, so that they may return there . . . the sheik would then send them wherever he wished as assassins . . . and if they were to die on their missions of murder they believed they would be returned to the garden paradise.

The very word "assassin" has its origins in the desolate Alborz Mountains, for it comes from the Persian *hashshashin*—hashish eater.

Polo correctly informed us that the suicide missions of these medieval terrorists eventually ended when their mountain fortresses were besieged and finally destroyed by the Mongols. We found evidence of the three-year siege, in thousands of broken pottery shards left behind by the Tartar troops near the ruined fortresses high up in the cliffs.

When we had hiked back down again we needed to help our driver get his car out of the mud; he'd also cracked a tailpipe getting us there. His name was Mehdi, pronounced McD, and though I was revolted by fast-food burgers at home, every time I heard his name, I had a hankering for a Big Mac.

"Are you guys from L.A.?" he had asked when we met him. "I lived there for twelve years."

We had hired him to drive us in his 1982 Cadillac Seville, something he relished doing at close to a hundred miles an hour on Iran's well-paved roads, and we took to calling him Johnny Contradiction, because he was a blend of California liberalism and Islamic fundamentalism. But we liked him, and when we were pulled over and brought in for questioning by the religious police because it was Ramadan and they spotted me in the back of his car with my sleeves rolled up, McD stood up for us and even waited the six hours until they finally let us go.

"You're okay with that?" I asked, dumbfounded. "Why would you move back to a country that treats you like this?"

"That is so typical of you Americans, everyone should live like you. It is not your culture, you don't understand," he said.

"What about stoning women to death? Is that just a cultural difference we don't understand?"

"These stories are not true," he said.

"I'm sorry, McD," Fran said, pulling out an Iranian English-language newspaper we'd picked up in Tehran with an article about a woman who cheated on her husband, was buried up to her neck, and publicly stoned to death. "This is not American propaganda. It's in an Iranian newspaper."

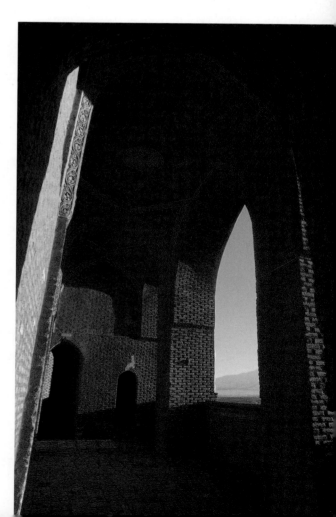

Oljeitu tomb in Sultaniya near Tabriz, Iran. Nowhere else was the Mongols' dramatic conversion to the religion of their subjugated vassals more evident than in Sultaniya, where in 1302 the Ilkhanates built this tomb in the Islamic tradition.

"Do you believe everything you read in the papers?" was all he could muster, and we left it at that.

馬哥孛羅

Delivering the princesses to the Khan of the Levant at the seat of his power in Tabriz in the north of Persia, Polo stresses the close bond that had formed between them.

> *We had watched over them and guarded them as if they had been our own daughters. . . . And the ladies who were very young and beautiful, looked upon us as fathers. . . . And I assure you in all truth that the now married queen Kokachin was so attached to us that when we left her to return to our country, she wept for grief at our going.*

Marco must have grieved too, for here he must have learned his hero, Kublai, was dead. What was he feeling? He was almost home, but just where was home? When he had left he had been a naive teenager, and now he was a worldly, middle-aged man who had spent most of his life abroad. What other loved ones did he leave behind in Asia? Just what awaited him in Italy? Were family and friends still alive? Would he be able, after a lifetime of adventures, to fit into the rigid constraints of Venetian society? Did he feel more Asian than European?

The Roman ruler Valerian kneels in surrender to the Persian king Shapur I in a relief carved in 260 at the base of older tombs belonging to Darius the Great and Xerxes in Naqsh-i-Ruslam, Iran.

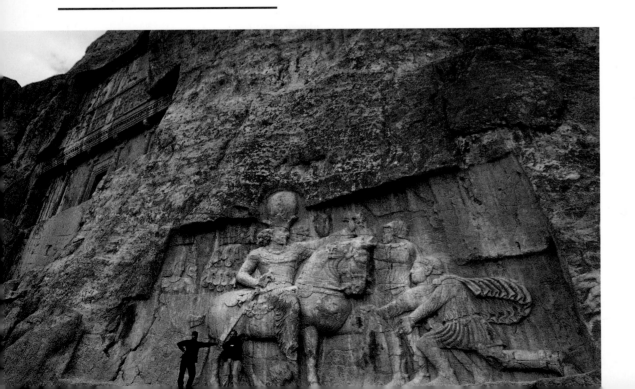

THE RETURN TO VENICE

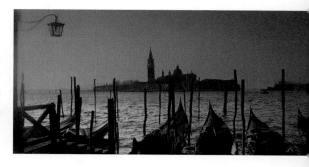

Coming Full Circle

CONTINUING WEST PAST THE SHADOW OF MT. ARARAT, we entered *Into the heart of Greater Armenia where there is a very high mountain . . . on which Noah's Ark is said to have rested . . . on the summit the snow lies so deep that it never entirely melts.*

We were not happy; it looked like the end of the journey had taken on all the flair and spontaneity of one of those organized tours for foreign dignitaries. "This area is under martial law," the Turks told us. "The Kurdish rebels kidnap and kill foreigners."

"No offense," Fran said, "but if you guys weren't here meeting us we would have passed through uneventfully, unnoticed."

The tourism ministers we'd met at the Silk Road conference organized a big reception for us at the border. Over a hundred people showed up, including television crews, newspaper reporters, local politicians, and armored vehicles with turret-mounted machine guns to escort us. We stood out like sore thumbs and thought for sure if the rebels were going to hit any target that day it would surely be this circus.

If Iran was the last piece of the Polo puzzle then Turkey meant we had come full circle. We had made it. Tired, and anxious to see family and friends who were making arrangements to meet us in Venice to celebrate, we capitulated, resigning ourselves to their five-star hotels, private cars, and gourmet food. We felt like Turkish rock stars as we made our way slowly toward Istanbul before being whisked through customs and put on a ship into what Marco said was *The sea that is crossed by ships sailing to Christendom.*

The domes and spires of serene Venice slid past us as we leaned over the deck rail and took a deep breath. We couldn't say too much to each other, each grappling with the end differently. I was excited to see the people who meant the most to me but felt like turning back, really not wanting it to end.

Italian officials put us into a grand regatta of gondolas reserved for heads of state. The bow of one, a Chinese dragon, was rowed by a phalanx of men dressed in yellow silk, another reserved for the doge was draped in cardinal red, and the last, manned

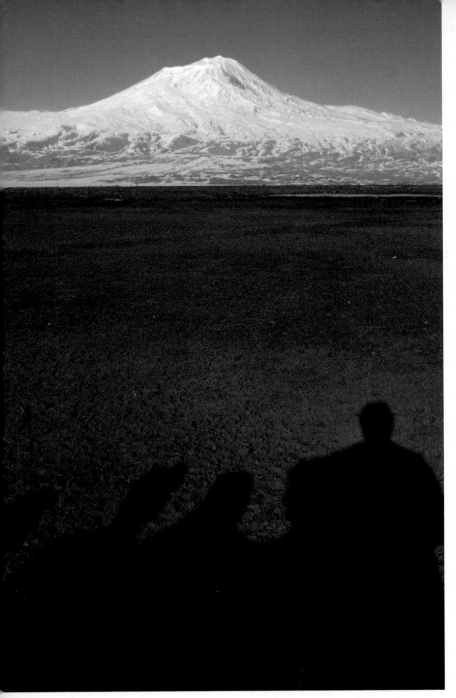

by sailors in traditional Venetian gear, rowed us down the Grand Canal to St. Mark's Square, where the bells of the basilica were rung in our honor. When our feet hit the square, we were met by the mayor of Venice and the press and the cheers of tourists, family, and friends.

My mom nearly tackled me and wouldn't let go for the next hour or two. My dad was there, taking his first airplane ride in over thirty years, a big step for him after surviving a helicopter crash in the army. Crowding around were aunts and uncles; Fran's mom, sister, and niece; and friends, even a couple we'd met in China a year before. It was surreal. We were numb.

(opposite page) The Venice the Polos came home to had become the most prosperous city in all of Europe.

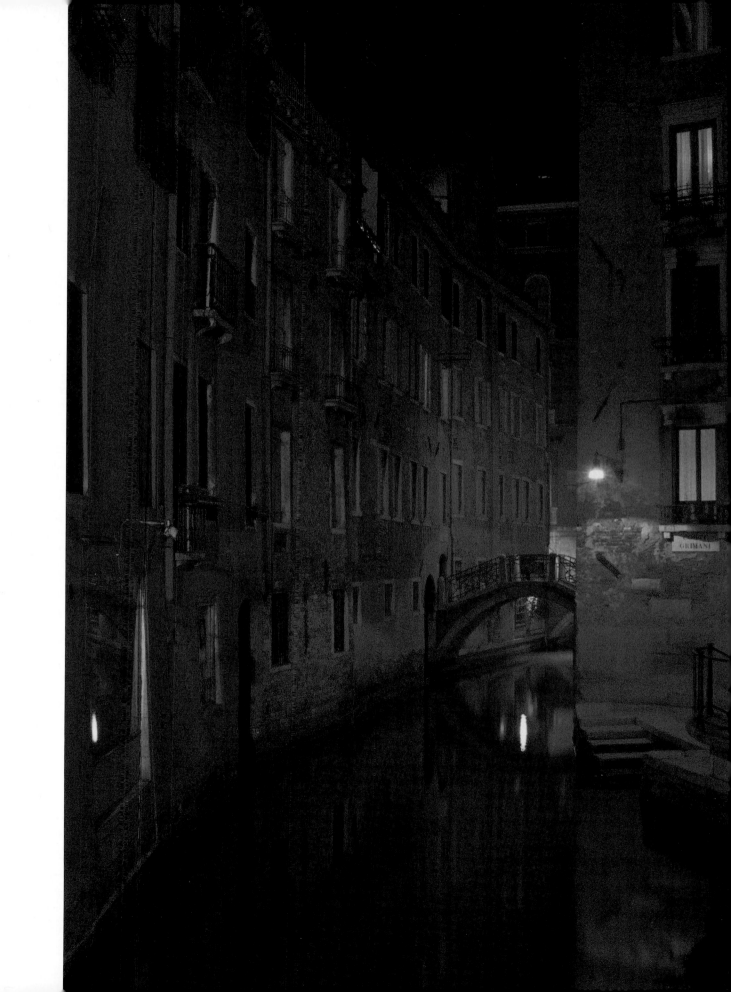

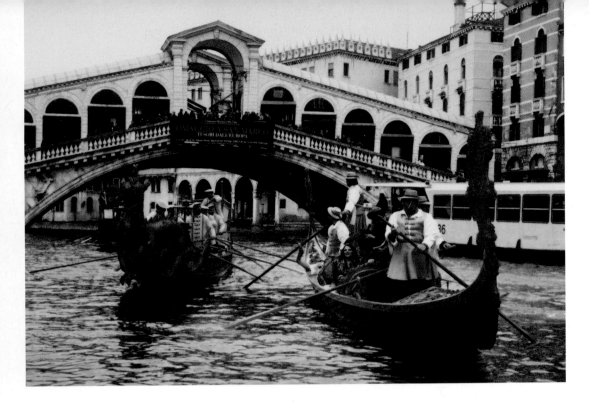

Our royal regatta of gondolas passes under the Rialto Bridge, not far from the Polos' home.

They walked us past commemorative posters with our names on them plastered on ancient walls and brought us to the Olivetti gallery in the square, which was having a show of my photographs that had been chosen from the film we'd sent home.

After a press conference, there was a banquet in our honor at the mayor's palace. "What can we, the citizens of Venice, do for you, two Americans who have taken such a stake in our history?" the mayor asked.

"Just one small thing, Your Excellency. We'd like to see Marco Polo's last will and testament."

It was served to us on a silver platter.

It was not an accident that our return to Venice was completed almost seven hundred years to the day of the Polos' homecoming in 1295. But unlike us, the weary travelers arrived home unannounced after being away for twenty-four years. They weren't given a regatta of gondolas and sailed down the Grand Canal. The bells of St. Mark's weren't rung in their honor, and officials of the Republic didn't receive them to celebrate their return. Instead, legend has it that their relatives, who had thought them dead for years, didn't recognize them, *For they had a certain smack of the Tartar about them, in both air and accent, having all but forgotten their native language.*

It wasn't until they ripped open the seams of their robes and diamonds, rubies, and pearls came pouring out that they were finally believed to be the lost Polos.

Drawn up just a few days before he died in 1324, Marco Polo's will releases his Tartar slave, Peter, and bequeaths to his wife and daughters his earthly goods, including a gold tablet given to him by the Great Khan.

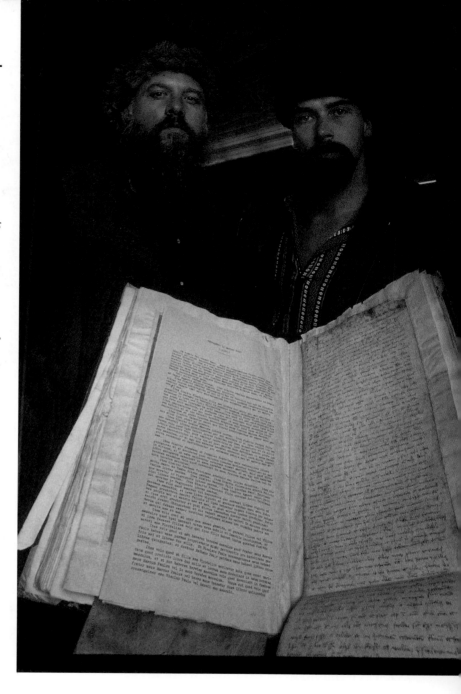

Home for a few years when hostilities broke out with Genoa, Marco jumped at the chance for adventure and led a war galley against Venice's ancient rival. He was captured and imprisoned for a year with Rusticello of Pisa, where he enthralled the ghostwriter with his unbelievable stories.

In his mid-forties when his account first appeared, Marco would go on to international fame as his work was translated into all the major languages of Europe, an unheard-of feat for a living author of his time. His book was even chained to the Rialto Bridge for everyone to read.

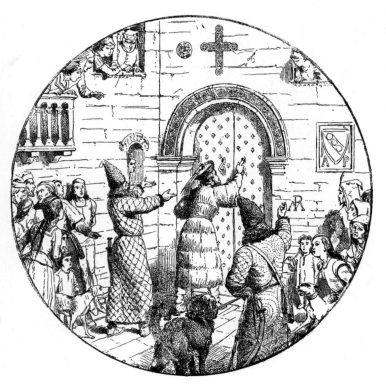

He married a woman named Donata, who bore him three daughters, and he seemed to have settled down at home in Venice, passing his time in the humdrum dealings of imports and moneylending. Occasionally a scholar or traveler heading east would call on him for consultation and advice, and we could imagine the old man reveling in the tales of his youthful travels.

When Polo drew up his will in January 1324, just days before his death at the age of seventy, he left the bulk of his worldly goods to his wife and daughters. Listed as his most prized possessions were a set of Buddhist rosary beads, a lady's golden headdress inset with precious stones and pearls, a silver belt worn by Tartar knights, and one golden tablet given to him by the Great Khan.

馬哥孛羅

So, did Marco Polo make it to China? From the comfort of their armchairs, scholars have been debating that very question for seven hundred years.

Having spent two years and roughly twenty-five thousand miles in his footsteps, and finding his descriptions come to life—literally jumping off the pages of his book—we know in our hearts that Marco Polo's book is true.

It is time for Marco Polo to take his rightful place as Europe's greatest explorer. For unlike those he would go on to inspire, Marco Polo never planted an imperial flag or tried to convert the people in his path. Instead he meticulously tried to relate what he

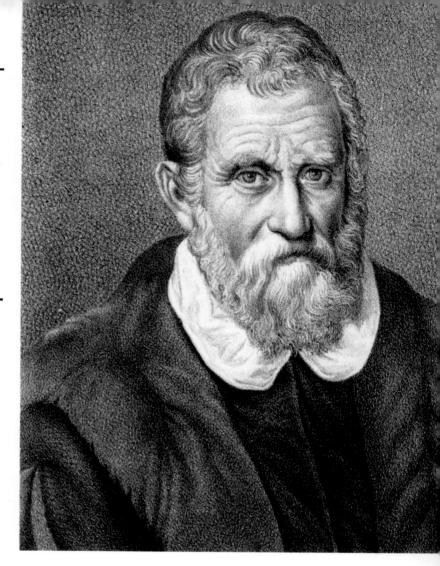

There are no surviving contemporary images of Marco Polo. This famous portrait of him as an older man, Yule tells us, was "copied with permission from a painting in the Gallery of Monsignore Badia in Rome."

encountered without being too judgmental, documenting a world outside his own and sharing it.

What's most important about Marco Polo isn't that he was the first European to reach China and the Far East—he wasn't even the first member of his family to do that. It is that by writing about it, he opened up a whole new world for the West. For the truth of the matter is this, never before or since has one man contributed more to the knowledge of geography. This then is his legacy and he knew it. *For I believe it was God's will that we should come back, so that men might know the things that are in the world.*

Marco Polo's book made the world a smaller place, more so than it had ever been, and yet seven hundred years later it seems that our divisions are just as great. When you see our planet from space, there are no borders and you don't need visas. As a species we like to separate ourselves from each other, whether it's along tribal, religious, or nationalist lines, and all too often it leads to fear and mistrust.

Polo lived during a time of extreme ignorance, when a handful of religious fanatics incited civilizations to clash by breeding hatred and intolerance, all in the name of God.

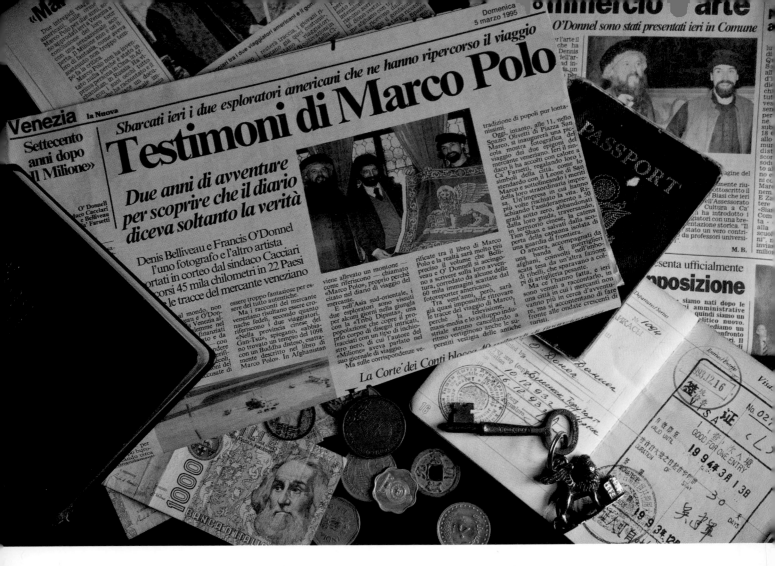

As was true then so it is today. It is easy to hate someone you've never met.

A wise man once said, "Travel is the enemy of bigotry." We believe Marco Polo understood this as well, which is why he remains so relevant today.

The most important thing we learned from this experience is that we must preserve the cultural differences that make our world so interesting, but at the same time agree to unite to end poverty and to sustain the health of our beautiful planet. A quest to retrace Polo's path led us down our own and to a deeper understanding of the need for respect and compassion for others. We are all the same. There is only one human race.

So, although we had no diamonds, rubies, or pearls sewn into our clothes, like Marco, we did return home richer men.

I haven't told you half of what I've seen.

EPILOGUE

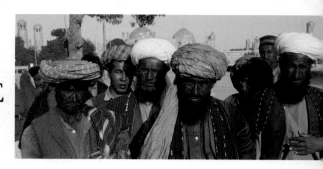

PEOPLE OFTEN ASK US if it would be harder to make the journey today, post 9/11. "It's a different world now," they say. How do you answer that?

On the one hand, by taking our eye off the ball in Afghanistan and invading Iraq, we have reversed a hundred years of the world's goodwill toward the American people; on the other hand, even though they are grossly undermanned and security is tenuous, there are thousands of Western troops in Afghanistan, making the country a hell of a lot safer than it was in 1993.

We found out that Mr. K was Massoud Kahlili. He was in Washington, D.C., when we met him, trying unsuccessfully to convince the Clinton administration not to abandon Afghanistan to the wolves. Two days before the 9/11 attacks, Mr. K was in Afghanistan, standing next to Ahmad Shah Massoud, the "Lion of the Panjshir," when Al Qaeda suicide bombers assassinated him. Despite losing an eye and a leg in the blast, Mr. K is now serving as Afghanistan's ambassador to India.

Commander Atta, his beard closely trimmed and wearing a suit and tie, has become an outspoken advocate for Afghan women's rights and has opened schools for girls in Balkh, where he is now governor. He keeps an uneasy peace with Dostum, who has also held on to power.

The Tibetans and Uighurs are still aching for freedom. Intolerance still rears its ugly head in Sri Lanka and other places we passed through. Yet we still believe, as we did then, that there are far more good, decent, and honest people out there than bad. The bad just get all the press.

When we came home we needed a break—from each other, from Marco Polo, from Asia. We hardly spoke for months, assimilating back into our old lives with varying degrees of success. I had an especially hard time with the wastefulness I encountered, most notably of food, after I'd seen painfully thin kids going through garbage dumps to find scraps to eat.

With my mom acting as matchmaker, our pal Shawny ended up marrying my cousin Samantha, Rob's sister, and they are now expecting their first child. If nothing else came from our journey that would have been enough.

We gave slide shows and lectures, were invited to join the Explorers Club, and were even signed by a big-name literary agent. We had fits and starts, some promises, and a few deals fall through before we decided to shelve the project for a few years and get on with life. "The Wakhan Corridor was easy compared to navigating New York's publishing world," I told Fran after one such occasion, the canyon that is Fifth Avenue reminding me of the remote Afghan passageway.

But, as you have no doubt figured out after reading our story, if nothing else we are stubborn and tenacious, and we never gave up. So, in a way the journey hasn't come to an end until now, as I sit here and write these last few lines after putting the kids to bed.

Oh yeah, that's right. My beautiful wife is indeed a strong and supportive person, and we have two boys who are being well educated, just as the Brahmin priest had foretold.

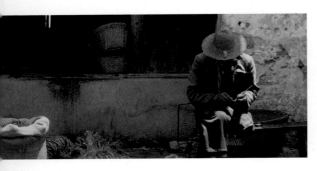

BIBLIOGRAPHY AND SUGGESTED READINGS

BIBLIOGRAPHY

Larner, John. *Marco Polo and the Discovery of the World*. New Haven: Yale University Press, 1999.

Rashid, Ahmed. *Taliban: Militant Islam, Oil, and Fundamentalism in Central Asia*. New Haven: Yale University Press, 2000.

Wood, Frances. *Did Marco Polo Go to China?* Boulder, CO: Westview, 1996.

Polo, Marco. *The Book of Ser Marco Polo, the Venetian, Concerning the Kingdoms and Marvels of the East*. Trans. and ed. Henry Yule. London: John Murray, 1871. All Marco Polo quotes we have used have been taken from this edition of *The Travels of Marco Polo*.

SUGGESTED READINGS

In chapter 1, we refer to three attempts and subsequent books that fell short in retracing Marco Polo's complete route. These are:

Dalrymple, William. *In Xanadu: A Quest*. New York: Vintage, 1990.

Rutstein, Harry, and Joanne Kroll. *In the Footsteps of Marco Polo: A Twentieth Century Odyssey*. New York: Viking, 1980.

Yamashita, Michael S. *Marco Polo: A Photographer's Journey*. Vercelli, Italy: White Star, 2004.

In our research for our trip, we read several books that are not mentioned in the text. The books by Tim Severin and Jean Bowie Shor attempt to retrace Polo's steps, the book by Italo Calvino is included for its beauty, and the remaining books are of general interest:

Calvino, Italo. *Invisible Cities*. Trans. William Weaver. New York: Harcourt Brace Jovanovich, 1974.

Hedin, Sven. *Across the Gobi Desert*. Trans. H. J. Cant. New York: Dutton, 1932.

Hopkirk, Peter. *The Great Game: The Struggle for Empire in Central Asia*. New York: Kodansha International, 1992.

Humble, Richard. *Marco Polo*. New York: Putnam, 1975

Moule, A. C. *Quinsai, with other Notes on Marco Polo*. Cambridge: Cambridge University Press, 1957.

Olschki, Leonardo. *Marco Polo's Asia; an introduction to his "Description of the World" Called "Il Milione."* Trans. John A. Scott, and rev. by the author. Berkeley: University of California Press, 1960.

Pelliot, Paul. *Notes on Marco Polo*. Paris: Imprimerie Nationale, Librarie Adrien-Maisonneuve, 1959–1963.

Polo, Marco. *The Description of the World/The Travels of Marco Polo*. Trans. and annotated by A. C. Moule and Paul Pelliot. 2 vols. London: Routledge, 1938 [Reprint: New York: AMS Press, 1976].

———. *The Travels of Marco Polo*. Trans. Ronald Latham. Middlesex, England: Penguin Classics, 1958.

Rossabi, Morris. *Khubilai Khan: His Life and Times*. Berkeley: University of California Press, 1988.

Severin, Tim. *Tracking Marco Polo*. 1st American edition. New York: Peter Bedrick Books, 1986.

Shor, Jean Bowie. *After You, Marco Polo*. New York: McGraw-Hill, 1955.

Spence, Jonathan D. *The Chan's Great Continent: China in Western Minds*. New York: Norton, 1998.

Stein, Aurel, Sir. *Innermost Asia: Detailed Report of Explorations in Central Asia, Kan-su and Eastern Iran Carried Out and Described under the Orders of H.M. Indian Government*. 4 vols. Oxford: Clarendon, 1928.